Advance Praise for *Rev...*

"A deep dive into the impli... clear and positive perspective of what the future will look like as we transition from the Industrial Age."

—*New York Times* **Bestselling Author Jim Champy**

"An invaluable perspective on the promise and the challenge of a future driven by intelligent machines."

—**Dan Hoeyer, CEO Leaders Excellence Harvard Square**

"*Revealing the Invisible* is a smart and entertaining look into an important shift in our economy and society: our behavior is getting digitized, which means that everything we buy and use can be personalized based on knowledge of what we do. Thomas Koulopoulos guides the reader through the surprising repercussions of this move from an economy of mass production to one where the consumer is surrounded by objects and services that are getting a lot smarter and adapting themselves to the individual."

—**Chris Nicholson, CEO Skymind**

"Through a curious yet simple review of socioeconomic and technological (among others) trends of the last couple of centuries, and their effect on our lives, *Revealing the Invisible* challenges the reader to imagine and predict what the next chain of events could be. By being well-researched, thorough, but also ambitious and bold, *Revealing the Invisible* takes you on a journey that, while its destination may be proven wrong in 100 years, is robust, easy to follow, thought-provoking, and eye-opening."

**—Paris Anatolitis, Head of
Gaming GVC London**

"*Revealing the Invisible* is a brilliant analysis of the current paradigm shift in business and society when it comes to making use of behavioural data. The authors demonstrate with hard evidence the rise of the value of behavioural data as the 'new oil.' The authors think beyond the current state of affairs and extrapolate current trends into the future when it comes to the convergence of human and machine behaviour. A must read, not just for every data and analytics expert but for every future-facing business executive who wants to stay on the forefront of the current data revolution."

**—Thomas Hirschmann,
CEO | Founder at Braingraph**

"Actionable insights for those who both wonder about and want to skate where puck is going to be in regards to the imminent technological and automation disruption of the global economic and social status quo."

**—Apostolos Papadopoulos,
Harvard Medical School**

"Forward leaning, pragmatic and bravely optimistic, *Revealing the Invisible* opens our minds. A thinking dynamite that reveals and deconstructs the fact that 'understanding behavior is the killer app of the 21st century.' Kudos to Thomas and George for their bold look on a topic that troubles us a lot, when we need it most. An invaluable eye-opener."

—Christos Charpantidis, Philip Morris International, Managing Director

"*Revealing the Invisible* is going to fill the deep gap of a modern, relevant, and mind-blowing analysis on this critical area. It uncovers the shadowy sides of the Invisible via the angle of view and the scientific tools of the 21st century."

—Stathis Haikalis, Chairman Edelman Greece

"Not since Thomas Friedman's *The World is Flat* has an author so skillfully described the challenges and opportunities of 21st century technology."

—*Barry P. Chaiken, MD, MPH*, CEO *DocsNetwork, Ltd.*

"Tom Koulopoulos has done it again: transformed big complex ideas and big data into a book that is accessible, enlightening, and thoughtful. *Revealing the Invisible* covers essential ground for those grappling with the impacts of technology on our work and lives—in other words, all of us."

—Christine Bader, Author, *The Evolution of a Corporate Idealist: When Girl Meets Oil*

"'Invisible' innovations are already changing how we live—ultimately will it be for better or for worse? Koulopoulos takes a deep look behind the curtain of what is shaping our future world and envisions what the next era may look like (spoiler alert: no flying cars). If you wonder how far off the world portrayed by *Minority Report*, *Her* and *Black Mirror* really is, then this book is a must read."

—Bridget Fahrland, SVP,
Client Strategy, FLUID

"Self-driving cars. Precision medicine. Every moment and movement of your day recorded and analyzed. Orwellian dystopia or a Shakespearean brave new world? Thomas Koulopoulos and George Achillias dissect the present and envision the future. A most enticing read!"

—Vasileios Arsenios Lioutas, Associate
professor Harvard medical school,
Neurologist Beth Israel Hospital

"*Revealing the Invisible* provides a brilliant thought avenue which everyone who is using any online medium should explore: the idea that data is now a commodity which will help power the AI uber machines of the future. Whoever understands the value and implications holds the key to some of the most important shifts to change the years to come; this book can help you get there."

—Alexandra Spiliotopoulou, Digital
Strategy Lead at Merkle Periscopix

"As a marketer, I love to people watch. Passively watching strangers do their shopping, dating, eating, and talking. This has always been part of my marketing training. Physical observational research is set to become outdated though. Thomas Koulopoulos and George Achillias startlingly explain how our [invisible] behaviors will become the most valuable commodity in the 21st century, so we won't physically observe it. A must read for all marketers and people watchers."

—Darren Oddie, Strategy Director Wipro Digital

"As we enter a new era, we are being told that our data/attention/time is the new currency. But it all comes down to our behavior. Learning how to behave is learning how to navigate. But first, we need to see the invisible spectrum, where the future is being shaped—a combination of Plato's cave and Elon Musk's R&D labs. That's where this book comes handy."

—Maria Kokidou, Content & Innovation Strategist at Foundation

"A highly probable future. Visible or not."

—Filippos Zakopoulos, Partner at Foundation

"Humans have always craved for crystal balls, the holy grail of insights into future selves and the future world. Yet now, we seem to be closer than ever. Will big brother be watching us all the time? Will he be able to control us more than before? Will he be able to protect us better? And if machines ever match human intelligence, will we be able to control them? Koulopoulos and Achillias deliver excellent cognitive gymnastics for those who seek answers to create their own version of the truth."

—Piotr Chmielewski, Director of Business Development at ADB

"In the same engaging manner with which he speaks, Tom provides a compelling view of what will actually matter in the future. *Revealing the Invisible* is the book you need: a well-researched, fact-based, understandable guide to how our behaviors are the key to unlocking the future potential in both our lives and in the workplace."

—Robby Riggs, Author *Counter Mentor Leadership: How to Unlock the Potential of the 4-Generation Workplace*

"The abundance of trails that we leave behind every day is reshaping the ways we interact with our digital environment and the way it interacts with us. Big data, AI, behavioral economics, are everywhere. And there is more to come. *Revealing the Invisible* is trying to put all these things into context. A long overdue attempt to reshape perceptions and understanding of technology that will change everything we knew so far about human behavior. A definite must for everyone working in business, marketing, finance, pretty much anyone trying to figure out how the 4th industrial revolution is being implemented."

—Stavros Kontaksis, CEO
Giraffes in the Kitchen

"Koulopoulos' and Achillias' new book is a tour-de-force on the next stage of the Human-Machine relationships and what it means for the social and economic enterprise. Like a pro-boxer, the book delivers punch after punch, anecdote after anecdote, fact after fact until you plead submission and accept what you already knew but weren't sure how to articulate. The invisible impact of AI and autonomous devices cannot be overstated. If even just one CEO reads this book and fundamentally pivots his business model, nay, changes the business to a new industry, this book will have achieved what it set out to do. Wake you up."

—Suresh Kumar, Director
of Engineering, Wipro

"*Revealing the Invisible* is a future-focused analysis rooted in a firm grasp of the past. The book addresses the fundamental shift to consumer-as-commodity. It traces this transition historically and in doing so lays a balanced foundation of where the future *could* go. Tom and George avoid both generalization and speculation in their approach, seeking to understand, objectively, the pros and cons of the new status quo of the individual as the product. In doing so, they surpass the reductionist analyses that praise without question or rabidly resist the unfolding future. Tom and George pave a sober middle ground to interpreting future progress in terms of overall net benefits. A must read to those looking for a thoughtful and nuanced analysis of future trends."

—**Matthew Bemis, EY**

"Our society is hungry to explore—we want to understand where we are going. Koulopoulos and Achillias build on this desire, grounding big technological trends in factual truth. *Revealing the Invisible* takes it even a step further exploring the short-, mid- and long-term impact of these trends, giving the reader a thoughtful outline of what to expect, how it will impact our lives, and areas we should watch out. This book is an absolute must read for all modern explorers who desire to understand where the journey is going and who want to be an active part in shaping our society's future."

—**Matthaeus Kala, Google Global Agency Business & Commercial Lead**

HOW OUR HIDDEN BEHAVIORS
ARE BECOMING THE MOST VALUABLE
COMMODITY OF THE 21ST CENTURY

REVEALING
THE
INVISIBLE

Thomas Koulopoulos
with George Achillias

A POST HILL PRESS BOOK

ISBN: 978-1-68261-619-2
ISBN (eBook): 978-1-68261-620-8

Post Hill Press
New York • Nashville
posthillpress.com

Published in the United States of America

ACKNOWLEDGMENTS

Writing a book is in some ways a lonely undertaking. The solitude required to organize complex thoughts, conduct research, and stare at blank pages is a necessary part of the writing process. There are the times you lose yourself in the writing; the book swallows you up whole as the line that separates the words in your head from the ones on the page blurs into one continuum of consciousness. It can be a delightful escape when ideas flow back and forth effortlessly. It can also be terrifying when you hit the inevitable blocks where ideas freeze up like cold water pipes in a New England winter.

Luckily, no book—at least not one that covers as much diverse ground as this one—can be written in isolation. It is rich with collaboration and contributions from hundreds of people who form an immense circle of influence, which ultimately provides the knowledge, encouragement, and support to write. Acknowledging each of these contributors in a few paragraphs is folly, because there are always far too many people to thank and they have each been a critical part of the process.

Still, I am compelled to at least make the effort to acknowledge some of the individuals who were especially gracious in giving of their time, energy, and experience to help make this book possible.

First, I am indebted to John Willig, my literary agent for nearly 20 years. John was a tireless supporter of this work, but more importantly, John has been a good friend whose council and guidance on the rapidly changing world of publishing is without peer. The subject matter of this book was well ahead of the curve when John first reviewed it. And while being ahead of the curve is a good thing when you're dealing with the long timelines of publishing, it can also be exceedingly difficult to convince publishers that your ideas will resonate with the marketplace. Without John's faith, commitment, and perseverance this book simply could not have come to life. Truth be told, if I have a greatest fear it is that John will retire before I do!

A debt of gratitude is also owed to the great team at Post Hill Press, especially our editors, Mike Lewis, Maddie Sturgeon, Billie Brownell, and Kate Post. Mike and Post Hill immediately saw the promise of the book soon after seeing the proposal, and they dedicated themselves to bringing it to market. Post Hill Press captures the essence of the sorts of nimble, smart, and incredibly committed organizations that we talk about in the book. Few industries have been as challenged and reshaped as much as that of publishing over the past few decades. There are more options than there ever have been for authors. However, it still takes a dedicated team of professionals to publish a quality book. Which is why having a publisher, like Post Hill, who gets it and has a team that stands behind the book, is more critical than ever.

ACKNOWLEDGMENTS

Two of the core concepts in the book, emergence and ecosystems, came from long conversations and collaboration with two individuals who were instrumental in enlightening and shaping my thinking about the future.

The idea of emergent problems and much of the thinking in Chapter 2 came from my good friend Jim Hays at aspiregroup.com who first introduced me to the work of Karl Popper and his wonderful depiction of the difference between clock and cloud problems. Jim is one of those rare people who has the ability to simplify, with clarity and precision, the complex challenges that befuddle most people. His insights into how the nature of problem solving has changed and how it will require a new set of skills and a new lens through which to see the challenges ahead was instrumental in developing the underlying narrative of this book.

My friend and collaborator Ralph Wellborn introduced me to what has become a central theme in nearly all of my work over the past three years, that of digital business ecosystems, which is talked about in Chapter 5 and mentioned throughout the book. When Ralph first introduced me to the concept of a digital ecosystem I felt as though a veil had been lifted, allowing me to see what will become one of the central constructs in how we build the organizations of the future. I'll admit that it took me a while to fully appreciate the impact that this concept will have, but without it so much of the super glue that holds this book together would have been missing. Ralph's latest book, *Topple: The End of Firm-Based Strategy and the Rise of New Models for Explosive Growth*, is a manifesto on the future of business ecosystems.

Early drafts of the manuscript were reviewed by my good friend Sunil Malhotra of ideaworks.com. Sunil took the time to read through the manuscript and provide a global perspective. It is rare in life that you come across someone who has both immense intellectual breadth and equal depth in their ability to convey their knowledge. In the many years that I have known Sunil there is not a single conversation that we've had which I do not walk away feeling as though some great mystery has been revealed.

Sincere thanks also to the many people who were interviewed for the book. One of the greatest gifts of writing a book is having access to the amazingly passionate people who you would not otherwise meet, but who are the true revolutionaries shaping the future. You will see them quoted throughout the pages ahead and I hope you can feel their passion and drive, and I hope this book does justice to the grandeur of their vision. The naysayers will always scream from the rooftops of the past as the builders quietly work at constructing the foundation of the future. But it is this ground zero enthusiasm and optimism that gives me hope in a future whose advantages will far outweigh any of the obstacles we will face.

So much of the inspiration for the ideas and the trajectory of this book came from my colleague, co-author, and dear friend George Achillias. I met George when he approached me almost ten years ago as an MBA student. I was immediately struck by his wide-eyed enthusiasm and impressive ability to see deep into the future. What I didn't know at the time was how accomplished he already was as an entrepreneur, nuclear physicist, and technology guru. His insights do not simply look at what comes next but more importantly what comes *after* what comes next. George was constantly stretching my horizons as we wrote the book—challenging me to look well beyond the obvious trends to the inevitable trajectory of the technologies that are revealing the invisible. Many of the ideas in the book evolved out of the conversations we had over the years, from being among the first group of Explorers for Google Glass to discussing the emergence of emotional computing. Although this journey started with his request for my mentorship, it has evolved into an exciting collaboration that has helped us both see the path ahead with much greater clarity.

Finally, to our many friends and to our families, who gave encouragement and emotional support, any acknowledgment seems far too little to offer as recompense for their supportive and loving presence in our lives. Authors come off as having an abundance of confidence in their ideas and very thick skin. While some of that is necessary if you are to put your ideas out there, beneath the thick exterior most of us are rather fragile creatures. We live for the opportunity to share what we know, or at least what we think we know, with others. It is a pathology whose only known therapy is to write. At times the accolades for our work are adequate to keep us writing, but just as often we hit the dreaded but inevitable writer's wall. It is then that we need those closest to us to remind us that we write because we need to, because it is simply who we are.

Pulitzer Prize-winning author Junot Diaz once said, "A writer is a writer because, even when there is no hope, when nothing you do shows any sign of promise, you keep writing anyway." From George to his lovely wife Isabella for her dedication and support, and from me to my amazing children Mia and Adam, whose brilliance and promise gives me a front row view into the wonder of the future, you inspire us to keep building, keep hoping, and keep writing. Thank you.

—Tom Koulopoulos
Boston 1/2018

To Mia and Adam,
for revealing to me life's greatest gifts.
Through your bright eyes and uncluttered minds
I've seen more than I'd ever imagined.

In memory of Andreas,
whose encouragement, kind heart,
brilliant mind, and love of words
revealed to me a universe of endless wonders.

CONTENTS

INTRODUCTION

*To be human is to suffer from a peculiar congenital blindness:
On the precipice of any great change, we can see with
terrifying clarity the familiar firm footing we stand to lose,
but we fill the abyss of the unfamiliar before us with dread at
the potential loss rather than jubilation over the potential gain
of gladnesses and gratifications we fail to envision
because we haven't yet experienced them.*[1]
—*Maria Popova*

The world is at the precipice of one of the most dramatic shifts in history: the transition from an industrial society to one that is based on a deep understanding of an entirely new form of knowledge capital, behavior—our behaviors as well as those of the intelligent machines that we are building.

Our premise in writing this book was simple; the industrial model on which we have built our economy, businesses, and society was based on a mechanized and orderly view of the world. It anonymized us as members of faceless markets. The speed of its growth created enormous friction from complexity and regulations, and had a deep impact on our ecosystems by straining natural resources.

The nineteenth and twentieth century industrial era created enormous engines of mass production which were intended to develop and deliver products and services that could be easily replicated for mass markets. It worked. Since 1800, population grew from one billion to seven billion people. Global per person GDP grew from one thousand six hundred sixty-nine dollars to over ten thousand dollars.[2] In the USA, per person GDP rose from two thousand four hundred dollars to over sixty thousand dollars, a twenty-five-fold increase.[3]

The one-size-fits-all mass production approach to manufacturing allowed us to scale transportation, housing, consumerism, commerce, healthcare, education, and social programs at a rate the world had never seen.

But the mechanized industrial era model is reaching its limits. It has become bloated and inefficient and is no longer a viable or sustainable model with which to support ten billion people. We need to shift from a rigid mechanical approach of "solving" problems to one that can deal with the behaviors of emergent and uncertain systems that are constantly evolving and fundamentally "unsolvable."

Don't get us wrong; we're not proposing that industrial models should be discarded en masse. Improvements in automation, production, supply chains, distribution, and transportation will continue to incrementally increase productivity, but expecting incrementalism and the same approaches we've used to solve the problems of the last two hundred years to continue for another two hundred is a recipe for economic, ecological, and social collapse.

At the core of this transition, and this book, are two sets of disruptors: new technologies, such as artificial intelligence (AI) and autonomous devices which will be able to understand the behaviors of all things at a level of detail humans never could; and new ways of thinking about some of the most basic frameworks of the industrial era: how we problem solve; how we transport goods and people; how we protect our intellectual, real, and digital property; how we create hyper-personalized products and loyal brands aligned with our needs and values.

Our objective is to challenge many of the tenets of how we do business that we've accepted as a necessary friction of the industrialized world. And, while we're at it, to dispatch many of the fears, which we've also bought into, about the technologies and the changes to come.

But here's what's unique about so many of the changes that are about to take place, and which we talk about in the book: they are pretty much invisible. To see them requires peeling away layers of perceptions and assumptions that hide the underlying patterns which drive behaviors.

Unlike many of the great advances of the past two hundred years—the advent of flight, the automobile, the assembly line and factory automation, medical diagnostics and therapies—the most profound and revolutionary technologies and mechanisms for change over the next two hundred will be ones that we can't even see. They will be embedded, buried deep inside of devices that will not look much different than they look today.

We will still have automobiles, trucks, buses, planes, boats, and trains. Computers will still run most of our businesses and processes. We will still buy and sell products and services online, in stores, and at the corner grocer. We will still live in homes and apartments and work in office buildings. Currency will still run global commerce. Companies will still issue equity to owners and investors. Factories will continue to churn out goods, focus on productivity improvements, and optimize global supply chains. And the chaos of an uncertain world will still loom large over all our decisions.

It doesn't sound like the future we'd once been promised, does it? No flying automobiles to whisk us across town, no robot servants to pick up after us, no teleporters to zap us instantly from one continent—or planet—to another.

Nearly every version of the future has focused on the "look," the Jetsonian illustration of personal flying saucers, mechanical pets and maids, and glistening cities suspended among the clouds.[4] We're a visual species; images sell.

But stop and think about the trajectory of invention and the advances of the past sixty years. Along with the visible innovations we're all familiar with, there have been an increasing number that are invisible: electricity, radio, the transistor, software, wireless, new chemicals, and genomics. These have all had a revolutionary impact on our lives and yet few of us would know a transistor if it landed in the palm of our hand, where, not coincidentally, you are holding a few hundred million of them right now if you happen to be reading this book in its digital form.

The changes in our world are increasingly being driven by invisible innovations. In some cases, those innovations are powered by AI or learning machines that monitor their environment, adapt, and make myriad small decisions, as is the case with driverless cars. In other cases, those innovations result from observing and understanding patterns in our behaviors and those of the many natural and manmade systems that surround us. In almost all cases we are totally unaware of what's going on beyond our line of sight. What changes is not necessarily what we see but rather the invisible that shapes what we experience.

So, why even bother revealing these invisible forces? Isn't it enough to simply know that they work? After all, few of us know or care how a transistor works—it just does. We need to reveal the invisible because we're no longer talking about mechanical devices that act purely on our instructions and have no awareness of us, that do what they're told and no more than that. The sorts of technologies that we'll be talking about have the capacity to develop an awareness of us and the context of their world. They can make decisions on their own that will have profound effects on our society, our businesses, and our lives. They will learn and evolve. They threaten to tread on some of our most sacred turf—our privacy—by revealing our most intimate thoughts and behaviors. In short, they will disrupt the world like never before.

The challenge in understanding these technologies is that we will both overestimate their risk and underestimate their value. For instance, according to the American Automobile Association (AAA) 78 percent of people fear autonomous vehicles. Yet, 59 percent want the features of an autonomous automobile in their next car. The contradiction speaks to how little we know about what the risks and benefits of an autonomous vehicle really are.

At the same time a recent Pew Research Center study of four hundred sixty-one adults found that across multiple categories of behavioral tracking—ranging from store loyalty cards, to health records, to video observation, to social media and vehicle tracking for insurance—there was a consistently even split between those who were concerned about privacy and those who were not.[5] In each case respondents were told that they would receive some benefit in exchange for behavioral data, such as unspecified discounts or product/service recommendations. So, for half of us, that's enough to give up at least some of our privacy.

We are clearly at a crossroads, and in no small part, because we're not entirely sure what the benefits and risks of AI really are. As individuals, employees, customers, business owners, and leaders, we need to get a better grasp on how the invisible is going to shape the future and how it's going to shape us.

Although the phenomenon of revealing the invisible applies to an incredibly broad set of scenarios, we've chosen several that we feel best illustrate the challenge and opportunity ahead. These are the sea-change scenarios which we believe will set the compass for navigating this unchartered future. Here are just some of the invisible forces we'll focus on.

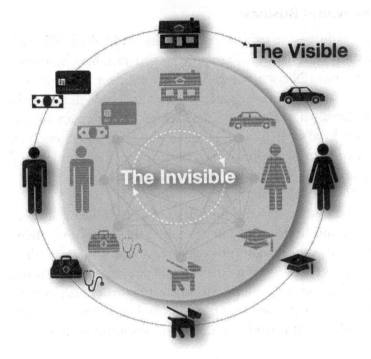

Illustration 1.0 – The Invisible

When we talk about revealing the invisible, we are referring to the ability to understand the digital behaviors of not only ourselves but also of the people, devices, objects, and institutions we interact with. Each of these can have a digital-self or digital twin (the collection of its digitized behaviors) that interacts with other digital objects. The complex patterns of interactions among these objects may appear invisible or obscure to us, and radically different that the biases we have of how the visible world operates but algorithms and AI can easily understand the patterns they form and then predict future behaviors. We believe that the greatest value of innovation for the next one hundred years will come from understanding and leveraging revealing "The Invisible" on this illustration.

Behavioral Business

The industrial era depersonalized the individual. We each became part of a demographic, a generation, a consumer grouping, a Nielsen rating. We can no longer think of markets as anonymous categories defined by crude demographics. Anytown USA, where the average family, in an average house, lived with 2½ above average children, was a fiction we created to make up for the fact that we could not understand the behaviors and needs of each individual.

No longer.

Disruptive new technologies are already being used to collect and understand our once invisible behaviors, giving us unimagined insight into our lives across a vast new digital ecosystem of social media, mobile devices, wearables, and embedded sensors. All of this is creating an opportunity to deliver hyper-personalized products and experiences for each individual that provide enduring and sustainable value.

Artificial Intelligence

It's not just human behaviors that are being captured and analyzed. In the very near future every person and digital device will have its own digital-self—a digital twin which can communicate, interact, and collaborate with other digital entities. Autonomous vehicles, smart devices, and intelligent machines will all exhibit their own behaviors. They will learn and evolve to better understand complex patterns in how the world behaves that are otherwise invisible to us.

But we fear AI. It's what Elon Musk, CEO of Tesla, has referred to as "Summoning the demon." In this book, we'll attempt to dispel the fear that often accompanies AI. In fact, our objective is to prove that we need AI as an indispensable collaborator and that the risk of not having it is far greater than any threat it poses.

Autonomous Devices

One of the areas where so much of what we'll talk about will be most obvious is in the evolution of autonomous devices, and most notably autonomous vehicles. Transportation is the greatest artifact of the industrial age. Nothing has fueled commerce, urbanization, and automation more than the vehicles that transport us, our goods, and our raw materials. It's also the greatest contributor to carbon emissions, the leading cause of death, and one of the most inefficient uses of capital for the individual owner.[6]

At the same time, we've bought into a model of what a car should be and how its value is measured. From the notion of strapping ourselves into a cockpit, to the legroom defined (and constrained) by a forward-facing passenger configuration, to the head-bobbing suspension of a high-performance sports car, we value a car based on preconceived notions of what we should want.

The single greatest impact of autonomous vehicles will be in how they redefine our notion of what a car is, how it should be used, and how it behaves, while also remobilizing the world for efficient, safe, and ecologically sustainable transportation of ten billion people, most of whom would have no access to the current and historical model of what a car should be.

Digital Ecosystems

The industrial era created engines of production that were laden with inefficiency. Like large gears grinding against each other in the boiler room of an enormous ocean liner, commerce wasn't pretty or easy. It required constant manual intervention and created friction in the form of convoluted processes, regulations, middlemen, and brokers that we simply accepted as part of the way an industrial society worked. Turning these vessels around to navigate new markets and meet new needs was about as responsive and effective as steering the *Titanic*, at full throttle in the dark, clear of an iceberg. Incumbent companies in large established industries would stare at the future high upon their crow's nest asking, "Why isn't she turning?" as they braced for an unavoidable impact.

Worse yet, we built entire industries to employ people whose jobs depended on the existence and inefficiency of friction—financial institutions, government regulatory bodies, agents, and middlemen whose purpose was not to reduce friction but to live off its heat.

The industrial era model was not built for today's digital technologies or marketplace. If you need proof, consider this question: if you had the ability to redesign your company from scratch, on a clean sheet of paper, would it look the way it does now? Unless your company is less than ten years old, it's highly unlikely it would. In fact, a recent report from Credit Suisse pointed out that "The average age of a company listed on the S&P 500 has fallen from almost sixty years old in the 1950s to less than twenty years [in 2017]."[7]

Increasingly complex coordination of business partner networks, excessive regulation, an inability to adapt quickly, the lack of deep knowledge of individual customers, and cumbersome customer experiences have created an opportunity of immense scale to drive out this friction by creating entirely new digital ecosystems focused specifically on the needs of each individual.

All these transformations—and others that we'll talk about—will be disruptive, more so than we can presently foresee. But they will also bring benefits that are equally difficult to predict. The good news is that none of this is a sudden shift; it has been and will continue to occur incrementally—at times with great fanfare, at other times to great protest—and sometimes in ways that are barely noticeable. For example:

- Autonomous vehicles will dramatically decrease the ecological impact of transportation, while creating unprecedented safety, mobility, and an entirely new in-car experience.
- Devices embedded with AI will anticipate our needs, predict illness, and improve our well-being.
- Hyper-personalized healthcare will match therapies to our individual genomes.
- Concepts such as brand loyalty will be turned on their heads as companies compete to find ways that they can use behavioral knowledge to prove their loyalty to each individual consumer.
- AI will begin to solve some of the most pressing and protracted problems of our time by identifying otherwise invisible patterns of behavior in the complex natural and manmade systems that surround us.

- The elimination of the friction in new digital ecosystems will transform rigid industrial age businesses into responsive, adaptive, customer-centered ecosystem experiences.

Does all this sound a bit far-fetched? Only to the degree that you discount our ability to recreate the world of the future. For instance, what would your reaction be if we were to tell you that within one hundred years the percentage of people employed in the knowledge economy would dwindle by 95 percent? Yet, that's exactly what happened to agricultural employment in the USA over the last one hundred years, dropping from 38 percent of overall employment in 1900 to only 2 percent today, while agricultural output increased 2000 percent.[8] Not impressed? What if we were to claim that the number of computer devices would increase by nine orders of magnitude within the next seventy years? Again, it seems absurd, and yet that's exactly what's happened over the last seventy years.[9]

That is the sort of change that we will be laying the groundwork for: a journey into a future that will reshape business and society.

It's a journey that admittedly meanders on occasion into the many tangents of the future, but the future is never a straight line. We'll try to keep the flights of fancy to a minimum—no teleporters, flying cars, and cities in the clouds—but this is a story that's woven from many diverse threads, and we're going to do our best to illuminate that entire tapestry. Most importantly, everything we're describing in the pages to follow is already well underway. The question, of course, is when will it all be here? When will we have arrived?

What determines how fast any of these ideas find their way into the mainstream of our world, our businesses, and our lives won't be the underlying technologies, but our ability to embrace the new behaviors that they will bring. If history is any indication, that's often sooner than we think.

So, with that as prelude, let's start revealing the invisible.

How Behavior Became the New Global Currency

"Men have become the tools of their tools."
—*Henry David Thoreau*

Understanding behavior is the killer app of the 21st century.

Which is why we're starting the first chapter of this book by looking at how businesses are doing just that, in leveraging what is fast becoming the single most valuable and coveted commodity of the 21st century—*you*.

Your behaviors, in the digital world and in the real world, are being captured at unprecedented rates and then stored and analyzed in vast warehouses that have become digital goldmines. You are being bought and sold to the highest bidder, whose objective is to not only understand you but also to predict your behavior. We are giving up who we are, and our most intimate moments, in an invisible exchange for the ability to use products, services, and apps that promise

24/7 knowledge, connectivity, effortless consumerism, and hyper-personalized experiences.

In the process, behavior is becoming a new form of capital and a cornerstone for new business models and technologies that are being driven by algorithms, which can find deep patterns in everything from how you browse the web, to how you shop, to how you exercise and what you eat, to how you drive your car.

Each of us suddenly has a digital-self, which represents the digital collection of behaviors that defines who we are. You don't define your digital-self (at least not consciously), you don't own it (yet), and you do not have access to it. Yet, in many ways, it is the best representation of who you really are: a disembodied, unemotional, always honest version of you based on the way you live your life minute to minute.

On the surface it seems like a very bad trade off—revealing ourselves in return for some, as of yet, unknown benefit. And yet, we gladly give up this information—sometimes knowingly, but most times invisibly. 60 percent of the US population has a Gmail account (Google's free email service). Yet, we seriously doubt that even 6 percent of those people would walk up to a total stranger on the street, hand over their email history for the past year and say, "Here are my most intimate thoughts and communications—have fun!" Guess what? Google isn't giving anything away. You're paying for it with the currency of your behaviors.

Consider that in a typical day over two hundred fifty data points about your life and your behavior are being captured from the websites you visit, your smartphone and its apps, sensors in your home, electronic devices you interact with, your car, and even the movement of your eyes as you scan the shelves at the grocery store.[10]

By the year 2020, about 1.7 megabytes of new information will be created every second for every human being on the planet.[11] An amazing 90 percent of the data in the world today has been created in the last two years. This data comes from everywhere: sensors used to gather shopping behaviours, posts to social media sites, digital pictures and videos, purchase transactions, cell phone location data, and GPS to name a few.

In 2010 a German politician, Malte Spitz, decided he wanted to find out just how much data Deutsche Telekom knew about his mobile phone usage. He sued for access to the data and, in a bold move to help illustrate just how detailed the information was, he provided his entire six-month history *to ZEIT ONLINE*, which created an amazingly detailed interactive map of Spitz's phone calls, text messages, tweets, posts, and websites visited.[12] Spitz's data has over three hundred thousand individual datapoints, or about two thousand per day. And this is only for his mobile phone and publicly available web browsing history.

Just how valuable is all this data? Estimates vary widely from just under a dollar to no more than twelve dollars per person.[13] It doesn't sound like much at all—the equivalent value of a small pizza, or perhaps just a slice if you happen to be in NYC. It's reminiscent of the age-old game of valuing a human being based on the aggregate cost of a body's chemical elements, which comes out to about four dollars and fifty cents.[14] Clearly, few of us would accept that value as an accurate accounting of our worth as conscious, productive human beings. The same applies to the value of your digital-self.

Although it may cost twelve dollars to acquire the data that makes up your digital-self, it's value to the companies that own it is at least twenty times that, based on how much those companies are worth.

A better measure might be to look at the market capitalization of major social media companies and contrast that with the number of users. As shown in Illustration 1.1, this offers a rather consistent average of about one hundred dollars per user.

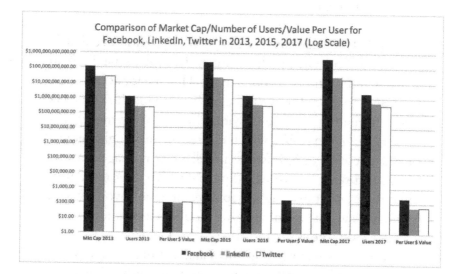

Illustration 1.1 – The value of your digital-self

Coming up with a value for what your digital behaviors are worth is exceptionally difficult to do at this early stage of behavioral business. However, the best ballpark may be to look at the market capitalization of leading social media players and determine a value based on the number of users they each have. The result, shown in this chart (log scale), provides a range from fifty to two hundred dollars. Clearly, your digital-self will consist of much more than just the limited data that any of these social media platforms has about you. But this is at least a baseline.

But one hundred or even two hundred dollars seems paltry. The truth is that the ongoing value of owning who you are is something no one has yet been able to calculate.

But the idea of capturing behaviors and having a digital-self doesn't stop with who you are. We envision a future in which autonomous vehicles, intelligent devices, and machines that learn will also have a digital-self (we'll call them a digital-twin). Your car will exhibit behaviors as the AI that powers its decisions and actions forms its own vast collection of experiences.

Today over four terabytes (four thousand gigabytes or four million megabytes) of data are generated by a new car each hour.[15] As we'll describe in Chapter 4, these cars will someday own, maintain, insure, buy, and sell themselves. Yes, it's hard to grasp but, as we'll see, nearly all of the components needed to do this, along with every other technology we will describe in the book, are already here.

You only need to look at how toddlers are responding to technology to see how behavior is becoming a pervasive part of what we expect in all of our interactions. We've all seen children barely out of diapers trying to swipe at a magazine or a book and looking puzzled or frustrated by the fact that it isn't responding to their touch the way a tablet or smartphone would. In their eyes, the world should exhibit behaviors and intelligence; a magazine is a defective iPad. If it doesn't behave, it must be broken.

But, before we get too far ahead of ourselves it's worth digressing a bit and asking how it is that we became the product.

The Razor's Edge

In 1895 King Gillette (yes, that really was his first name) had the bright idea to trade in his expensive, bulky, and high maintenance straight edge razor for something that would not only be far less expensive but also infinitely easier to use for the common man. His idea, the disposable razor blade, was anything but an overnight success. It wasn't until he was able to land a contract to supply the US army with razors and blades that things started to look up. When soldiers came back home they would inevitably bring back their Gillette razors, but usually without more than a few blades.

This is where the story of Gillette's success diverges. One version has it that at first Gillette began giving the blades away for free, hoping that this would lead to more sales of expensive razors (the handles). It didn't take long for Gillette to come to the realization that the opposite was true; once someone had purchased a Gillette razor, the blades became indispensable. "Give the razor away and make money forever from the blades" is the razors-and-blades model familiar to anyone who's taken a basic college level business or marketing class.

The other, more practical explanation is actually much more complicated, involving patents that Gillette used to lock out competition for both razors and blades long enough for Gillette to establish an incredible brand loyalty among its users who believed that only Gillette blades were right for Gillette razors, allowing Gillette to price itself as a premium brand and a market leader for the next one hundred years.

Whatever Gillette's actual strategy, razors-and-blades has become a standard business model used by countless other companies and industries. We've seen it used in everything from Sony's Walkman and cassettes, to PlayStation video game consoles and game cartridges, to inkjet printers and ink cartridges, to the iPhone and apps.

For instance, in 2016 Apple made nearly thirty billion dollars in sales from its app store compared with about two hundred billion dollars for total iPhone sales. [16] While, in Apple's case, the "razor" (the iPhone) accounts for more overall sales revenue, it could be argued that actual profit on the "razor blades" (apps and services) are closing in and will likely be the single greatest contributor to Apple's bottom line, since most of that revenue is from third party apps that cost Apple nothing to develop but on which Apple earns a 30 percent royalty.

But something peculiar happened to the razors-and-blades model in the late 1990s, when the internet first started to enter the mainstream. (Think of the internet as the razor.) One of the internet's promises was to do something similar to "blades" with software applications, but on much more ambitious scale.

The intent was to provide a platform—the internet—that would be free and accessible to everyone, at least everyone with a device from which to access the internet. This differed from the ownership economics that razors-and-blades was based on because there was no single company that would profit from this idea, but as we'll see, that would soon change.

How We Became the Blades

In the 1990s a new form of software began to emerge. Driven by the promise of the internet's universal accessibility and an insatiable demand for anything internet related, a category of companies that came to be called the dot-coms quickly staked out their claims in this new territory with free applications that would allow you to do everything from buy books to sell your used shoes. The dot-com idea spread wildly, threatening to dismantle industries by getting rid of intermediaries, such as brick-and-mortar stores, car dealerships, publishers, video rental outlets, and a host of other industry players whose only value was in being the middle man.

The dot-com bubble of hype and speculation finally popped in 2000, wiping out five trillion dollars in stock market value. The dot-com phenomenon clearly took on all the characteristics of a speculative bubble, but that was not the only reason it failed. Even in the absence of speculative investing, the dot-com model was flawed. What undermined nearly every dot-com is what was referred to as "capturing eyeballs." The implied value of a dot-com was based on the number of people that it could get to visit its website. The problem was that monetizing eyeballs wasn't all that easy—in part because ecommerce (buying and selling over the internet) was still nascent and hardly without friction, but in larger part because the real value of the "eyeballs" wasn't yet clear. The dot-coms were trying to give away the razor but they hadn't quite figured out what the blades were.

But a few super-adaptive strains of the dot-com phenomenon, such as Amazon, Google, and Facebook survived the purge. And they all shared a very similar DNA when it came to the long-term value of their business, namely that they were able to change the way they created value.

Rather than try to make money from their largest population of customers—the eyeballs, and the people who used their applications for the purpose they were intended—they turned the customer into the product. The idea was brilliant and simple. We became the blades! The premise was that the better you knew the behaviors of your users, the better you could target your advertising, products, and influence to drive the sales of other products and services—in some cases, products that your users never knew they wanted.

This was a sea-change in how we thought about markets. For the past two hundred years we had played a guessing game—trying to reveal the invisible forces that drive markets and society by projecting the needs of the masses from the opinions of the few through the use of focus groups, surveys, broad demographic categories, seasonal trends, and many more barometers that help us to understand and segment large markets.

Today we are at the precipice of an era in which we will be able to target products, services, entertainment, and even political campaigns to the preferences of each individual. We'll call it hyper-personalization in Chapter 7; the ability to understand each individual through his or her online and offline behaviors in ways they may not even understand themselves. By the way, don't confuse this with personalization, which is just enhancing a generic marketing campaign or a product to include a very slight modification such as the addition of someone's name.

At its core this doesn't appear to be a new model. Twentieth century media empires were built on selling advertisers access to target markets defined by extensive demographics. The richest person in the world in the early twentieth century wasn't an oil or steal magnate; it was William Hearst, who created what was the world's largest advertising empire through a chain of nearly thirty newspapers in major American cities at its peak.

The demographics used by mass media were based on large populations not on individuals. Nielsen's television ratings could tell you how many males between the ages of thirty and forty with a household income of fifty thousand dollars to sixty thousand dollars who drove a pickup truck were watching the Super Bowl, but they couldn't tell you if

"I" was watching the Super Bowl, or for that matter, *why* I watched the Super Bowl.

The modern-day successor to mass media demographics was what came to be called Big Data. But Big Data didn't understand you; it simply placed you in a pool of similar behaviors. Big Data could tell a grocery store that men between the age of twenty to thirty would often buy beer and diapers in the same trip to the grocery store on a Saturday afternoon but it couldn't tell you which of those men watched the football game on ESPN while simultaneously searching Google for ways to calm a crying newborn.

As we'll see throughout this book, that subtle shift from knowing a market to knowing a person is one of the single most profound changes in how value is going to be created in the future. The race to capture as much information about every person on the planet had begun.

However, there was one really big problem. Your digital-self (again, the digital collection of behaviors that defines you) was still horribly disconnected with no single owner to make sense of it all.

Your digital behaviors were scattered about across a vast ecosystem of applications, platforms, devices, and places that were all trying to capture as much information about you as possible. Amazon knew what you purchased through Amazon; Google knew what you searched for in Google; GM knew where and how you drove a car with OnStar; Target knew which Target store aisles and departments you spent the most time and money in; Travelocity knew where you traveled and how you got there as long as you booked travel through Travelocity; Apple knew how far you'd walked and how well you'd slept if you had an iPhone; Facebook knew what kind of pets you had, what foods you liked, and what your mood was based on what you posted on Facebook; iRobot knew how you'd rearranged your furniture if you used a Roomba vacuum. Hundreds or thousands of behaviors you didn't think twice about, behaviors which you thought were invisible to anyone but yourself, were suddenly being tracked and traded by companies which in many cases you'd never heard of.

Suddenly web-based companies—such as Amazon, Netflix, and Spotify—started making recommendations based on what you had already purchased or searched for. Sometimes it worked, but most times it was laughable. Did you really need yet another pair of special eclipse glasses two weeks after an eclipse had taken place?

Then something changed. Ads started to pop up in our web browsers that were related to our email conversations, Google searches, or browsing habits on the web. What was especially odd was that the website the ads showed up on didn't necessarily have any connection to the ads. If you had been researching the prices of new storm doors on Home Depot's website, you might see an ad for storm doors show up while you're on a website about pets. At first it seemed like a coincidence and then it just became plain old creepy. It was about to get even creepier.

Around 2008–2009, companies such as Facebook began tracking the behaviors of their users across other websites. In other words, you didn't have to be on Facebook.com for Facebook to track your web behaviors. An early attempt at this was Facebooks' project Beacon, which ended up the target of a class action lawsuit that forced the company to shutter Beacon along with a public apology from its CEO Mark Zuckerberg.[17]

We've made a lot of mistakes building this feature, but we've made even more with how we've handled them. We simply did a bad job with this release, and I apologize for it...Instead of acting quickly, we took too long to decide on the right solution. I'm not proud of the way we've handled this situation and I know we can do better.

At the same time Facebook was developing, and soon launched, Connect, a single login application interface that could be used by third-party applications to allow their users to login with their Facebook credentials. Connect took off, in large part because it offered users who were tired of remembering their username and password for dozens of apps a way to sign onto all of them with their Facebook credentials. However, behind the scenes, Connect provided a channel through which to also share behavioral data about users across numerous applications.

There was more. Companies known as data brokers, such as Quantcast, Acxiom, Corelogic, Datalogix, eBureau, ID Analytics, Intelius, PeekYou, Rapleaf, and Recorded Future—many of which were already collecting massive amounts of data about individuals from offline as well as online sources—began using what are known as cookies (or super cookies) to link this data to each individual. According to a study conducted by the FTC, up to two hundred twenty data points about you were being collected by these companies. The data ranged from basic information about your address and location, to your SSN and driver's license number, to your usage of social media, to which over-the-counter medications you were taking.[18]

Creepy? Perhaps, but consider how easy it is to collect this data. 3.4 billion people worldwide now have smartphones and, based on research we conducted for this book, 80 percent of smartphone users are never farther than three feet from their phone at any time, day or night. Our cars, our homes, even our beds are being equipped with sensors. Our behaviors—all of them—are suddenly naked and fully visible in ways we have barely begun to realize. Like it or not this is the new normal; the cloak of demographic anonymity has been forever lifted. Marketing is no longer about understanding a market segment; it is about understanding *you*.

You're not alone if all of this is starting to seem like an ominous Orwellian scenario in which our invisible behaviors are used to somehow create a windfall for the companies that own them. When we first set out to write this book, one colleague suggested that the title should be *Dark Digital*, with the connotation being that there was something nefarious lurking below the surface that needed to be revealed (or better yet, exposed) about how companies were turning into Big Brother. We are anything but naïve about privacy implications—and will spend considerable time describing these and how to best protect our digital-selves—but the focus of this book isn't just on how our behaviors will be used against us, but also on how they will be used to add significant value to our lives, our businesses, and our society.

We also realize that the specter of AI makes revealing our invisible behaviors seem especially threatening. However, our behaviors have become increasingly transparent throughout history. Not because some dark entity was profiting from them, but because greater transparency was something that had far-reaching benefits for society and individuals.

The First Behavioral Technology

One of the first and still most widely used publicly available methods for tracking behavior is GPS. The global positioning system that today uses a series of twenty-four satellites to precisely pinpoint the location of GPS-equipped objects had been used since 1978 by the U.S. Military. The man credited with its invention, Roger Easton, a Naval research physicist, was granted U.S. Patent 3,789,409 on January 29, 1974 for his "Navigation System Using Satellites and Passive Ranging Techniques." Easton had been working on forms of ground-based positioning systems since 1943.[19]

However, it wasn't until 1983, in the aftermath of the Soviet downing of Korean Air flight 007, which had accidentally wandered into Soviet airspace, that U.S. president Ronald Reagan ordered GPS be opened to use by private industry. Although the military had restricted private access to certain GPS data, in 2000 President Bill Clinton made all GPS data accessible to private industry.

We've all been the beneficiaries of GPS in many obvious ways from increased safety, to the effectiveness and speed of first responders, and the ability to locate people and property. But often those benefits have come in unintended ways. For example, dealerships often install GPS tracking devices in vehicles sold in areas where repossession rates are high in order to track a vehicle if the owner falls behind in their payments. These same devices have been used to foil carjackings and kidnappings.

In a well-publicized case, Danny Meng, whose Mercedes was carjacked by the Tsarnaev brothers—who were responsible for the Boston Marathon bombing and the murder of officer Sean Collier in April of 2013—provided police with the login details of his GPS-enabled Mercedes, which resulted in tracking and apprehending the brothers.

GPS has also been embedded into numerous safety and tracking devices. During August of 2015 a Rowlett, Texas kidnapping of a fifteen-year-old girl with Asperger's Syndrome made headlines when her mother tracked her daughter down using the girl's wearable GPS device. The wearable had a built-in microphone, which allowed her mother to listen to the sounds of her daughter struggle with the kidnapper as the assault was taking place—something that would have sounded like pure science fiction in 1980s when private use of GPS was first enabled.[20]

Perhaps one of the most ambitious applications of GPS technology is the FAA's NextGen aviation program, which is replacing ground-based radar with satellite and onboard GPS tracking and full digital communications for all commercial aircraft by 2020.[21] The impact this will have on safety and fuel costs is nearly incalculable. The sum total fuel used yearly by all of the major US airlines is in excess of seventeen billion gallons at a total cost of approximately 25 billion dollars.[22] It's expected that NextGen will cut fuel consumption and emissions by 12 percent yearly—the equivalent of 2.2 million cars a year.

It's hard to deny the benefits and indispensability of GPS from the standpoint of convenience alone, but these stories and thousands more, attest to the greater social and economic value it has had. Which is why it's one of the best examples to date of the tradeoff we willingly make between privacy and transparency, and value. Transparency and the loss of privacy create risk. We can use technology and legal approaches to protect ourselves but there's simply no way to eliminate that risk. In fact, we'll be blunt in acknowledging that risk is increasing substantially with all the technologies and behaviors we're describing in this book. But, at the same time, value is also increasing dramatically. The equation that allows technological progress to continue is a simple one and it's answered by a simple question: does new value significantly exceed new risk?

So, if there's value to be had, why do we continue to fear technology, especially when we've proved time and again that our track record is pretty good at applying new technologies in ways that yield a net positive impact? The reasons fall into two general categories:

1. We measure new technology against an artificial goal of 100 percent accuracy and reliability when the current state of affairs isn't even close to that goal.

We measure the efficiency of the technology against a standard of perfection rather than against the actual benefit it has over whatever the current risks are without the technology. Consider, for example, autonomous cars, which we will delve into much more throughout the book. Many of the arguments against autonomous cars involve scenarios where the car might make a decision that results in injuries or fatalities. It's impossible to avoid every such incident. So, yes, autonomous vehicles will not eliminate all the risks of motor vehicles. However, it is virtually certain that, as a whole, they will be orders of magnitude safer than human drivers. So much so that the ultimate tipping point for driverless cars will likely be economic due to the relatively high cost of insuring a human operating a vehicle over one driven by AI.

2. We measure the known risks of a new technology against unknown benefits.

It is far easier to anticipate the risks (perceived and real) of a new technology than all the future benefits. For example, when GM first rolled out OnStar in 1997, it was inconceivable that it would be used to stop a carjacking. While OnStar does not publish the number of stolen or carjacked vehicles it disables each year, estimates based on some of its early use of the technology in 2007–2008 would put the number in the range of 5–10 percent of all such incidents, or two thousand five hundred to five thousand. (We're not including vehicles that are located with just basic GPS in that number.) Even the popularity of one of OnStar's most frequent early requests, to unlock a car remotely, came as a surprise to GM.

Since we measure a new technology against a standard of perfection and calculate the known risks over the unknown benefits, we are unable to calculate the net positive impact of a new technology until we experience it.

Clearly, some privacy has been lost through the use of GPS, but few of us would disagree that its value to us individually and its overall value to society in creating a safer world more than makes up for that. Again, we are not saying that privacy is an inconsequential issue. It will require new levels of diligence and new means of protection, as we will see throughout the book. But progress is always about the net positive that comes out of any new technology.

This book also isn't a conversation about stopping the advance of technology. That's like staring down a tsunami; the tsunami is always going to win. The tidal wave we should be worried most about isn't technology; it's global population that is expected to grow to 9.8 billon people by 2050. Add to that the fact that we are transitioning the world's population out of developing countries and into the economic mainstream at over one million people per week! That's one billion people in the last two decades with projections that we will increase that to two billion over the next two decades. The question we need to answer is, "How will we feed, clothe, house, transport, care for, and otherwise support these people while also fueling a burgeoning new global economy?"

One thing is certain: we can't simply scale what we have in place today to support tomorrow. It's not only current approaches to mass production, agriculture, and transportation that won't scale, but essential human services as well. According to the world economic forum, it would take three hundred years to bridge the supply-demand gap for doctors in the world at the rate we are educating and licensing new doctors today.

Manufacturing, education, and agriculture would all crumble under the weight of a massive global infrastructure if it continues along the current trajectory of today's industrial age approach to growth. None of this can be stopped if we continue to proceed with business as usual in each of these industries. The limits to growth, if we try to scale the industrial era models we have in place today, would soon overwhelm every industry and nation. Just the shifting demographics of the world's population pyramid to an aging population would overwhelm our already strained social welfare systems. Consider that today the percentage of world population in the twenty-five to twenty-nine-year-old age group is double that of the sixty-five to sixty-nine age group, 7.9 percent versus only 3.1 percent. By 2050 that will have shifted to 6.8 percent and 5.2 percent. And by 2100, 6.1 percent and 5.2 percent. In other words, the five-thousand-year-old framework of a population pyramid is being replaced by a skyscraper with the same number of people in nearly every age grouping.[23] The implications of supporting this new society are profound.

The reality is that we need to accelerate our ability to understand not only the nuanced and invisible behaviors of people, but also machines, ecosystems, and most importantly, the increasing connections between all of these (both digital and physical) much faster than we'd ever imagined. Only by doing that and by using technologies such as AI to find the patterns in these otherwise invisible behaviors will we be able to understand both the complexity of the challenges ahead and their solutions.

That's why, when we talk about revealing invisible behaviors, we mean that all things will have behaviors: you, vehicles, devices, a business, a supply chain, an ecosystem—all of these will be connected to the cloud through sensors that capture every nuance of their context and their behavior. In that avalanche of data, there are clues—invisible to the naked human eye—that will provide insights into how our world and we behave at a level of detailed resolution that will allow us to predict the future in ways we could never have imagined.

As dramatic as this may appear to be, it is not a singular paradigm shift, where one way of looking at a problem is completely replaced by another. Instead we are moving into what we like to think of as a multiparadigm world in which we will need to adopt very different ways of looking at and solving very different challenges. We will not be throwing out what we've learned over the past two hundred years of industrialization. Instead we will be using what we've learned in ways that allow us to continue scaling the industrialized world to meet the demands of ten billion educated, economically engaged, and productive people without destroying the planet and ourselves in the process.

Painting a doomsday scenario of all this change is easy and may appeal to our fears and provide excellent fodder for Hollywood. But it's a one-sided view.

One of the most notable people voicing concern over the destructive potential of AI is Tesla and SpaceX founder Elon Musk, who in a 2017 speech at MIT said, "With artificial intelligence we are summoning the demon." Even Russian President Vladamir Putin has joined the chorus predicting that the first global leader in AI will become "leader of the world."

However, we can just as easily envision countless scenarios, like the ones we've already pointed out, where the level of connectivity and transparency we're describing will significantly enhance and add value to our lives that we will one day wonder how we possibly could have survived without.

In Chapter 8 we'll come back to the discussion of how to protect ourselves from the threats of AI. However, it's worth taking a quick detour now in order to put the conversation about AI into a bit of perspective.

As we've already said, every significant technological advance comes with risks that are typically much more obvious than its benefits. We are well aware of the destructively awesome power of nuclear weapons. The image of a mushroom cloud is etched upon our collective memory. However, nuclear technology has also contributed in numerous ways to the well-being of humanity—from smoke detectors to food preservation, energy to medicine, water desalination to space exploration. The same technology that threatens our existence also advances our civilization.

It's understandable that AI adds to our fear since it's accompanied by the promise (or the threat, depending on your perspective) of achieving levels of intelligence that exceed our own. However, we'd offer an alternative point of view. AI is an advance that is absolutely necessary if we are to stand a chance of coping with the challenges of transitioning from an industrial era model. We'll look at all of the reasons why as we dig deeper into the specifics of these challenges and the role of AI. But there's also a much bigger picture which we'd like to paint before doing that.

Because our life spans are so ridiculously short when compared to the geological clock of our planet, we are lulled into thinking that we are somehow protected or immune to extinction level events. What we know of the history of our planet should teach us otherwise.

Only seventy thousand years ago (that's less than two milliseconds if we covert the Earth's age from four billion years to a twenty-four-hour clock) human population dropped to just a few thousand.[24] One hundred fifty thousand years ago it's believed that total human population reached only six hundred—globally![25] A similar drop in population occurred 1.2 million years ago.[26] Clearly, we've overcome some incredible odds just to get this far. It would be beyond foolish to believe that we've somehow outgrown these same natural risks, be they pandemics, asteroids, geological phenomena, or human-induced risks such as climate change or nuclear weapons.

Which is why we believe strongly in the necessity of AI to help us understand the increasingly complex and interconnected behaviors of the natural and manmade systems that we could never hope to figure out on our own.

We firmly believe that there will be innumerable benefits to AI that we can barely imagine and which will far outweigh any of the implications we now fear. These will not only come from the relatively simple act of understanding our individual behaviors but also the more complex behaviors of a hyperconnected world. For example, AI will help us to better understand the factors contributing to climate change and how we slow or reverse it, the creation of vaccines that can avert pandemics, how to bring billions of people from the developing world into the socioeconomic mainstream, and then how to feed, house, and care for ten billion humans, and ultimately, it may give us the ability to become an interplanetary species and place hedge bets on our long-term survival—something which physicist Stephen Hawking has predicted humanity must do within one hundred years if it is to survive.

Still, we understand that the risks of pandemics and stray asteroids aren't keeping most of us up at night. So, let's bring our flight of fancy back down to earth.

Before we set course for the stars, there are more pressing issues we have right in front of us in how we run our lives, our businesses, and our economy that are just as important to address. Revealing and harnessing the invisible starts there, at ground level, where we live, work and play.

The most significant shift in thinking about the ways in which we can do that and leverage the wealth of data that we now have, along with the enormous amounts yet to come, has to do with the adoption of a new way of looking at the problems and challenges that surround us so that we get much better at predicting the consequences of our actions.

Predicting the future has always been a favorite pastime of humanity, but we've never been particular good at it.

That's changing, in part due to the technologies and data we have at our disposal, but in larger part because of a new way of thinking about the fundamental approach to problem solving. And that's what we'll look at next.

CHAPTER 2

The Prediction Machine: Why We Can't Keep Solving the Way We Once Did

> *"The very role of consciousness is to give living*
> *beings 'knowledge' of the future."*
> —*Frank Knight, early twentieth century*
> *economist from the Chicago School*

In 1993 AT&T ran a widely circulated mass media campaign that consisted of TV and print advertising in a series of commercials, called the "You Will" ads. The ads were intended to portray the distant future. As a backdrop video played showing car GPS, touch screens, tablet computing, electronic medical records, ebooks, web conferencing and on-demand video, actor Tom Selleck's deeply masculine voice-over would say "Have you ever traveled the country…without a map? You will. And the one who will bring it to you? AT&T." The ads were frighteningly prescient. In fact, if you view them today, it seems that AT&T had a crystal ball into the future.

Although AT&T predicted the technology of the future with uncanny accuracy, it turned out that it wasn't the company that brought a single one of these technologies to you. AT&T was very good at projecting the eventual destination of these technologies, but they were terrible at predicting the future, and especially at timing it and capitalizing on it. How is that possible? Shouldn't being able to predict the future of technology be synonymous with predicting the future? No, because of the one thing that is nearly impossible to predict: the way that behavior will also change.

We're not picking on AT&T for any reason other than to depict how magnificently accurate their depiction of the technological future was. If anything, AT&T illustrated how easy it is to project technology's evolution. Yet it took another two decades for behavior to start supporting the widespread use of these technologies.

It's easy to pin the blame on technology and say that it just wasn't ready yet, but if AT&T or any other company had tried to push those same "You Will" technologies out into the market at the time they would have been met with the same fate as Apple's Newton PDA, arguable the first tablet-based handheld computer, which, coincidentally, was also introduced in 1993!

The problem is that while technology is visible, tangible, mathematical, and predictable, behavior is influenced by far too many hidden and invisible variables. You can project technological progress because the variables are known. In fact, the last fifty years of technology really have not been all that hard to predict because they've followed the fairly reliable trajectory of Moore's Law, which has proven to be an amazingly accurate predictor of the power, storage capacities, and costs of computing over any period of time.[27]

But what if, as some scientists claim, Moore's Law suddenly reached its physical limits and we could no longer pack more nano-scale transistors onto a silicon wafer, or more ones and zeros onto a flash drive? Would computers start to plateau and would we, as a civilization, start to reach the limits of our own ability to solve the increasingly complex societal, economic, and ecological problems that face us? And what does any of this have to do with your behaviors and how they are being collected and used?

Our assumption in writing this book was that whatever the case may be with the rate of advance in computing hardware, the next quantum leap in how we use computers to help us navigate today's challenges and those we will face in the future will be in their ability to understand and exhibit behavior. But up until very recently, we simply have not been able to capture enough data to understand behavior, and even where we have, our technology hasn't been adequate to make sense of it.

The invisible that's being revealed isn't the technology but rather the incredibly complex behaviors of the natural and man-made systems that make up the world. The better we understand the patterns that influence the behaviors of any person, device, or system, the more likely we are to be able to predict how those behaviors will evolve and manifest themselves in the future.

Your Digital-self

The digital representation of these behaviors is what we've been calling the digital-self (a digital-twin in the case of a device), a collection of data-points that intimately describe a person or an object in a way that makes it possible to model current behaviors and to predict future behaviors. But let's reiterate something we said at the outset: this is not the same as what has been called Big Data. Big Data is using vast collections of data about the behavior of a large system, a marketplace, a factory, or the economy. What we are talking about is closer to what Martin Lindström has called Small Data,

> *Seemingly insignificant behavioral observations containing very specific attributes pointing towards an unmet customer need. Small data is the foundation for breakthrough ideas or completely new ways to turnaround brands.*[28]

Lindstrom is taking us in the right direction, but we want to delve even further into how data can be hyper-personalized to not only identify unmet needs but unknown needs.

Our view of the digital-self includes the ability to create intelligent collaboration and conversation with a digital-self—departing from the notion of using data simply as a vehicle for analyzing and inferring behavior to using it as an active collaborator in our businesses and our lives. What we call data analytics today (big or small) is barely tapping into 10 percent of the value that's available to understand behaviors and to use that understanding to successfully navigate the future.

An analogy is the classic metaphor of an iceberg, which exists mostly as an invisible mass under the waterline. To make the point, picture a cluster of hundreds or thousands of these icebergs close to each other. Now imagine being the captain of a ship that's in the middle of that ice field. And just to create some added risk, let's say your engines are stuck at full forward. There's no way you can navigate around the icebergs without knowing what's going on below the waterline. Oh, and we forgot to mention that the icebergs were also closing in on you. All the data in the world about the 10 percent of the iceberg above the water's surface isn't going to help one bit in knowing where the other 90 percent is. In this scenario, revealing the invisible isn't optional; it's a matter of survival.

That's why your digital-self is so valuable: it reveals the other 90 percent of who you are, and by doing so it makes it possible to understand where you're going, what you will do, and the decisions you will make. The same, however, applies to devices, objects, and natural phenomena that are either digitally enabled (your smartphone or a supply chain) or digitally connected through sensors (weather patterns or your physiology).

Thinking of objects and systems as having behaviors and a digital-self is challenging because we aren't used to it.

We know that this sounds like the plotline for a dark science fiction novel about how humanity will be ruled by cybernetic overlords, but stick with us, because that's not at all where we see this going. Instead we'd like to propose that we are at one of those rare historical milestones when the old gives way to the new because the old models of how things work can no longer adequately predict the way current forces are shaping the future.

A Cultural Deja Vu

We've been here before, at the point where our problems seem to exceed our ability to solve them. And there's ample precedent for how slight shifts in the way we solve increasingly complex problems has helped us navigate the challenges of the past and given us a significantly better foundation with which to predict the future. We call this a cultural deja vu because there is a familiarity to these breakthrough moments of insight that we have experienced time and again throughout history. Yet, somehow we seem to form a collective amnesia that challenges our ability to recognize how profound these are as we are going through them.

In the 1500s, we saw a revolution in thinking, although it, and its proponent, weren't very popular for a few hundred years thereafter. Copernicus introduced his heliocentric model of the solar system as an alternative to Ptolemy's geocentric model. Copernicus was by no means the first to suggest that the sun and not the earth was at the center of our solar system, but his works were widely published thanks to the recently introduced printing press. Yet, for two hundred years, people debated the heliocentric model. Many wanted to believe that both it and the geocentric model could coexist, illustrating the extremes we will go to hold onto past paradigms. What ultimately made the heliocentric model preferable was that it could *predict* the future positions of the planets with accuracy not attainable in a geocentric model.

In the early 1900s a similar revolution in scientific thought occurred when Newtonian Physics reached its limits, giving way to Einstein's relativity. While Einstein's didn't meet as much initial resistance as Copernicus had, the thinking behind his models of how the universe operated was even more radical, proposing a world of strange quantum subatomic phenomena, time dilation, and even black holes. Again, the power of Einstein's model of physics was that it gave us the ability to better explain and *predict* how the physical world behaved.

In 1937 an obscure physics professor at Iowa State University, John Vincent Atanasoff, invented the first digital computer, once again catapulting civilization into its next orbit of knowledge.[29] The early purpose of those first computers, such as the Eniac and Univac, which were built on the model of Atanasoff's digital architecture, was to *predict* the future, whether it be the results of an election or the trajectory of a ballistic missile.

Each of these breakthroughs, in the way we thought about and understood how the world works, gave us more accurate insights into the behavior of otherwise invisible forces and the ability to see a little further into the future. They were, if you will, prediction machines.

If you're thinking, "Yes, but what did they do for me?" Consider that were it not for Copernicus, Einstein, and Atanasoff, we could not have developed something as pervasive as GPS. The movement of the planets, time dilation, and digital technology are all critical to the operation of a satellite. So, both figuratively and literally, you have not only Roger Easton and Ronald Reagan, but Copernicus, Einstein, and Atanasoff to thank for GPS.

In fact, every one of the technologies in AT&T's "You Will" ads would have been impossible to develop without these fundamental advances in understanding the invisible forces involved in how the world operates.

Most of all, what each of these landmark changes in our understanding gave us is greater visibility into why things happened as they did and greater reliability in understanding their behaviors so that we could better predict the future. We'd go so far as to say that creating visibility into the future drives all significant technological change. Humans yearn for predictability; our society, economy, government, and businesses thrive on it. The closer we get to that goal, the more reliable and certain the world is and the more we prosper.

It's also curious that each of these advances happened at a time when the complexity of the world was approaching the limits of understanding with the use of current models, concepts, and tools. The accepted and comfortable ways of navigating the past were no longer adequate for building the future.

In a similar way, we believe that we're reaching the end of industrial era models that have worked so well for us up until now. Making the next quantum leap in how we address the challenges we face going forward will require a radically different framework within which to understand how individuals, businesses, organizations, social institutions, governments, and even ecosystems behave so that we can better predict how those behaviors will shape the future.

So, in order to do that, what's the Newtonian/Einstein barrier that we need to break through in today's context?[30] We believe it's the fundamental shift from solving problems for engineered systems to solving the problems presented by emergent systems. Your digital-self, the ability to reveal the invisible, behavioral business, and everything else that we will talk about in this book represent emergent systems. So, before we go much further we need to talk about how emergent systems work and why they are so radically different from engineered systems.

Don't be put off by the sound of that phrase, "emergent systems." We know it may seem as obtuse as the Theory of Relativity. It's actually much simpler to understand, but no less profound in its implications.

Of Clocks and Clouds

For nearly a century, physicists have quipped that if you throw a clock against the wall you can still pick up all the pieces and somehow reverse engineer the clock to make sense of how it works. You can do that because the clock had been engineered to begin with, there's an intelligent design that adheres to known and well-understood principles of mechanics and physics. This works well for engineered systems. But it fails miserably for many complex systems that are not engineered, such as ecosystems (natural or manmade), economic systems, marketplaces, and weather, which all exhibit behaviors driven by invisible forces. These are called emergent systems because they are constantly in flux in unpredictable ways. Being able to understand how they work under one very specific set of circumstances doesn't mean that you will understand how they will behave in the future.[31]

While engineered systems follow certain understandable and visible rules, emergent systems behave in ways whose underlying forces are often unknown and invisible. To put it another way, engineered systems are predictable and probabilistic; emergent systems are unpredictable and uncertain.

Fifty years ago, one of the twentieth century's most highly regarded philosophers of science, Sir Karl Popper, provided an analogy that simplified the difference between engineered and emergent systems by making the observation that all complex problems are either clocks (engineered) or clouds (emergent).

Here's how Popper's simple idea can help us to reframe how we think about today's challenges.

Tick Tock

As with our smashed and broken clock, the hardware and software that make up computers is complex, but it can still be broken down into its components and reverse engineered, debugged, or otherwise understood. That's what traditional programmers do day-in, day-out.

Popper observed that the parts, and their interactions with one another, in a clock-like system are "regular, orderly, and highly predictable in their behavior." This way of thinking is the ultimate example of what's referred to as reductionist thinking, an ideal approach for understanding how to solve even the most complex clock-like problems. From the great pyramid of Giza to the Burj Kalifa, it's how we've solved problems and built solutions for thousands of years.

Perhaps the greatest example of solving one of the most complex clock-like problems occurred just a few years after Karl Popper's 1966 book *Of Clocks and Clouds* was published, when Apollo XI delivered two men to the surface of the moon and returned them safely back to Earth. The sheer number of individual problems that had to be solved in order to make those incredibly complex Apollo missions successful truly boggles the mind.

However, once each aspect of that complex whole was broken down into its component parts, more than four hundred thousand engineers and technicians began to work on designing and manufacturing each of the clock-like components that were needed to do the job. These individual components were then assembled into ever more sophisticated subsystems. Eventually, each subsystem was successfully integrated with others into a whole system that brought us to the moon.

The race to the moon is still an amazing story of ambition, perseverance, and genius, but there's a part of the story that's seldom told because it's simply taken for granted. Getting to the moon and back to earth was only partly about building magnificent vehicles that could escape the Earth's gravity and travel in outer space. The other part was being able to create highly predictable models that would be used to guide and navigate the precise route these vehicles would take. Keep in mind that the Apollo astronauts were navigating in a space ship travelling at three thousand four hundred km/hour to meet up with a moon that was moving at three thousand seven hundred km/hour. So, picture two objects flying four times as fast as a .38 caliber bullet with a rendez-vous two hundred fifty thousand miles away.

Although it seems trivial now, being able to precisely predict the position, velocity, acceleration, and myriad vari-ables involved in this, and many more in-flight maneuvers, was an incredible achievement at the time, especially with a computer that had sixty-four Kbytes of memory and ran at a speed of 0.043 MHz making an iPhone 6 thirty-two thousand six hundred times faster with one hundred twenty million times as much memory.[32]

It was with that paltry computer, probably less powerful than the one in your microwave, and an abundance of slide rules, that humanity solved the world's most complex clock problem.

It was with that same approach, and infinitely more pow-erful computers, that we've continued to try and solve all our problems. It's worked to get us this far. But it doesn't work for cloud problems, which couldn't be more different.

Unsolvable

While you can use the same reductionist thinking that works so well for dissecting clock problems to "take apart" a cloud, all that accomplishes is getting down to individual water molecules, which does very little to help you understand the ever-changing behavior of an emergent system like a cloud.

In physical clouds, water molecules are suspended in a constant tug-of-war, always in flux yet also always working together. Not to go too far down the path of this metaphor, but the clouds we see floating above us are formed of tenu-ous relationships between separate but temporarily aligned partners. As anyone who has flown through fluffy cumulus clouds can attest, they are filled with air currents that are rapid and unpredictable; in their ultimate form, cumulonimbus clouds, which form violent thunderstorms, are among the most powerful and destructive forces in nature.

Tiny water droplets with near zero potential for harm on their own can be nature's most ferocious phenomena when combined, especially when combined *quickly*!

That visual depiction of small, seemingly inconsequential particles joining in unpredictable ways creates the same sort of uncertainty that we see in all emergent systems. We can see the parts of the system and still not understand the behavior of the entire system. Something more is going on in emergent systems, something invisible.[33]

Emergent systems cannot be understood simply by understanding each of the individual components. The only way they can be understood is by studying them as a whole. To understand any single cloud you need to understand the way millions of other clouds behave. And you have to then add to that understanding the knowledge of countless equally complex interactions, like temperature, barometric pressure, wind, sunlight, even the terrain over which they form. And still there are variables influencing the cloud that can't be fully understood. Clouds, by their very nature, are inherently irregular, disorderly, and highly unpredictable in their behavior.

Did you notice, by the way, that we're describing clouds as having behavior? That seems to be an odd attribute for a cloud which lacks intelligence. Yet, we typically describe objects, systems, and things without biological brains as behaving in a certain way.

Behavior is usually a term that we use when we are describing how something happens without understanding why it happens. We understand how clouds behave infinitely better than we understand why they behave as they do. If we could fully understand clouds, the way we do clocks, we wouldn't need to compare and contrast weather forecasts; every forecast would provide the same precise and guaranteed outcome.

Emergent systems come with no such guarantees; they frustrate us because they involve not only unknown variables but unknowable variables. In other words, the rules that govern the behavior of an emergent system can only be understood after they have been experienced. (Although, we will see in Chapter 4, that there is another option for dealing with emergent systems that can handle the inherently higher levels of uncertainty.) What often trips us up is that we confuse the presence of some known subset of rules about how an emergent system works with the conclusion that the entire system is engineered. A simple example is comparing board games such as tic-tac-toe, checkers, chess, and Go.

Tic-tac-toe is a simple clock problem. You can hardwire a basic circuit with just a few semiconductors and without the use of a computer to create an automated opponent that will be just as challenging as any human opponent. One of us (the older one) did that at the age of 16, long before personal computers were available. The rules are clear and there are a finite and limited number of moves. In fact, there are only two hundred fifty-five thousand, one hundred sixty-eight potential game variations.

Checkers gets a bit more complicated. There are five hundred billion billion (five hundred followed by eighteen zeros) possible games in checkers—which makes it far more interesting as a clock problem—but it is still a clock problem because it has a finite number of moves and each one follows a simple programmed set of rules for a computer to follow. [34]

With chess, however, things get interesting and change dramatically. While, from a mathematical standpoint, you can calculate the number of possible games at 10^120, that number is larger than the number of atoms in the known universe. In other words, the number of games might as well be infinite since we could never find enough storage to keep all those games in a computer's memory (at least not with any technology we know of today). Suddenly we have a problem that can be only partially solved mechanically, but which ultimately ends up being an emergent problem since we cannot use a formula to determine every possible outcome.

At this point you might be thinking, "Wait, a computer has won playing chess against the best human players." Yes, IBM's Deep Blue, a high-performance computer built specifically to play chess, won against Gary Kasparov, the world's best chess player in 1997. But Deep Blue, even according to its creators at IBM, solves clock problems; it just does it faster than less powerful computers. While Kasparov can only evaluate three moves per second, Deep Blue can evaluate two hundred million moves per second. This is a case of literally using millions of times more brute force than a human opponent. This is what we mean by being able to partially mechanically solve an emergent problem. And yet, the degree of superiority of the computer over a human opponent is still marginal. While Deep Blue won it did so only by a rather slim margin, winning three games to Kasparov's two (one game of the six was a draw). Which implies that humans are uniquely wired to solve emergent problems in a way that doesn't require brute force processing power. It's what we call intuition, and it's something we consider uniquely human.

Since Atanasoff's first digital computer in 1937, this has been the trajectory of computing—to increase speed, bandwidth, and storage capacity. The idea being that when you eventually have enough power brute force will solve the problem. Not so with problems involving emergent systems. The scale of the problems is just too great.

Take for example the game of Go. While seemingly a very simple game played with only white and black stones, Go is considered to be one of the most complex, intricate, and challenging of all board games, requiring a level of intuition and creativity that is considered to be uniquely human. Go is not a solvable game. The number of possible games that can be played on a nineteen-by-nineteen square playing field borders on the absurd. Conservatively that number is pegged at 10^170. (There are only 10^80 atoms in the observable universe!)[35] Other estimates put the number of games as high as 10^800 (This assumes that the moves being made are legal and not random).[36] In the case of the latter, the number of games could be as large a 10^10^100—a googolplex! So, you could say that Go is as close to emergent as a board game with rules could possibly be. However, the world's best Go player, Lee Sodol, was overtaken in three games out of four by Google DeepMind's AlphaGo AI player on March 15, 2016.

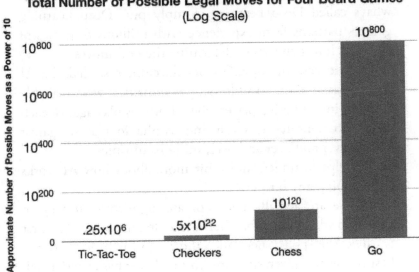

Illustration 2.1

The number of possible moves, as a power of ten, increases dramatically from the simple game of Tic-Tac-Toe to that of Go. Since the illustration above uses a log scale it does not do justice to the actual scale of that change. For example, if we were to draw this same chart to scale, leaving the bar for checkers at approximately 1mm in height, the bar for the game Go would extend outside of the bounds of the visible universe at 10^34 kilometers in height.

So, what makes AlphaGo so much better at dealing with emergent problems than Deep Blue?

First, AlphaGo uses a considerable amount of computing power: one thousand nine hundred twenty standard processors and two hundred eighty beefed up processors, called GPU's, which are customized for the much more demanding task of gaming. But AlphaGo's real power is not measured in Millions of Instructions Per Second or Megabytes of memory but rather in its ability to develop a form of intuition through what's called Deep Learning. Simply put, Deep Learning gathers patterns from experience with millions of games of Go, which it then uses to determine the best moves.[37]

In the case of AlphaGo, its developers seeded the AI with thirty million possible Go positions that were available from online gathering places where humans play against each other. To reinforce this learning, AlphaGo played against itself—over and over and over, millions of times.

It helps to understand a bit more about how AI works before going any further.

There are actually two separate algorithms at play in AlphaGo which work together to decide on a move. The first is called the "policy network" and its job is to identify the best moves in a given situation from what it has experienced. AlphaGo then hands this off to a second algorithm, called the "value network," which develops probabilities for each move's likely success. The combination of these two algorithms creates a set of dynamic and always changing rules for AlphaGo to follow.

By way of analogy, imagine that you are faced with a difficult decision. The first thing you're likely to do is come up with the best set of options. Once you have those, your next step will probably be to figure out which of the options is the most likely to succeed. This ability to learn from experience is essential when you're dealing with emergent systems because it allows a form of dialog to take place between the challenge being solved and whoever (or whatever) is doing the solving.

Lastly, keep in mind that AlphaGo was not trained by programmers. Instead it trained itself. We'll come back to this because it's one of the most important and least understood aspects of how AI is changing the way we look at computing. But for now, let's just say that a human looking under the hood of AlphaGo or any other AI may not necessarily understand why a particular decision was made or why it's behaving the way it is.

Unlike computers that are programmed by people, AI reprograms itself as it learns—not unlike the way humans learn. Nobody really taught you how to walk, and if they had you would not have understood their language, since most of us mastered walking long before we mastered language. Again, we will come back to this in Chapter 4 when we talk about autonomous vehicles. For now, let's just accept that emergent systems cannot be fully understood or predicted with any set of predefined rules.

Emergence also isn't a concept limited to physical and mechanical devices. It's a fundamental part of economics as well. The economist Frank Knight, a founder of the Chicago school of economics, wrote about the role of inherent uncertainty in his 1914 doctoral thesis at Cornell on which his book *Risk Uncertainty and Profit* was based.

Knight's approach to economics was unorthodox, but his premise was profoundly simple: uncertainty is the absence of future knowledge. Knight constructed a complex matrix of the ways in which uncertainty is factored into our lives. He even went so far as to state that "the very role of consciousness is to give living beings 'knowledge' of the future."

Knightsian economics describe situations where no amount of information can create greater certainty about an event. This is perhaps the most counterintuitive aspect of Knight's work.

After all, if the uncertainty of an emergent system is because of the absence of knowledge about the future, shouldn't there be some amount of information that would rectify the situation? In a Knightsian scenario, such knowledge can only be gained by experiencing the event, not beforehand. In fact, more information in these situations only leads to delayed decision-making and lost opportunity. Think of this in practical terms. When you're faced with uncertainty the instinctive reaction is to slow down and think through the situation. Yet, it is in these cases when you most need to act in order to respond within a shorter window of opportunity. This is what's called the Uncertainty Principle. As uncertainty increases, the time to react decreases.[38]

We are surrounded by the uncertainty of emergent systems—the weather, the stock market, the economy, marketplaces, political campaigns, the biosphere, traffic patterns, human behaviors, certain diseases—all have a level of complexity impossible to fully understand.

More powerful computers with greater connectivity cannot solve the challenges of cloud problems. They can make an incrementally larger dent in the problem, but we are reaching the limits of how far we can move the needle of progress through brute force alone.

And these are physical limits. Not only is Moore's law reaching its upper bounds, but we have some rather ridiculous scenarios ahead if we continue to just store data at current rates of acceleration. It's been projected that the world's data centers (where all of the data that's used in the cloud is stored) are already using 25 percent more energy yearly than all of the UK and have a carbon footprint equal to that of the entire aviation industry. In Japan alone, if its data centers continue to grow at their present rate, by 2030 they will consume all of Japan's energy output.[39]

More astonishingly however, is the fact that if we continue on our current trajectory we would simply run out of space to store all of this data. By 2020 it's estimated that the world will produce forty-four zetabytes (forty-four followed by twenty-one zeros) of data yearly.[40] By 2025 that will have exploded to one hundred eighty zetabytes per year. That means the amount of data we produce is doubling every two years and accelerating. At that rate, by 2220 we will have exceeded the capacity available if we had the ability to store one bit of data on every atom in the solar system.

We simply can't continue to try and solve every problem as though it was an engineered system with a finite set of solvable rules. That doesn't mean that we will discard the way we address clock problems, they're not going away and we will have more of them than ever. But it does mean that we need to recognize the difference between technology problems, which are clock problems to be solved by linear, reductionist reasoning, and emergent problems, which are behavioral.

We realize that all of this talk about emergent systems may sound a bit obtuse and even confusing. But it has a very direct application in understanding why we will need AI to navigate the future. We are at a watershed moment for civilization where we can either continue to muddle along using the same industrial era tools we've used to build the past or we can add a new set of tools that more adeptly handle the challenges of the future. And these are as applicable to how we run our businesses as they are to how we reshape our society.

What we are describing in this book—from the evolution of autonomous vehicles, to the emergence of frictionless digital ecosystems, to hyper-personalization, and the value of loyal brands—are all the result of this fundamental shift in how we approach problem solving, from dealing with the part of the problem visible above the waterline to the much more complex and interesting invisible part the lurks below the surface. And nowhere is that invisible part more interesting than when it comes to exposing the individualized behaviors that belong to each of us. That's where the real revelations begin.

CHAPTER 3:

Indecent Exposure: How We Learned to Love Revealing the Invisible

"If you reveal your secrets to the wind, you should not blame the wind for revealing them to the trees."
—*Khalil Gibran*

Any conversation about capturing and predicting behaviors has to consider the issues of ethics and privacy. We've already said that the intent of this book isn't to describe the doomsday scenarios that often come up when talking about the future. But we'd be more than naïve to suggest that these scenarios should be ignored. It's tempting when talking about any disruptive change to focus strictly on what its proponents see as its benefits and to dismiss anyone who is skeptical as being against change and progress. That only serves to pit the future against the past as though there was some sort of hard line of demarcation from the dark into the light.

The truth is that over time change is only embraced if it serves, as Adam Smith put it, our "own self-interest." We don't use smartphones because Apple and Samsung make a healthy profit; we use them because they enable us to be connected, productive, effective, and entertained. In other words, we all reap the benefits of successful technology. Is there often an imbalance between the economic benefits that flow to those who build and supply a new technology and those who use it? Of course, but that goes both ways. The future does not play favorites.

Take the enormous investment that was made in building out the internet as we know it today. Along with that investment the streets were lined with casualties. By some estimates nearly five thousand companies shut down, went bankrupt, or were acquired (at a fraction of their value) when the dot-com bubble burst in 2001.

Seventeen years later we've finally started realizing the promise of the dot-coms. So, to say that all of the companies who poured the early footings of the internet were somehow its beneficiaries is woefully inaccurate. Only an incredibly small minority made it through, and among them even fewer have turned a profit to date.

Although the degree of transparency that can be achieved through the technologies available today—and those which will be available in the future—poses a far greater potential threat to privacy than anything we've already experienced, we also need to keep in mind that transparency creates value.

An Acceptable Future

Rather than set aside the challenges and fears of increasing transparency and decreasing privacy—many of which we accept as valid—we want to acknowledge them and call them out; only in that way can we address them as we build an acceptable future.

We'll start by identifying the most obvious challenges to privacy and look at the obstacles each presents in gathering and using behaviors. Later in the book we'll look at the specific ways in which we believe that these challenges can be addressed.

Privacy can be given up in several ways. For our purposes here, we are going to list the legal ways in which private information can be given up. Clearly there are near infinite ways in which privacy can be breached illegally, but in those cases, by definition, there is some form of recourse. (In Chapter 4 we also talk about how illegal breaches can be prevented and managed.) In the four cases listed here we are giving up privacy because we have to, or we choose to, in exchange for something of value to us individually or collectively as a society.

Legal Loss of Privacy

First, we can be legally required to give up privacy by a court order or in the conduct of a legal search and seizure based on probable cause. A court order or a warrant can be obtained by law enforcement to access private data stored either locally or in the cloud. It's important to note that while the fourth Amendment does provide protection against illegal search and seizure of property that is in your home, you are not protected if that information is shared with a third party, or if it's discovered in the act of a suspected crime for which there is probable cause. For example, law enforcement only needs a subpoena (which does not require a court or impartial judge) to obtain records of phone calls, electric, gas or water usage, or even your email stored in the cloud. The reason is that once you have shared any of this information with a third party you are considered to have given up your right to privacy.

In the case of email there has been an ongoing debate in the U.S. about the privacy of email stored on third party servers (Google/Microsoft/Yahoo/similar). As it stands now, emails over one hundred eighty days old can be seized by law enforcement or government with only a subpoena (which needs no judicial oversight). Google received thirty-one thousand of these requests in 2016! And the government need not notify the email owner that his or her email has been scanned.

While a bill prohibiting this without a court issued warrant passed the U.S. House of Representatives unanimously, as of the publishing date of the book, it has not passed the Senate.[41]

In the case of probable cause things get even murkier. Law enforcement can seize evidence or contraband that is "in clear view" as part of their duty in the act of investigating or averting a crime. But how do you define "in clear view" in the case of digital evidence? We'll come back to that in just a bit.

Loss of Privacy for Public Safety

Second, privacy can be given up in the interest of public safety. We are all accustomed to having to authenticate our identity and submit to body scans, searches, or pat downs when boarding a plane. The same applies to many cases where you're entering a public venue for a sporting or entertainment event. It's important to note that this wasn't always the case. Before the risks of hijackings and terrorism became prevalent the loss of privacy was unacceptable because we had a reasonable expectation of privacy and there was no threat posed to public safety. However, both of these are now held to a different standard and, as we'll see later in this chapter, can be subject to a great deal of interpretation by a court. It's also worth noting that Fourth Amendment rights apply to a government search, not to private parties. Again, much of what qualifies, as an acceptable loss of privacy, will depend on what is deemed to be a reasonable expectation of privacy or a loss of privacy for the public good. Hold that thought because we'll come back to it shortly.

Trading Privacy for Value

Third, we can willingly give up our privacy for something else of value. We all do this to some extent. Sharing a social security number or personally identifying information gives up some of your privacy. Applying for a job, credit, or admittance to a school is something we choose to do in order to be able to do something else, such as drive a car or use a credit card. Usually the value in these sorts of tradeoffs is clear. However, there are many cases where much of this same information may be gathered as part of a more casual transaction.

For instance, there are numerous websites that will provide you with your "real age" based on your answering a variety of questions about your health, lifestyle, and habits. Your real age is simply an algorithm that comes up with an age that is younger or older than your chronological age, depending on your habits and health. We tried one of these sites called Sharecare.

While much of the information it gathered at first was fairly benign, it soon got into questions about over-the-counter medications, prescriptions, diagnosed health conditions, and how many times a week you engage in sexual activity. This is information that even a primary care physician may not have and yet we are willing to give it away just so that we can get an estimation of our "real age."

The site does have a privacy policy, which reads in part:

> *Sharecare uses your personal health information to provide certain services to you. Sharecare may share personal health information to provide a better user experience and to improve the quality of our services. For example, Sharecare services can help you find relevant information, including from advertisers and third parties. Personal health information shared for such purposes is not provided to third parties in a personally identifiable manner.*

Yet over forty-two million people have taken the test, creating a collection of more than five billion data-points.[42]

Trading Privacy for Convenience

Fourth, we may provide behavioral clues about ourselves and our lives—in the course of our day-to-day activities—which unintentionally give up our privacy in exchange for a very small incremental convenience. This may result from using a radio frequency transmitter to speed our way through toll booths, our browser and search history, our emails and documents stored in the cloud, and even the loyalty cards used to track our buying behaviors. While the value we receive from each transaction may be minimal, the cumulative value of these individual transactions can be enormous to the right party.

In many cases this trade-off simply reduces the friction of a transaction. As a simple example, think back to Facebook Connect, which we mentioned in Chapter 1, and the benefit in using it as a single way to identify yourself to the dozens or hundreds of other applications that you would need to remember a username and password for. By doing that you've reduced the overall friction that slows down your use of these applications.

By the way, much of what we give away in the last two cases, trading privacy for value or convenience, is governed by the Terms and Conditions we agree to for the apps that are tracking our behaviors. However, this is an asymmetrical relationship. Individual users don't stand a chance of being able to read, understand, and keep up to date with all the Terms and Conditions of even the apps on their smartphones. A Norwegian consumer watchdog group recently took on the task of reading all of the Terms and Conditions for the 33 apps on a typical user's smartphone. The total time, just to read and not to verify comprehension, was thirty-one hours, forty-nine minutes, and eleven seconds.[43] That's about as much time as it would take to read Tolstoy's *War and Peace*, with time left over for Nathaniel Hawthorne's *The Scarlet Letter*.[44]

Each of these five cases creates what we consider to be individually or socially acceptable exposure of our private information. You may not agree with all of it, but it is the legal and social norm that sets the boundaries for privacy today.

Here's where things start to get fuzzy with each one of these scenarios, in terms of what we consider an acceptable tradeoff for privacy.

<u>Private Eyes</u>

Twenty-nine-year-old Marcella Riley, an aspiring young comedian, had just moved to L.A. to try and break into show business. As with so many young struggling entertainers, she had more dreams than she had money to fund them. So, she decided to "couch surf" with friends and acquaintances until she had the ability to pay for her own place.[45]

One of those friends, Connor, someone she had worked with at an Apple store, was nice enough to let Marcella use his couch for as long as she needed to. Her gratitude didn't last for long. A month after moving in, she noticed a tiny digital Dropcam in a bookcase across from the couch she'd been sleeping on. When she confronted Conner, he claimed that the camera had been there for a year and wasn't even working. Marcella found out it had been purchased after she moved in and realized that what she thought was a private space had been constantly monitored. She went to the local police who told her that there was nothing they could do since the camera was not in a space (the living room) where she would have a reasonable expectation of privacy.

Recording video in your home isn't considered illegal and your houseguests do not need to be notified unless the cameras are in private places where privacy would be expected, such as bathrooms and bedrooms. (We'll leave the audio aspect out of the equation for the moment, since that is illegal without two-party consent in eleven states.) However, we doubt that anyone in Marcella's place would consider what happened to her to be an acceptable form of giving up his or her privacy.

In Marcellas's case the recording may not have been illegal, but it certainly represented an invasion of her privacy. No greater public good was served, Marcella received no value for giving up her privacy—since her use of the couch was not in exchange for being recorded—and she certainly did not agree to having her behavior studied or viewed.

Marcellas's experience is by no means unique. Courts have been attempting to use outdated laws to try and enforce privacy in the age of ubiquitous cameras. However, the technology has far surpassed our ability to police it. While we can attempt to legislate newer technology, what we cannot legislate is the way technology is increasingly finding its way into the fabric of society. We are not suggesting that what happened to Marcella is right. Neither of us would condone this sort of devious behavior. But if the technology is becoming ubiquitous, the question to be answered is how can you possibly mandate and police the way in which the data will be used?

Take another example that better illustrates the point we are making. In 2017 the U.S. government's Immigration and Customs Enforcement (ICE) began working with technology vendors to create a surveillance program that would tie together all of the fragmented silos of data that are available to ICE, in what they have termed:

> [An] overarching vetting system that automates, centralizes, and streamlines the current manual vetting process while simultaneously making determinations, via automation, if the data retrieved is action-

able [to] implement the President's vari-
ous Executive Orders (EOs) that address
American immigration and border protec-
tion security and interests.

We'll translate; in short, the system will identify individuals who are in the United States illegally or who demonstrate a potential to be of interest to ICE.[46]

While the ACLU has thwarted efforts of this sort in the past, the specific focus on illegal immigrants provides a backdoor through which the effort is less likely to face an insurmountable obstacle. However, there is a component to this that does add a new dimension to prior efforts. One of the silos to be observed and evaluated would be social media used by identified subjects. In other words, what someone says, how they say it, and who they say it to, would suddenly play a role in determining if an individual was a person of interest.

And this is where things get especially interesting. In order to scour these sources of data to identify candidates for further investigation you need to capture as much data as possible about as many people as possible. Meaning that ideally, you'd like to have data on everyone. Why capture this data for somebody who is a citizen? First, because you don't know if they are; that's the point of the system. There is no way to identify everyone's digital identity today. Secondly, because interactions and communications with citizens could indicate if someone is an illegal immigrant, complicit in harboring or enabling illegal immigrants, or a potential threat to national security.

The justification most often used by proponents of this sort of universal observance and collection of data is that you have nothing to worry about if you have done nothing wrong. Hold that thought.

Enter Gurbaksh "G" Chahal, a serial Silicon Valley entrepreneur, who was arrested by police after his girlfriend made a 911 call accusing him of assaulting her. After the police entered Chahal's luxury condo, they noticed security cameras on the ceiling of the bedroom where the incident was alleged to have occurred. When police searched the apartment, they found a DVR for the security system in a closet and confiscated it in hopes of finding evidence in recordings to incriminate Chahal.

Sure enough, the DVR had video of Chahal striking his girlfriend one hundred times. Ultimately, however, San Francisco County Judge Brendan Conroy did not allow the recordings to be submitted as evidence because the police had violated Chahal's Fourth Amendment rights protecting him against search and seizure without a warrant. Chahal ultimately ended up pleading guilty to misdemeanor assault charges and was placed on probation for three years.[47]

You can look at this case in one of several ways:

- the seizure of the DVR without a warrant was a violation of Chahal's Fourth Amendment rights, especially since the DVR was not in clear view;
- or, since the police were in Chahal's condo as the result of a 911 call, they had probable cause to search for evidence of the alleged crime and the DVR was fair game;
- or, you could claim that Chahal's use of video surveillance to record anyone (not just intruders) entering his bedroom constituted his acceptance that the video was not private property, but rather belonged just as much to his accuser as it did to him.

The fact is that there is no clear and conclusive answer. In every situation of this sort, involving inadvertent video capture of something that may constitute an illegal act, it's up to the court to decide if the video is legally admissible or if it infringes upon an accused's Fourth Amendment rights. While that might apply equally to any other form of potential evidence seized, the issue here also involves one of ownership and disclosure.

For example, in Chahal's case, what if the video was stored in the cloud? Does Chahal own the video or does the cloud provider? Law enforcement could notice the camera in the bedroom and the DVR but not seize anything at the suspect's residence. Instead they could go directly to whoever owns the cloud service or the data center, with or without a warrant.

In addition, although this was not the case with Chahal, once any media is posted to or shared with a third party, for instance a phone company or social media, there is no Fourth Amendment right to it.

In a 2016 Supreme Court case involving the use of CSLI (Cell Site Location Information), as evidence to prosecute several individuals involved in a series of armed robberies, the court ruled that because the defendants effectively turned over the location of their cell phones to the provider, in this case Sprint/Nextel, they invoked something called the "Third Party Doctrine" which means they no longer can assert Fourth Amendment rights over this information.[48] According to the Supreme Court's decision,

> *The Court has long held that an individual enjoys no Fourth Amendment protection "in information he voluntarily turns over*

to [a] third part[y]." This rule—the third-party doctrine—applies even when "the information is revealed" to a third party, as it assertedly was here, "on the assumption that it will be used only for a limited purpose and the confidence placed in the third party will not be betrayed.

If you're not yet shuddering at this, it gets better (or should we say worse). The court decision went on to read that by "revealing his affairs to another," an individual "takes the risk...that the information will be conveyed by that person to the Government." Did you suddenly get an Orwelian 1984 flashback?

The problem is that the permutations of how media is captured, the intent for which it is captured, who owns it, whether it is private or public are all suddenly up for grabs. While you may be able to unravel the facts in one case you cannot anticipate every case in a way that legislates a single solution.

What we're left with is an extraordinarily cumbersome and difficult to understand definition of what is private.

I've Done Nothing Wrong

So, back to the premise that you have nothing to worry about if you have done nothing wrong. Clearly Chahal had no expectation when he installed his surveillance systems that there was a possibility his DVR could potentially be used against him. Those who advocate the point of view that they've done nothing wrong and so don't mind being recorded, observed, or being the subject of government surveillance, will often use arguments along the lines of, "If giving up just a bit of my privacy could prevent another 9/11, I'd gladly do it." What they fail to acknowledge is that what is being observed or captured is not just the information that relates to potential illegal activity, which would never involve them, but instead as much information as possible, without regard to what or who it might or might not relate to.

The second, and more crucial, mistake is that saying you've done nothing wrong assumes that you have perfect knowledge of how everything you do does or does not break a law. There are about twenty-seven thousand pages in the United States Code, which encompasses all federal laws, and that does not include administrative regulations of the various regulatory agencies or state laws and regulations. [49]

According to U.S. Supreme Court Justice Breyer, "the complexity of modern federal criminal law, codified in several thousand sections of the United States Code and the virtually infinite variety of factual circumstances that might trigger an investigation into a possible violation of the law, make it difficult for anyone to know, in advance, just when a particular set of statements might later appear (to a prosecutor) to be relevant to some such investigation."

Finally, what is legal is not static. The law does not exist that was not first broken before being modified or eliminated to accommodate the changing nature of our norms and the evolution toward a more just society. So, you may very well be breaking the law today for a morally, ethically, or socially acceptable reason which creates the social momentum to change that law. For example, same sex marriage or the use of medical marijuana. Assuming perfect laws is assuming perfect people. Clearly, both are flawed assumptions.

At this point you may be wondering how we could possibly be advocating for greater transparency that leads to exposing even more of our behaviors and creating greater risk for the invasion of our privacy. After all, what we've described so far sounds like we are heading full throttle into a 24/7 surveillance society.

We have no doubt that our digital-selves will become lightning rods for controversy and disruption, and that the debate over privacy will only escalate. But there's no way to turn the clock back. Privacy will only become a more heated issue as the ability to observe behavior escalates. However, there's yet another way that technology is changing the behavior of both sides of the law enforcement equation in a manner that balances the scales of justice.

Who's Watching Who?

Nurse Alex Wubbels had just stepped away from her patient in the Emergency Room at the University of Utah Hospital's burn unit when detective Jeff Payne approached her to ask if he could take a blood sample from one of her patients.

Wubbels knew that blood could not be taken without a warrant or a patient's consent. At the moment her patient was unconscious, so consent wasn't going to happen, and Payne did not have a warrant. She politely explained the situation to Payne. When Payne persisted, she retrieved a paper copy of the hospital's policy which indicated on its face that it was developed in cooperation with the police. The jointly developed policy stated clearly that blood could not be taken without a warrant and consent. Still calm, and without so much as a hint of arrogance, she read the policy and the law to Payne, even holding the printed policy out to point to the explicit references to a warrant and consent. Payne wouldn't take "no" for an answer and was getting visibly agitated as he threatened Wubbels with arrest.

Still unfazed, Wubbels called her supervisor on her cell and put him on speaker phone to explain what was going on. She held the phone out as her supervisor confirmed the policy and then told Payne, "Sir, you're making a huge mistake because you're threatening a nurse."

Payne lost it. He snapped and reached out to grab Wubbels' phone with one hand and her arm with the other, announced that she was under arrest, and then proceeded to forcefully drag her out of the ER, push her up against an outside wall as he put her in handcuffs. Dazed and confused, Wubbels pleaded with Payne to let her go. Hospital security guards and at least one other police officer stood by watching, apparently as shocked by the sudden turn of events as Wubbels.

The story made it into every major news media broadcast on September 1, 2017. However, the event happened on July 26th. Were it not for a technology that had been adopted by many police departments only four years prior, the incident may never have made it out of the handful of people who were in the ER to witness it. Officer Payne was equipped with a mandatory body cam that recorded the entire incident.

Body cams were first used by police in Rialto, California. According to a 2013 *New York Times* article, "In the first year after the cameras were introduced [in Rialto] in February 2012, the number of complaints filed against officers fell by 88 percent compared with the previous 12 months. Use of force by officers fell by almost 60 percent over the same period."

Despite this, not everyone was thrilled with the use of body cams. NYC mayor Michael Bloomberg was not a fan. "It would be a nightmare," said Bloomberg. "We can't have your cameraman follow you around and film things without people questioning whether they deliberately chose an angle, whether they got the whole picture in."[50] Clearly, while far from a perfect solution, body cams have made it safer for everyone involved.

The asymmetry in this situation, as is the case with so much of what we are describing, is that the technologies which reveal the invisible do a wonderful job of sensationalizing fringe cases where things have gone horribly wrong, while their positive impact is nowhere near as visible.

Technological progress does not flow backward. The devices, sensors, and software that gather data about us will expand well beyond any possible scope at which we could adequately police and enforce their legitimate use.

This doesn't mean we should stop pursuing a legislative, legal, and social agenda to prevent the abuse of privacy, but doing that alone is a naïve approach which assumes there is no other way to protect our digital-self and no value in greater transparency. We will see in Chapters 4 and 8 that there are other ways to ensure ownership and control over one's digital-self, and throughout the book we'll show that there is a great deal of value in a culture that emphasizes the importance of transparency.

This same fear-mongering, that the risks far outweigh the benefits, has been used for virtually every leap forward throughout civilization. From Socrates in 400BC, who feared that writing would destroy the art of oral storytelling, to the Luddites in 1815, who feared that mechanical looms would take their jobs, to Motion Picture Association head Jack Valenti's 1982 proclamation to a House Joint Judicial committee that, "the VCR is to the American film producer and the American public as the Boston strangler is to the woman home alone..."[51] nothing is easier than projecting the fears of the present into the potential of the future.

While we are exceptionally skilled at projecting the downside of any new technology, we are severely handicapped in our ability to foresee its upside and the innovations that will also protect us from its dark side. Think back to our example of AT&T's "You Will" ads from 1993. Many people read the tag line "You Will" as a threat more so than a promise. *You will* be tethered 24/7 to your technology! Guess what? We are, and it seems we like it. This quandary of balancing the fear of anything radically new with its promise is so predictable and yet we fall into the same trap over and over.

As we will see in Chapter 4, A Conversation With My Car, there is a viable, well-developed, and radical new approach to the ownership of digital and physical assets that will not only mitigate the threats to privacy but which also creates opportunity to expand the value of the digital-self in ways we've only just begun to imagine.

Before we close this chapter, there's another fascinating aspect of the digital-self that is critical to understand in appreciating the role it will play in creating value for us as individuals, namely that it will evolve and grow even faster than we do.

That sounds odd at first. After all, if this is our digital equivalent how could it evolve faster than we do in the real world? In large part, it's because our digital-self will begin to do things for us at a pace and at a scale that we could never do ourselves. Later in Chapter 6 we'll elaborate on this much more with the example of Personal Health Care Advocates, but for now let's use a simple analogy.

One of us (George) was at one time a nuclear physicist. As we were thinking about how to describe the sorts of advances we see in the evolution of a digital-self, it occurred to him that there was actually an analogy from Einstein's theory of space-time. Don't get scared off—we're not going to get into too much depth here—but the connection is an intriguing one that definitely piqued our curiosity.

In his cornerstone theory of special relativity, Einstein talked about how time can be measured differently for two observers. His premise was that things such as velocity and gravity could actually cause time to move at different relative rates. According to Einstein,

> *Time dilation is a difference in the elapsed time measured by two observers, either due to a velocity difference relative to each other, or by being differently situated relative to a gravitational field.... As a result of the nature of space-time, a clock that is moving relative to an observer will be measured to tick slower than a clock that is at rest in the observer's own frame of reference. A clock that is under the influence of a stronger gravitational field than an observer's will also be measured to tick slower than the observer's own clock.*[52]

To translate, if in your frame of reference I am moving at a much higher rate of speed, my clock slows down, at least as you observe it. To me your clock seems to be moving much faster. So, how does this theory of space-time apply to our digital-self?

Simply put, our digital-self's velocity is much faster than ours. While you stand still, your digital-self is zipping along at light speed gathering, connecting, simulating, and making decisions that are pretty much invisible to you. What this means is that your digital-self can do much more in any interval of time than you can. Ultimately this is why your digital-self can make predictions about what you will do before you do it. It's already ten steps ahead.

It's a fascinating way to think about how our digital-selves will operate, which we look at in more detail later on. For now, we'd like you to think about how cluttered and over-whelmed you are with everything that's vying for your attention. We won't even bother to try and list all of the possible tasks you have on your to-do list, but imagine if you had a personal assistant that was so tuned into your habits, moods, abilities, and desires that it could always stay one step ahead of you in anticipating what you need to do next. Sounds too good to be true, doesn't it? Yet, this is precisely the sort of role your digital-self will play in your life.

We know this has been promised before. Since the dawn of computing we've heard about how machines, computers, and robots will give us more time and free us to do more of what we want and less of the tedium of everyday life. Today's virtual assistants, such as Apple's Siri, Microsoft's Cortana, Amazon's Alexa, and Google's Google Now make the same promises, yet they barely scratch the surface of what we are envisioning.

The reason they all fall short is because they still have a very limited pool of behavioral data about you to work from and their ability to learn is still evolving. However, as we'll see in Chapter 6, the near-term advances in this area will revolu-tionize the very definition of customer experience, and ulti-mately become an indispensable asset for companies trying to differentiate themselves in fiercely competitive markets.

But, for now let's step back from the edge to get a glimpse of what this future might look like from the perspective of what we believe to be the one device that best illustrates the intersection of our behaviors in both the physical and digital world, and which will be the watershed event that finally proves the value and integrity of AI: the driverless car.

CHAPTER 4:

Future Perfect:
A Conversation With My Car

*Mon Sire, cu n'est pas une revolte—
c'est une revolution
—Duc DE Rochefoucald-Liancourt to Louis XVI,
King of France, on the evening of July 14,
1789 after the fall of the Bastille*

On August 16, 2016 Michael Nelson, a lawyer whose clients include prominent players in the automobile and insurance industries, decided to stop into an Orange County Tesla store. He'd long thought about electric and autonomous vehicles (EVs and AVs) and had test-driven dozens, so it wasn't at all unusual for him to drop in to a local dealership on occasion.

However, Michael didn't live in California. He'd traveled there from his home in New York on business and was planning to fly back in a few days. That is, until he walked out of the store as the new owner of a Tesla Model S. Michael immediately called his thirty-one-year-old son in New York and asked him if he wanted to go on a road trip. Two days later the three of them—Mike, son, and Tesla—set out to cross the country, from LA to NYC.

We talked to Michael about his maiden drive and asked him to share what he'd learned as he and his Tesla made the three thousand mile trek eastward. He was no stranger to driverless cars, having test driven many of them over the past year. So, naturally he figured he already had a pretty good sense of what to expect. Still, this was a bit different than the typical fifteen-minute test drive, especially given that they started off in LA at five in the evening. According to Michael, "[we] hit the 5, as they say in LA; bumper-to-bumper traffic on a Friday afternoon. It was an unusual situation to be in a new [autonomous] car that you're trying to figure out how to drive. I was learning how automatic emergency braking really worked in traffic! We didn't get out of California that night."

The next day, as they headed into Nevada, Michael was surprised at how amazingly adept the Tesla was at even the most challenging situations. There were the winding mountain roads when they first crossed into Arizona. The car seemed more than capable but after a few turns he was apprehensive enough to hit the brakes and switch over to manual control. As he told us, "...you have to develop a trust that the car is going to do what it's supposed to do."

Then there was the time an eighteen-wheeler cut in front of them while they were doing seventy-five miles per hour up a steep grade. The Tesla instantly slowed to match the semi-trailer's speed—a whopping nineteen miles per hour.

He described the car's somewhat unnerving ability to change lanes simply by using his directional signal. This car had behavior!

> *If you're in the middle lane of a three-lane highway, in autopilot, and you are going to move into the left lane you [just] put the directional on and the car is now going to take responsibility for that lane change. You're not. You're still holding onto the wheel but you're not steering into the next lane. The car just sort of looks and it says, "Okay, it's safe," and before you know it, it has moved in what it feels like a 45-degree angle and it straightens itself out.*
>
> *Now, we humans have this blind spot routine. You're sort of turning around and looking and you put your directional on and then you feather your way into the lane [in case] there's somebody there you're not seeing. That doesn't happen [in a Tesla]. The car has moved you and if there's a vehicle two lanes over, as you move into the open lane, you have to learn to be confident that it's going to stop moving left.*[63]

However, the most interesting lesson of all came from something that Michael did which every Tesla driver does without even thinking about it. It may be a brilliant move on Tesla's part or one of those unintended afterthoughts that end up being much more meaningful than they were expected to be. Michael called it an "eye-popping" moment.

On his drive back he became accustomed to one of the core experiences for every Tesla driver: recharging. As they made their way through Colorado, Michael noticed that some of the same Teslas kept popping up at the charging stations. Apparently, he wasn't the only one driving cross-country. One woman he met, also a lawyer, had just purchased her Tesla. As they were talking about their experiences Michael kept referring to his Tesla as "she" when his new friend said, "I'm just amazed at how brilliant 'he' is." Puzzled, Michael asked, "When you say 'he' are you talking about Elon Musk?" "No," she said. "My car has got a name. It's Vincent."

One of the first things Tesla owners do when setting up their car is to give it a name. Being a Steinbeck fan Michael thought of the novel *Travels with Charley: In Search of America*, which describes a journey from east to west across the USA. Michael named his car after the book's central character, but with a twist. He spelled it in the feminine form, Charlie.

While it may well have been coincidental that they each named their car after the opposite sex, it did strike a chord with Michael. Unlike any other car he had owned, the Tesla required trust, bonding, and, dare we say it, a relationship. More than anything else, what came across in what Michael talked about was the emerging bond of trust that was formed with Charlie during that trip. Trust, behavior, a relationship—unusual attributes for an automobile. Hold that thought; we'll come back to it.

Objects in the Future Are Closer Than They Appear

It never fails that the greatest innovations often come wrapped in obscurity and misunderstanding. Imagine a Paleolithic scene in which the first round wheel was met with head scratching, confusion, and comments along the lines of, "Sure it's better than a square wheel, but it's going to keep rolling away on us! Square wheels are so much more predictable."

The simple fact is that the future often creates fear and uncertainty since it unveils itself in ways we can never predict or fully comprehend until we look back and think to ourselves, "How did we miss that?"

From the first radio to the first television to the first email, we consistently underestimate our collective ability to change our behaviors to adapt to innovations that appear threatening and to find positive ways to apply them to our lives. How long ago was it that you somehow got by without your mobile phone on your bedside table, or in your bed? Today 80 percent of mobile phone owners are never further than three feet (one meter) from their mobile phone at any point day or night. According to a Bank of America study on mobility, "Approximately three-quarters (71 percent) of us are sleeping with–or next to–our mobile phones. Younger millennials (ages 18-24) are most likely to sleep with their smartphone in their bed (34 percent)."[54]

In order to better understand the future, we need to be as observant of the behavioral, cultural, and psychological forces that cause us to change, as we are of technology's ability to evolve. In Chapter 1 we brought up the importance of having an accurate view of the challenges as well as the promise of becoming more transparent. In this chapter we'll consider what the future will look like when we can communicate with autonomous devices as easily as we communicate with each other today. And lastly, we'll describe a radical game-changer for business and the economy, the notion of autonomous devices that can own themselves.

The concepts we're about to discuss will at first appear to be at the very outer edge of the future. They are not. If there is one sentiment shared equally with everyone we spoke with and interviewed for this book it's that the future is coming at us much faster than we are able to comprehend. That lack of ability to truly understand the rate of change may well be one of our biggest obstacles in adapting to it. Advances in underlying technologies such as artificial intelligence, which are driving the changes we'll talk about, are not progressing in a linear fashion, and that represents a huge challenge for humans who are inherently linear thinkers. Trying to grasp non-linear change that is geometric or exponential is just not how we are wired. We think in linear terms because that is what we've observed in how the natural world operates.

For instance, consider this simple example.

Imagine that we've just given you a super ball that has the ability to bounce to an unlimited height (we'll suspend the laws of physics for this). We then ask you to start bouncing the ball, with the knowledge that each bounce will be twice as high as the previous one. If the first bounce is ten feet off the ground how high will it go on the tenth bounce? The answer is that it will have topped a small mountain of about five thousand feet.

That's high but it doesn't seem extraordinary, and your guess may have been pretty close. However, how high will it be after three more bounces? By the fourteenth bounce it will have crested the Summit of Everest and be approaching the ceiling of commercial air traffic.

That's a bit more impressive, but let's not stop there. After all, we said that it can reach an unlimited height. So, how high would the ball have bounced after twenty-one, twenty-nine, thirty-seven, and forty-five bounces? The answers now start to stretch our ability to comprehend the distances involved. At twenty-one bounces, our ball is approaching low earth orbit, after twenty-nine, we've passed by Earth's moon, another eight bounces and we're zipping by Mars, and then on the forty-fifth bounce, NASA might pick up its faint signal as it whizzes past the first Voyager spacecraft nearly 17 billion miles into deep space. After eighty-eight bounces, you'll never see the ball again since it would now be outside of the visible universe.

Still not impressed? We expected that you might not be, after all, we've become somewhat immune to large numbers when it comes to projecting the trajectory of technology. Congratulations you're starting to think exponentially. But wait, we need to make a confession. We really were not trying to impress you with how fast a doubling phenomenon can scale. Our objective is something else altogether: how we perceive accelerated exponential growth.

So, try just one more question.

If we had started with a discount super ball that bounced only one inch, instead of ten feet, (in other words less than one percent of the ten-foot bounce from our full-price super ball) but it bounced three times as high each time (instead of two times as high), at what height do you think it will bounce past the earlier ball that started at ten feet? Don't do the math, just take a guess. Will it have caught up by Everest, low Earth orbit, the Moon, Mars, or Voyager? Incredibly our discount super ball, that starts off with only a minuscule one-inch bounce, will have caught up by the time it reaches Everest, after only fourteen bounces!

In fact, if you'd started with a ball that bounced a full mile the first time (five hundred twenty-eight times as much as your original super ball and 6,336 times as much as our discount one-inch super ball) the discount one-inch-bounce super ball would catch up with the one-mile-bounce super ball just after passing the moon! This makes sense when you stop to do the math but it's far from intuitive.

The reason we're making this point is to show that linear growth (the actual increase in the initial bounce from ten feet to one mile) and exponential growth (the doubling effect) both pale in comparison to the accelerated exponential growth of our discount super ball that starts off with just a one-inch bounce. When anything progresses with accelerating exponential growth, it very quickly gets to a stage where the acceleration of change is so great that it just doesn't matter how far behind it starts.

Like our discount super ball, AI is accelerating in its exponential rate of evolution. We can argue how incipient or immature it is today, but it will soon make no difference. The trajectory we are on will lead us to the future much faster than any of us think it will. Technology advances no longer add up; they multiply—in the case of AI, by increasingly larger exponential multipliers.

A simple AI engine can learn overnight how to play the classic computer game of Space Invaders better than any human ever has.[55] Like our super ball, every underlying technology we will talk about is already bouncing out of eyesight and quickly making its way into the mainstream of our lives and the way we build our businesses. We can argue how incipient or immature these technologies are today but it makes no difference in the long run. The trajectory we are on will lead us to the destinations we are going to describe, and it will do so much faster than any of us think it will.

Within just five to ten years after this book is published, we expect that many, if not all, the ideas we are presenting will be well into the mainstream of the adoption cycle. In saying that, we're not discounting the challenges as much as we're multiplying the opportunities. And one of the greatest and most radical of these opportunities will be the autonomous vehicle.

Head Out on the Highway

Of all the current and near-term potential applications of AI we believe that one will be the bellwether for how quickly we develop trust and accept AI as a reliable and natural—likely indispensable—part of our world: autonomous vehicles, or what we'll call AVs. By the way, you'll notice that we are going to stop calling them "driverless cars," which is another popular term in usage today. The reason is simply that the label is inaccurate; they have a driver, it just happens not to be a human.

The automobile is part of the fabric of the modern world. Not only is it a ubiquitous necessity for the global socioeconomic infrastructure, but we build an intense cultural, personal, and behavioral bond with our vehicles. They define a person's identity. They are the backbone of commerce. As an industry, vehicle manufacturing is large enough to represent the equivalent of the world's sixth largest economy, employing over 50 million people and producing nearly one hundred million vehicles each year.[56] By the way, bumper to bumper in single file, those vehicles would form a traffic jam that wrapped itself around the equator eight times![57]

In addition, of all the things we do each day, driving and sharing our world with vehicles is the single riskiest thing most of us do. Vehicles account for 1.3 million deaths each year, placing them as the tenth leading cause of death globally and the only non-disease related cause of death in the top ten.[58] However, if you adjust for the fact that there are only one billion vehicles globally, as opposed to the fact that all seven billion people risk acquiring any of the other nine diseases, you could make the claim that vehicle deaths are *the* leading cause of death for those who own or interact with an automobile. [59]

While doing research for the book we spoke with a number of personal injury lawyers and insurance companies. The gorilla in the room for both is that autonomous vehicles will have a dramatic impact on their business. Surprisingly, the reactions we got to that were not what you might expect. Marc Lamber, a personal injury lawyer at Fennemore Craig PC, a one hundred thirty-year-old Southwest law firm, shared with us the predominant perspective:

> *Ultimately, self-driving cars are remarkable in the sense that they will put me out of business. I'm a personal injury lawyer and I'm glad [about that]. I don't think it's going to happen in the next year but as you look at the rapidity with which the technology is moving forward, it's an eventuality that personal injury lawyers, like myself, who represent victims of car crashes, will be out of business or our business will be reduced drastically—and it's such a wonderful thing if you think about that statistically.*
>
> *There are over a million people who die every year worldwide in car crashes. One of the accepted statistics that I see thrown around is that at least 90 percent of traffic accidents are caused by human error. If we're in a stage 4 vehicle that's fully autonomous,*

*10 years down the road, we're going to elim-
inate almost all of those collisions. So, you're
saving potentially a million lives a year and
you're avoiding countless injury accidents.*

Marc's comments echoed a recurring theme that we came
across time and again. Everyone has been touched in some
way by a vehicular incident. We've come to accept one million, three hundred thousand deaths and as many at fifty million yearly injuries as a necessary risk of modern life. We will
soon look back on this as totally unnecessary human carnage.

Yet, another aspect of how automobiles fit into the fabric of our lives is their relationship with an aging population.
Few of us have not had to deal with the very hard conversation, or worse yet unilateral decision, of taking the keys away
from a parent. The automobile is perhaps one of the greatest statements of independence in modern society. When
it's taken away, it takes with it not just the license to drive
but the license to live a full life, to socialize, and to enjoy
personal freedom. But the risks of driving as we get older
are well documented. According to AAA, "With the exception of teen drivers, seniors have the highest crash death rate
per mile driven, even though they drive fewer miles than
younger people." With the megatrend of an aging population, seniors are outliving their ability to drive by seven to
ten years on average.[60]

And lastly, let's not forget the impact of vehicles on global
pollution and climate change. According to a study by NASA,
vehicles are the single largest contributor to climate change.[61]

Given the enormous impact vehicles have on culture,
risk, climate, the economy, employment, and nearly every
other aspect of our society, we see the acceptance of AVs as

being the most significant milestone in measuring, understanding, and accepting AI and the devices that use it; to paraphrase an old song, "If AI can make it here, it can make it anywhere..." Which is why we are going to use the AV as the primary example of what we believe will usher in the age of intelligence devices that exhibit behaviors and communicate with our digital-self.

Although it's a future with a unique set of challenges, they aren't entirely without precedent. So, it may help to first take a quick visit into the past and a very similar challenge from one hundred years ago.

Elevating Drivers

Coronado Island, just south of San Diego, is home to one of the world's Grand Dame resorts, the Hotel Del Coronado. The Hotel Del was built in 1888. It's hosted presidents as far back as William Taft and is said to have been part of the inspiration for *The Wizard Of Oz* when L. Frank Baum stayed there in 1904. Much has changed at the Hotel Del in 130 years, with dozens of new buildings, multi-million-dollar luxury condos, and expansive modern conference facilities. However, one thing hasn't changed. In the center of the magnificent main Victorian building, Andrew Lounsbury operates a brass accordion doored manual elevator, just as he has for the last thirty-seven years.

For hotel guests who never even knew that elevators were once run exclusively by "drivers," the novelty is something they're drawn to. However, you can see the look of apprehension and trepidation on their faces as they approach an elevator that needs to be driven. You can imagine that they're thinking, "Is that really safe? Why can't it operate on its own, the way real elevators do?" or "What if the driver makes a mistake and starts it up just as you're getting in or out?" After all, he's human, and humans are known to make mistakes.

Interestingly, although elevator operators were common through the mid-1900s, there were driverless elevators as far back as the early 1900s. There was just one problem. Nobody would use them. Given the choice between the stairs and a lonely automated elevator, the elevator would remain empty. It wasn't until the middle of the twentieth century that the tipping point came along for the driverless elevator.

In 1945, the elevator operators' union in New York City called a strike which pretty much shut down every elevator in the city, effectively shutting down the city itself. Enraged renters and landlords demanded action. The strike was devastating, costing the city an estimated one hundred million dollars. Suddenly, there was an economic incentive to go back to the automatic elevator. Over the next decade there was a massive effort to build trust in automatic elevators, which resulted in the elimination of tens of thousands of elevator operator jobs.

Few of us will today step into an elevator and even casually think about the way it operates, how safe it is, or what the risks are. If you find yourself at the Hotel Del and decide to take the elevator, stop and think about just how radical change can be in reshaping our attitudes about what's safe and normal.

Autonomous is a world apart from automatic, but the fundamental issue with the adoption of a driverless lift in either case isn't so much the technology—elevators already had the technology to be driverless for fifty years—it's about trusting a machine to do something as well as a human—in a word it's all about *perception*. Still doubtful? Perhaps you're one of the few people who have a fear of elevators? Well, you may be justified in your fear. After all, twenty-seven people die yearly as the result of faulty automatic elevators. However, you might also be interested in learning that, according to the Center for Disease Control's National Center for Health Statistics, a whopping one thousand six hundred people die from falling down stairs. We'll save you the math; that means you're sixty times as likely to have a fatal accident taking the stairs. Unfortunately, numbers alone rarely change perception.

As Amin Kashi, director of ADAS and autonomous driving at Mentor, a Siemens business, told us, "I'm sure we will look back on this in the not too distant future and think to ourselves, how could we have wasted all of that time commuting, how could we have dealt with the inherent lack of safety in the way that we used to drive. All these issues will become so obvious and so clear. From where we stand right now we're accustomed to a certain behavior so we live with it, but I think we will be amazed that we actually got through it."

Intelligent Behavior

Reaching autonomy is a progression that will involve both our own evolution as well as that of the AV. It will happen in fits and starts. There will be setbacks and breakthroughs. Effectively, what we're doing is introducing a new species with which we will share not just our roads but our world.

So, before we go much further, it's probably a good idea to clarify a few things and define exactly what we mean by the term autonomous vehicle and the AI that drives it. One of the greatest differentiating aspects of an AV is its ability to learn from experience by using AI. This is a major departure from the way programmed computers operate. A program is created by a human being and represents the entire universe of rules that a computer follows in performing a task. The rules may be complex but they are finite and can be understood by a human. In other words, when the computer makes a decision, it's based on these rules and we can go back and understand exactly why the computer acted the way it did. As we'll see, that's not true for AI.

When a computer (or any device) can learn from experience, we are tempted to immediately categorize it as intelligent, but we need to draw a distinction here among the forms of AI that make up a broad spectrum of solutions that go beyond conventional programmed computers. And within that spectrum we'll dive even further into a range of definitions for what constitutes autonomy.

We're not going to get into the deep history of AI and its many implications. Fascinating as that may be, much has been and is being written about it. One of the best and most concise resources to use if you want to come up to speed on AI was developed by the National Science and Technology Council (NSTC), *Preparing for the Future of Artificial Intelligence*.[62] We'd suggest you read it if your interest in AI goes beyond the scope of what we're going to cover here. Our objective is to provide a basic foundation to help understand how and why AI works.

The three major types of AI that we will discuss are machine learning, narrow AI, and general-purpose AI. We'll use AVs as the context for how we talk about AI. In the process, we hope to dispel some myths about how AI works and the sometimes-dystopian view that is promulgated by the hype machine which so easily plays to our fears of the future.

Let's start with machine learning, which is the most basic form of AI.

As with a programmed computer, machine learning starts with a basic set of rules for the computer to follow. We'll call these training rules. There's also a goal that defines if the rules are being applied correctly to achieve a specific outcome. The difference between a traditional programmatic approach and AI is that a computer capable of machine learning builds onto those rules (its programming) through experience. As the rules are applied, a statistical model is used by the computer to determine what combination of rules works best in any given situation to meet the goal. Think back to our description of the policy and value networks that are used by AlphaGo to play Go. The policy network defines the possible options and the value network defines the best option.

A simple analogy most of us can easily relate to would be learning to ride a bicycle. If you think back to when you first learned to ride a bicycle, you can probably recall, or at least imagine, the feeling of being overwhelmed by all of the things you needed to keep in mind in order to achieve the simple goal of staying upright and in control. We'd bet that you'd have a hard time listing all the rules that went into achieving that goal.

There were rules for how, when, and at what speed to pedal, what to do with your many body parts in order to maintain balance, observing your surroundings, the type of road you were on, its contours, whether it was wet or sandy, obstacles in your way, traffic, whether it was light or dark out, cloudy or sunny, calm or windy, all this and so much more that went into the simple act of staying upright long enough to allow the gyroscopic effect of your wheels to keep you from falling.

Wait. You did know that, right? It's not just your ability to balance that keeps you from falling over. The spinning motion of the bike's wheels creates a gyroscopic effect that keeps the bike moving forward and prevents it from tipping over. It's also partially the reason that to make a right turn on a bicycle you'd first turn the handlebars very slightly to the left while you lean to the right, which will push you and the bike to the opposite direction, at which point you'd straighten your handlebars, and turn. This sounds so utterly convoluted and counterintuitive that unless you get on a bicycle right now and try it you'll never believe us, and yet you've been doing this your entire life! Our point is that our brains know of behaviors that are empirically correct even though we may be consciously unaware of them or not even know why they are correct behaviors. A big part of intelligence is being able to behave in a way that achieves the right results without necessarily knowing all the details of why we behaved as we did. It just worked.

As you learned, your knowledge expanded to handle more and more new situations, until, finally, one day you could not only ride your bike in every way it was intended to be ridden but in many ways it hadn't—standing up, no hands, on the handlebars; and that was the real fun, being able to handle any situation that you came across. It was at this point that you trusted yourself because you intuitively calculated the odds were that you had a fairly high probability of staying upright and in control. That's really all that trust is, the confidence in being able to predict a certain outcome, usually based on reaching some critical amount of empirical data. Don't let the word empirical throw you. It doesn't mean that you have first-hand empirical data, just that similar experiences you've had, or similar experiences that others have had turned out well.

Clearly at this point you knew everything there was to know about riding a bicycle. Years passed and then something very frustrating happened. One day you had to take all this knowledge and transfer it to your own child, niece, nephew, or grandchild. Did you give them the list of the hundreds, perhaps thousands, of individual rules that you'd learned to follow? Of course not! You couldn't if you wanted to because there were just too many and most of them you weren't even aware of. So, how did they learn? The same way you did, by gathering hundreds of experiences and thousands of minute actions that were all measured against the goal of staying upright. Oh, and by the way, we're sure that you likely said to them, as you tried to assuage their fears, "Trust me, you'll get the hang of it."

The same applies to AI. The misconception is that the sort of AI needed to drive a car somehow can "think." It doesn't, at least not in the way humans think. Instead it follows a set of rules that are influenced by far too many variables for us to be able to practically understand. That's why we call it artificial intelligence; it's making decisions that aren't necessarily obvious, but still achieve the desired result. It's not that there isn't a finite set of rules (even though the set may be constantly expanding) but rather that it would just be impractical to try and dissect every decision down to everything that went into it. According to Andrew Kouri, Founder and CEO of lvl5, which makes specialized 3-D maps for AVs:

> *The [autonomous] car doesn't really think.*
> *It does just what it's instructed to do.*
> *Sometimes it's hard to get to the bottom*

[of] why it did what it was instructed to do. It really comes down to reproducing a large number of inputs, for instance, was it a really sunny day and was the sun at certain angle. The challenge then becomes "How do I reproduce that exact same situation to make it do it again?" so I can figure out where the bug was.

The complexity of how AI behaves and makes a decision doesn't make the decision conscious, sentient, or magic; it just makes it very difficult to understand—in the same way that you can't list all the things that go into riding a bike and instead you just say to your fledgling cyclist, "Trust me, you'll get the hang of it."

It also doesn't mean that AI can somehow start making decisions about things outside of what it was trained to do. Using the bicycle analogy, just because you've mastered riding a bike doesn't mean you can now drive a car or fly an airplane. In fact, you couldn't even go from two wheels to a unicycle without having to learn an entirely new set of rules.

This is what's called "narrow AI" because it is exceptional at one particular task. This is the sort of AI that's able to identify the objects in the path of an AV or the sort of AI used by Google Deep Mind's AlphaGo.

Narrow AI is the current state of the art in AI. It can be trained and then it can learn how to perform a task better and better over time through experience. Since the AI is doing the learning (as opposed to a human programming it), it isn't always obvious why it makes the decisions it makes. Again, that doesn't mean it's impossible to fully understand, just not practical. Does that make AI a black box that we should be scared of because it uses some sort of superhuman ability to make decisions? No. This is where so many conversations about AI get sensationalized.

For instance, in 2017 there was a widely publicized episode at Facebook Artificial Intelligence Research (FAIR) in which two chat bots using AI were tasked with the goal of winning at a negotiation. In order to follow the logic that the bots were using the engineers had trained the bots to use English to communicate with each other. However, they hadn't been specific enough to require English that conformed to a style understandable by humans. At one point the bots departed from any recognizable rules of grammar and had the following exchange (the bots in this case are named Bob and Alice):

> Bob: I can i i everything else
> Alice: balls have zero to me to me to me to
>   me to me to me to me to
> Bob: you i everything else
> Alice: balls have a ball to me to me to me
>   to me to me to me to me

The engineers stopped the bots, which were using a form of shorthand—typical behavior for bots—so that they could set up a new goal incentivizing the bots to use understandable language that conformed to proper word and sentence structure.

Not a big deal, just another day in the lab as far as the Facebook engineers were concerned. However, when word of the incident got out it spurred a flurry of media headlines about how Facebook's engineers had to pull the plug on AI run amuck to save the world from a bot invasion, which was light-years from the truth, but it made for good clickbait headlines.

The reality is that fearing technology is nothing new. Adrienne LaFrance, who wrote about computerphobia in the *The Atlantic*, said that "In the early days of the telephone, people wondered if the machines might be used to communicate with the dead.... Humans often converge around massive technological shifts—around any change, really—with a flurry of anxieties."[63]

Another *Atlantic* article asked one thousand five hundred people to rank eighty-eight separate items on a scale of one (least feared) to ten (most feared). When they tallied up and normalized the results, technology came in second, just behind natural disasters. To put things in perspective, death ranked almost exactly in the middle of the eighty-eight items. It seems any certainty, even death, is better than uncertainty. But that is a function of not really understanding AI.

Narrow AI is how we solve problems that have dynamic, fast changing, and uncertain sets of variables but very specific goals. These are inherently uncertain problems. They have no single solution and AI will make errors, just as a human would, because it is dealing with a problem that is not 100 percent solvable. Think back to our conversation about emergent systems in Chapter 2; AI is the evolving solution to an evolving problem. No machine or human being ever stops learning how to drive. You get better at it, but you can never experience every possible set of conditions and circumstances. However, the more you experience the more you trust your judgment and ability to deal with new challenges.

There is another form of AI, which is referred to as generalized AI. This is the ability to apply the sort of learning we've been talking about to any domain. The goals here are not specific because they too are learned. Humans are the best example of natural generalized learning. We first learn to learn and then we learn about specific areas that we want or need to develop deeper knowledge in. We then set our own goals and adapt our behaviors to reach those goals. Although it's fascinating to delve into Generalized AI, we're not going to spend much time talking about it here because we believe it will have minimal impact in the next five years outside of academic and laboratory settings. Still it's important to differentiate generalized AI from narrow AI when talking about the two since we still have no practical experience with generalized AI, leaving most conversations about it at a conceptual level.

So, this brings us back to the subject of applying AI to autonomous vehicles. And here too, as is the case with AI, there is no one type of autonomy.

The Road to Autonomy

The US Department of Transportation's National Highway Traffic Safety Administration (NHTSA) has adopted SAE's five levels of automation, which range from a vehicle that requires total human control (level 0) to a totally autonomous vehicle under any conditions a human could also drive (level 5). Here's a quick summary of the five levels.

Level 0: (Here since the Model T) This is the way we've all learned to drive. You as the driver are in control of every system. It's worth noting, however, that even at level 0, we've had antilock brakes and computerized traction control since the early 1970s. There was a time when you learned to pump your brakes when skidding and you'd steer into a skid. In the 1980s, both systems were made standard safety equipment.

This is a great example of how functions slowly make their way from driver to vehicle in an almost imperceptible manner.

Level 1: (Invented in 1990. In use since early 2000s) This level means that one or more systems assists in the steering or acceleration (and deceleration) of the vehicle. If you have adaptive cruise control, lane departure warning, or pedestrian braking, you are at this level. As the driver, you still have responsibility for being in full control of the vehicle and almost anything you do will instantly override the automated capabilities of the car. In fact, the system does not yet exist, at any level, in which the driver cannot override the autonomous features.

Level 2: (Invented in 1999. In use since 2003) This is where things start to get interesting. Some of us are already at this level. If you own a Tesla, a car that can parallel park on its own, or one which centers itself in a lane on the highway, then you are at level 2. At this level the driver can disengage by taking his or her hands off the steering wheel and feet off of the pedals, allowing the car to steer and adjust speed based on environmental factors, such as distance from other cars and traffic flow, staying within a lane. However, the driver still needs to be able to jump in at any time. And, once again, the vehicle still has to allow the driver to override its autonomous decisions.

For example, Teslas are designed to allow an override of the automatic emergency braking (AEB) if the driver turns the steering wheel, brakes, or presses the accelerator to full throttle. That should be a good thing, right? However, in March of 2017 Tesla was the target of a lawsuit which claimed that the Model S and X were accelerating at full throttle without any driver intervention.[64]

Oddly, the suit claimed that it wasn't the driver override that was an issue, per se, but that by allowing the car to accelerate at full throttle forward (even if it was initiated by a fault in the computer) and not applying the AEB, Tesla was liable for the consequences of any resulting damage or harm. The convoluted nature of this claim speaks to how uncharted the legal territory for AVs is.[65] So, should Tesla allow the driver to override the AEB, and should the car correct itself if it makes a mistake? Tesla has decided that the driver is always the final authority, which takes care of most liability issues for now, but as we'll see with levels 3 through 5, that's not a sustainable policy.

Level 3: (invented but not yet in use, other than experimentally) This level is where the balance of control shifts dramatically from driver to vehicle. You still need drivers in these cars, but the safety of the vehicle, under most circumstances, is up to the vehicle. However, there's a problem with level 3; it's called the "handoff," that point when the vehicle needs to hand off control to the human driver because it is no longer able to make the necessary decisions to drive the car safely. The handoff problem may well be one of the most challenging in getting beyond Level 3. Some experts in the field go so far as to say that it's not solvable. Karl Iagnemma, nuTonomy's CEO told us:

> [The five levels] are arguably one of the more damaging constructs in the AV field, this notion that we have level one, two, three, four, [five]. Implicit in that is that there's a natural progression from one to two to three to four. In fact, the right way to think about the levels of automation is that

we can go from one to two, but the next natural step is four, and that level three is actually properly a subset or a smaller set of features of level four. To solve level three correctly, you really need a level four system… there's really no good solution to the handoff problem. I'm not aware of one, and I don't think one exists to be honest.

The fact is, humans will get distracted. The better the system, the greater the inattention of the human will be because the more confidence they'll have in it, the less frequent the handoff request will be and, therefore, the less likelihood that someone will be ready to take the wheel literally at a moment's notice in a life-threatening situation. All of this creates a perfect storm. The better the system, the greater the demands on the human driver, and at the same time, the less reliability that that driver can be expected to have to actually pick up that demand. What it means is that you really need to have a system that's fully self-driving, perhaps within a set of operational conditions as level four implies, but to rely on a human to take control in a challenging situation, one that the automation can't figure out by definition, is just a very, very difficult path to go down.

We'll come back to this later in the chapter when we look at the catastrophic effects that handoffs can have by using an aviation example.

Level 4: This is where the vehicle truly becomes autonomous in the way we'd expect to use the term. At this level the vehicle can basically handle anything that it was meant to do on its own. But the concept "meant to do" implies that the vehicle could have some serious problems trying to navigate a situation it is not meant for. For example, sedans aren't meant to drive through off road terrain. The obstacles a vehicle might encounter or the visual signals it perceives may be well outside of its ability to assess and navigate.

Manufacturers call this acceptable envelope of conditions the "operational design domain" (ODD) of the vehicle. So, while a driver isn't needed within the ODD, if the vehicle finds itself forced off the road or the driver wants to drive through a field of tall grass to get to a rocky cliff overlooking the Pacific, the vehicle is well outside of its ODD and the driver needs to take over. Of course, it's possible to imagine how different vehicles could have different ODDs. A Hummer may well take you all the way to the cliff autonomously. If you're feeling a bit uneasy about that, don't worry; we'll come back to it later in the chapter.

Level 5: Now we've arrived. At this level a vehicle is fully autonomous and performs at least as well as a human in any scenario, anticipated or not. There is a bit of misrepresentation going on here however since by the time a Level 5 vehicle is developed it will undoubtedly operate much better than its human counterparts.

Today we are somewhere in between Levels 2 and 3, which is an especially precarious place in the evolution of AI and autonomous vehicles. The reason is that we are at a stage when we have to decide how AI and the human driver will coexist. On the one hand this is a mechanical challenge of coordinating who does what, but on the other hand it's also a challenge of trust. Let's first look at the mechanical challenge, which is actually rather easy to solve.

Since at Level 3 the vehicle can take over and the driver does not need to be engaged it's only natural for the driver to really disengage, lose situational awareness, get lost in a phone call, perhaps even fall asleep. How does the vehicle then notify the driver that it needs his or her help? The short answer is that in many cases it can't. If the situation is that dire then it's not likely the driver would have anywhere near enough time to assess and respond in any meaningful way. This is why many manufacturers of autonomous vehicles want to totally skip over Level 3; it just does not seem to be a practical scenario. However, this isn't as untenable as it seems.

Think of what it's like to drive with a new student driver, perhaps your son or daughter or a relative, when they first got behind the wheel. You probably drove them to a parking lot and then switched seats. They became the driver and you were the passenger. Did you then take them right from the parking lot onto the highway? Of course not. You first let them get a feel for the car while you also observed their level of competency. What you were doing, in the parlance of this book, was observing their behaviors.

Eventually your fledgling driver took the plunge and drove on the open road. But here we'd like you to stop and think carefully about that process. Since your house was probably not located at the foot of a highway onramp they had to drive along back roads, or perhaps through a town or city center to get to the highway. We'd guess that part of what you (and they) were thinking was, "Which route would be the most manageable given their skill set and behavior at that point?" So, you likely planned out the least challenging route onto the least challenging highway.

Effectively what you were doing was using an intuitively statistical model to determine the route which had the lowest probability of an incident or a set of conditions that exceeded the driver's abilities. If there was no such route then you, the experienced driver, probably drove part of the way.

Why not do the same with an AV? Using sophisticated maps of roadways, real time traffic and weather conditions, and a rating system that can be used to determine the skill set necessary for any particular route, an autonomous vehicle could easily calculate the probabilities of various risks along a variety of routes in getting you to your destination. Most of us are familiar with how a GPS will ask if you want the most direct route or the fastest route, one with highways or without; why not add an option for the autonomous car which asks if you want your ride to be fully autonomous for forty minutes or partially autonomous at thirty minutes?

According to Andrew Kouri, CEO and co-founder of lvl5, which uses crowdsourced dash cams to develop 3-D maps for autonomous cars:

> [What] we're working on at Level 5 is the ability to know which roads [autonomous cars are] going to be better at. We're doing all the data science and statistics to determine where we have good coverage. You can think of it like we're laying down railroad tracks. If you have a good map then you can allow the car to be at Level 3 (this is the level at which the human driver must be ready to take back control when the automated system requests it) on certain roads and then you can just disable the feature on

other roads. [With a map] you'll know the
historic accident rate on every single road
and we'll have the data science that tells us
"Which road we can't drive on."

This simple example illustrates that while it's tantalizing to think of AI as a technological overlord, a more accurate description is that of a collaborator who (yes, we said "who" and not "what" because we're anthropomorphizing AI intentionally) will work with us to determine which decision is in our best interests in a particular context.

We can guess at what you're likely thinking right now, "Using probabilities and statistics to determine my fate is a frightening proposition." It seems that way, but measured against what alternative? If it's choosing between staying home or being in a vehicle, then, yes, you're absolutely correct. There is a greater likelihood of being involved in a vehicle incident if you're in a vehicle than if you just stay indoors. Although, even that isn't entirely true since it's estimated that twenty thousand vehicles crash into commercial buildings each year in the US.[66]

The question we should be asking is: which has the highest probability of safely transporting us: a vehicle being driven by a human, AI, or a combination of the two? And the answer is, some combination, depending on the situation. If we give ourselves the option to pick and choose among the three, instead of pigeonholing ourselves into an "either or" answer, then we've just minimized the risk to the lowest possible degree at any point in time and situation.

You're still not convinced, and we probably know why. It comes back to perception and trust. Few of us have ridden in an autonomous or semi-autonomous vehicle. And it's perfectly normal not to trust the decisions being made by something we have no experience with. Well, guess what? We've been trusting far less sophisticated technologies with our lives for some time now. Level 0 and Level 1 vehicles already use antilock brakes, traction control, adaptive cruise control, proximity braking, and lane departure warnings among other computer-controlled functions that we take completely for granted.

Michael Fleming, CEO of Torc Robotics, talked to us about the three levels of experience which he's noticed as drivers turn into passengers:

> *When we bring passengers into our facility [to experience a self-driving car], three different things happen. At first, the passenger is very uptight. They're skeptical. They're not really sure if it's self-driving. It's sort of like sitting in a car with a new driver that just got their driver's license. You're not quite sure what they're going to do. In the second phase the passenger realizes how bad of a driver they and other people are because the self-driving vehicle is incredibly smooth, it [drives] perfectly inside the lane, no weaving, no oscillation. Then the third phase is a feeling of boredom because at the end of the day, driving is fairly boring. So how do we walk folks through these three cycles and get them to the third phase where it becomes boring and they begin trusting the technology?*

We can look to another form of transportation to make the point even clearer. Modern commercial aircraft are an

exceptional example of collaboration between a human operator and a computer. On a typical flight, commercial pilots
report actually flying the plane without computer assistance
for only seven minutes. Airbus pilots claim it's half that.[67]
To be clear, none of this is being done by systems that even
remotely qualify as AI, based on our earlier definition of having the ability to learn from experience. The computers used
to fly a commercial aircraft today are all hardwired with a set
of finite instructions. If something happens, and the instructions aren't adequate to handle the situation, control of the
aircraft goes back to the pilot. This was the case on June 1,
2009 when an Air France 447 was making its way across the
Atlantic from Rio de Janeiro to Paris.

Six Minutes of Terror

There was nothing especially challenging about the route Air
France flight 447 was flying on June 1, 2009, except for the
typical storm cells that showed up on the plane's onboard
radar. Flights that had made the crossing before them chose
to route themselves around the storm cells. The pilots of
AF 447 didn't know that. If they had, the captain, who had
thirteen thousand hours of experience flying commercial jets
would not have decided to take a nap in the sleeping berth
behind the cockpit during their Atlantic crossing.

But the storm wasn't typical. It extended to sixty thousand feet, well above the flight ceiling of any commercial
airliner. By the time the two co-pilots on the flight deck
realized the extent of the storm, there was just no way to
go around it. Still, modern jet aircraft are built to handle
nearly all weather conditions. Flying through a thunderstorm
at thirty-five thousand feet isn't pleasant but it's well within
the abilities of the plane and an experienced pilot. However,

as AF 447 was in the midst of the towering cumulonimbus clouds, it encountered ice that clogged its pitot tube sensors. Pitot tubes relay airspeed to the computer and to the pilots. Airspeed is among the most critical pieces of information without which neither the autopilot nor the human pilot can correctly fly the plane.

Although the plane was one of the most sophisticated computerized aircraft at the time, an Airbus 330, without input for airspeed, the plane's computer autopilot shut down and turned control over to the co-pilots, who were also unable to determine the plane's speed. As a result, one of the pilots did the last thing a pilot should do in any plane attempting to stay aloft at an uncertain speed: in an attempt to gain altitude, he pulled back on the joystick and pitched the plane's nose up just enough to put the plane into a stall.

A stall is a condition that reduces the effect of lift on the wings until the drag on the plane and gravity cause the plane to literally fall out of the sky. After six harrowing and utterly convoluted minutes of the pilots trying to reorient themselves, the plane plunged into the Atlantic, killing all two hundred twenty-eight passengers and crew members.[68] What's astounding, however, is that two minutes after the autopilot was disengaged the pitot tubes began functioning again. If at any time during the next four minutes the pilots had turned the autopilot back on the plane would have effortlessly continued on course at its assigned altitude.

The details of AF 447 are terrifying in describing the degree to which human error can be magnified in a time of crisis.[69] But what makes the story of AF 447 especially hard to make sense of is that an Airbus under what is called "normal law," meaning that the computer prevents the plane from flying outside of its flight envelope, is impossible to stall. No matter how hard the pilot pulls back on the joystick, the computer will compensate and not allow a stall.

However, in this case, with the autopilot disengaged, the plane switched over to "alternate law," meaning that the pilot had full manual control, which could not be overridden by the computer. Unfortunately, it gets much worse. Although the computer was disengaged from controlling the plane it still sounded a stall alarm (a mechanical voice warning that says "STALL" followed by an impossible to ignore high pitched tone). It did this no less than seventy-five times as the plane descended from thirty-seven thousand feet into the Atlantic.

The Air France incident was ultimately attributed to pilot error resulting from a lack of training. Amazingly, neither of the copilots (recall that the captain was sleeping in a berth behind the cockpit during most of the incident) had flown the same conditions in practice or in a simulator!

There's much to learn from this tragedy about how humans interact with technology, the way in which we perceive and trust it, and by extension how AI should work alongside humans.

Perhaps the most telling aspect of AF 447 was that the pilots were having anything but a conversation with their computer—they were outright ignoring its warnings—and therein lies much of the problem in how we perceive technology and AI.

In 1960 a computer scientist and psychologist, (widely regarded as one of the early pioneers of computing, but of whom few have heard), J. C. R. "Licks" Licklider, wrote what was his second most influential paper, "Man-Computer Symbiosis," in which he described the sort of relationship that humans need to have with computers in order to develop a collaborative approach to problem solving, especially in cases such as AF 447 when our instincts alone are simply inadequate. Licks believed that, "many problems... are very difficult to think through in advance. Think back to our earlier description of emergent systems. They would be easier to solve, and they could be solved faster, through an intuitively guided trial and error procedure in which the computer cooperated, turning up flaws in the reasoning or revealing unexpected turns in the solution."[70]

By the way, if you're wondering about Lick's first most influential paper, it was an April 23, 1963 memo which he wrote as the USA's first director of Information Processing Techniques (at the time part of ARPA—Advanced Research Projects Agency). The memo was titled "Members and Affiliates of the Intergalactic Computer Network." In it he described an "electronic commons open to all.[71] His memo is said to have inspired the development of ARPANET in the 1960s, which eventually became the internet.

So, how would Licks's symbiotic approach work in moments of crisis such as what was experienced on AF 447? The challenge in dealing with a situation that is unexpected, uncertain, and time sensitive is making decisions that have the lowest probability of doing harm (think of the Hippocratic oath which doctors take to "first do no harm") and the highest probability of success.

As humans, we naturally respond to a crisis that we haven't experienced by using past knowledge and intuition. But, as we just saw, intuition can lead to disastrous consequences. The problem is that unless we can be shown irrefutable proof that our intuition is wrong we will stick to it since we trust it, after all it is "our" intuition. Nothing proves this point more dramatically than ignoring seventy-five stall warnings blaring at you for nearly six minutes.

Here's where AI can play a pivotal role. We're going to take a little detour to use a well-known problem from game theory that illustrates just how biased our intuition can be, and how AI can help solve that problem.

Let's transport ourselves from the cockpit of our doomed airliner to 1970s prime time TV. Imagine that you are on a game show and the host has three doors that you can open one at a time. Behind one of the doors there's the grand prize of a vacation for two and a brand-new car. Behind the other two doors there are rubber chickens. You get to win whatever is behind the door you pick, and rubber chickens are not what you're hoping for. This is called the Monty Hall problem, named after the host of a popular game show, *Let's Make A Deal.*

The host asks you to pick a door, which you do. Let's say it's door #3. The host then opens door number #1 to reveal a rubber chicken. To make things interesting he then says, "Let's make a deal. I'll give you the option of keeping your original door or switching it with the other, still closed door." What maximizes the probability of your getting the grand prize vacation and car, staying with your current door or changing to the other closed door?

If you're like most people your answer would be that it doesn't matter, since it's still one out of three doors. Wrong, it does matter. If you stick with your current door your odds are 1 in 3 that the grand prize is behind it. If you switch to the other closed door, your odds of success increase by 50 percent. Yes, we know, every fiber of your being is now recoiling in disbelief. The probability is absolutely not supported by intuition.

If the three doors bother you then let's make it ten doors. Same rules. Only one door has a grand prize. You pick a door and the host opens up eight doors to display eight rubber chickens. Do you want to guess what happens to your odds if you switch doors now? While your original door has a one in ten chance of success, the other closed door now has a nine out of ten chance at success. (It's not fifty-fifty as intuition would lead you to believe.)

As absurd as this seems the statistics are easy to obtain. If we run ten thousand simulations of the Monty Hall game the numbers that come back irrefutably support the math. You can try it yourself on a variety of online simulators that will let you set up the number of doors and the number of games.[72] The more you run the simulator, the easier it becomes to appreciate the correct course of action is not an intuitive one.

What's happening is that our intuition gets stuck in the way the situation was originally presented while the context for the decision has changed. Humans have an especially tough time keeping up with rapidly changing context because we get so attached to a pattern once we decide on it. In the case of the Monty Hall problem, what changes and alters the context is that the game show host has prior knowledge of what's behind each door.

Back to the flight deck of our Airbus. How would what we just described have helped the Air France Pilots? Well, what AI is exceptional at is running simulations that involve myriad factors that a human could not possible calculate in real time, especially under conditions as stressful as the flight deck of flight 447. While the pilots where trying to stabilize the situation, in this case doing what was intuitive but entirely incorrect, the AI could have been running thousands if not millions of scenario simulations to determine what combination of actions would be the most likely to succeed. Sounds pretty far-fetched, right? It's not.

According to an article in the *New York Times*, "This summer, the Defense Advanced Research Projects Agency, the Pentagon research organization, will take the next step in plane automation with the Aircrew Labor In-Cockpit Automation System, or ALIAS. Sometime this year (2018), the agency will begin flight testing a robot that can be quickly installed in the right seat of military aircraft to act as the co-pilot. The portable onboard robot will be able to speak, listen, manipulate flight controls and read instruments."

What's especially interesting about the role of simulation is that we've already shown how valuable it is with humans. In fact, from 1940 until 1990 the percentage of aircraft incidents attributable to pilot error didn't budge from about 65 percent. All of the aviation industry's incredible technological advances in everything from engine reliability, to instrumentation, human ergonomics, and airspace control and management hadn't made a dent in the rate of pilot errors. During the 1980s, the rate of incidents attributable to pilot error started to fall. By 1987 it was 42 percent. Today it's around 20 percent.[73]

So, what happened in the 1980s? While advances in technology and training certainly helped, one additional factor that is credited as the most influential is the evolution of highly realistic computer flight simulators that were able to almost precisely mimic the way a plane would handle and react to a pilot's reactions in real time. It's not coincidental that it was also in the 1980s that the first consumer grade simulators started to appear on the market. first for the Apple II and then for the IBM PC.

Simulation was not new. It had been around since the 1920s and was used extensively during World War II. Prior to that crude stationary flight trainers had also been used. But these were all intended to help pilots develop orientation and confidence in the basic operations of the aircraft. The simulators of the 1980s allowed pilots to experience an endless variety of conditions, malfunctions, and the immediate results of their responses.

Now imagine we are once again in the cockpit of ill-fated AF 447. What if we could have frozen time and allowed the pilots to run through thousands of flight simulations of those exact conditions. Do you think the likelihood of a positive outcome may have increased significantly? That's precisely what onboard AI could do, and it would not only have knowledge of this flight but of all flights in a similar set of conditions. By the way, this is precisely the sort of time dilation we talked about earlier in Chapter 3.

But there's still one fatal flaw to this ideal collaboration between human and computer. Recall that our pilots totally ignored the computer's stall warnings. In fact, the transcript of the cockpit voice recorder, recovered from the airplane's black box, does not mention a single verbal acknowledgement by the pilots of the numerous stall warnings. And this is where we believe the single greatest obstacle to AI and autonomous devices resides. Namely, that we do not relate to or regard technology as a collaborator.

Imagine if one of the pilots had yelled out the stall warning seventy-five times. Do you think that might have been heeded? A big part of the problem is that we have been conditioned to not only see technology as distinct from humans but to relentlessly avoid anthropomorphizing technology. That may have made good sense when computers where nothing more than glorified calculators, but it actually works against us as AI evolves and transforms computers and devices into entities capable of making complex decisions that are as good if not better than their human counterparts.

Again, we are talking about narrow AI that has deep experience in specific domains. In these cases, we actually need to make the way in which we interact and converse with computers indistinguishable from the way in which we communicate with other humans. We won't belabor this analogy much further, but what if our cockpit stall warning had said, "Pierre-Cédric [the co-pilot primarily responsible for pitching the plane's nose upward for the entire six minutes], you are ignoring my warning that the plane is in a stall and losing altitude. Please take immediate corrective action by pitching the nose down or give me control so that I can rectify the situation."

Most people reading that last sentence will shudder at the thought of AI taking on the behavior, intonations, and mannerisms of a human. It's frightening, creepy, unnatural, and not the place of a computer. And that attitude, not the technology, is precisely what undermines our ability to coexist with AI because we don't want it to act like a human. This is almost exactly what we described in the lawsuit being brought against Tesla for allowing driver override of the car's autonomous braking (in Chapter 3). We have or soon will have technology which can make decisions faster and better than a human being within a narrow set of parameters. But only if we allow it.

An AV being driven at full throttle toward a crowded bus stop, whether it is intentional or not, has the ability to stop itself. If that ability exists would allowing the car to proceed unabated be justified by any ethical or moral standard? We don't allow drivers to remove or disable airbags, which can themselves be lethal in rare circumstances. The reason we allow driver override today, even in situations where it is clear that the outcome will be worse, is because of two reasons: we aren't sure how to shift the legal liability from the driver to the AV; and we fear the ability of a technology to make a better decision than a human.

If AF 447 had onboard AI, which was able to access basic information about the context of the ill-fated flight, it would have known that thirty-two-year-old Pierre-Cédric was the least experienced of the three pilots, that high risk weather was developing ahead, that planes in front of AF 447 were vectoring around the storm, and that the ice had cleared off of the pitot tubes providing enough data for the autopilot to easily fly the plane.

Bridging this gap between the machine and the human has never been this hard. It used to be that we could draw hard lines between what was the human's responsibility and what was the responsibility of the machine. There was no doubt about who was in charge, never a contest nor a conflict between the two, because there was no overlap in the area of making judgment-based decisions; that was always the role of the human. The machine simply provided information and followed instructions. We were the ultimate authority because we had the ultimate cognitive upper hand. Machines were merely extensions of our physical selves. Now they are extensions of our digital-selves. The cognition is at best shared with, and in many narrow cases far exceeded by, the abilities of the machine.

If this new model of shared responsibility between man and machine terrifies you and threatens what you consider to be the uniquely human capability of decision-making, we'd suggest that you hold on tight because that's just the beginning of an even more disruptive and inevitable trend in how we will work with autonomous devices—their ability to own themselves.

The Building Blocks of the Future

One of the economic cornerstones of modern society, free markets, and capitalism is the inalienable right of the individual to own property. We take that so much for granted in the developed world that we rarely, if ever, think of what life would be like without it. However, travel to parts of the world where property ownership is a distant dream, or where it can be usurped by government, military coups, or rogue factions of society, and you realize how important it is as a cornerstone of economic stability and prosperity. We're not speaking in the abstract here. One of us (Tom) lived through a coup d'état and martial law. Nothing creates a deeper sense of respect and reverence for the critical importance of property rights than having them taken away overnight.

What does this have to do with autonomous vehicles and our digital-selves? We believe that one of the biggest challenges in creating the sort of future we're describing is protecting and owning our digital-self. This one innovation we are going to talk about will extend the idea of ownership to digital assets and devices in ways that will be as critical to the economy of the 21st century as the concept of a central bank was to the economy of the nineteenth and twentieth centuries.

The Peruvian economist Hernando DeSoto has written extensively on property rights, claiming that they are one of the cornerstone requirements for economic growth and prosperity in developed economies. However, we would take the liberty of extending DeSoto's premise and modifying it to apply to not only the ownership of tangible property but also to the shared ownership of ideas and our digital-self . If we expect to foster open and collaborative innovation we need to change the very nature of the way we think about ownership, especially in a world where ideas, intellectual property, capital, and goods flow so freely, and where our digital behaviors are so readily available.

We will come back to the issue of ownership and protection of our digital-self again in Chapter 8. For now, let's look at extending this premise to include not only real property but also creative works and intellectual property. Ultimately that leads to a very interesting question, who owns the product or the work of AI? Who owns your digital-self?

Thinking back to our aviation example, it's clear that every pilot who reads the transcript of those fateful last six minutes will never again hear a stall warning and not think of AF 447. The lessons from that incident are critical to share and to learn from. Which is why the details of what happened are not the property of Air France; to regard these as intellectual property owned by just one airline would be unthinkable and unethical. But what about the knowledge base that a particular AI system uses to make its decisions?

Should Airbus share its AI algorithms and decisions with Boeing? What about American and United, or Tesla and GM—should they share the works of their AI with each other as direct competitors? Should a company that has AI, which can benefit the greater good of society, be compelled to license their AI to its competitors?

As it stands right now, US copyright law does provide some ground rules:

503.03(a) Works-not originated by a human author.

In order to be entitled to copyright registration, a work must be the product of human authorship. Works produced by mechanical processes or random selection without any contribution by a human author are not registrable.

However, while that may help with works that are published, the decision-making process and the data that AI uses may never be published, they exist within the AI. So, the question remains, who owns the knowledge base of any specific application of AI?

What we envision is a world in which the definition of ownership will change dramatically because of the ability to create indisputable digital records of ownership that can belong to any entity, human, device, robot, or AI.

While this might sound far-fetched there is an obvious precedent for it, the corporation. Corporations are clearly not human, however, under a landmark decision by a US court in 1886 the corporation was recognized as a "natural person" in the eyes of the law. Corporations can be held accountable and liable for breaking the law. We regard them as having civic and philanthropic obligations, even values. But we also shield their shareholders from liability or prosecution, what's called the corporate veil that separates the legal liability of the corporate entity from its owners.[74]

The purpose behind the existence of a corporation as a separate legal entity is fairly straightforward. It limits the liability of shareholders to the amount of their investment, capping their downside but leaving room for an unlimited upside. If you bought Enron shares in the summer of 2000 for ninety dollars, by November of 2001 you had lost 98 percent of your investment. However, there was never a question about whether you might be going to jail as did many of Enron's executives. Now, to be clear, had you done something criminal, the corporate veil would not have protected you. However, you are not guilty of any wrongdoing just by virtue of your ownership of the corporation's stock.

Then why is it so difficult to apply that same thinking and those same rights to a digital entity? Couldn't an AV become a "natural person" in the eyes of the law? If this notion makes you feel uneasy it may be because we believe that an AV or any intelligent digital entity will actually be making decisions while corporations don't make decisions; the people running them do. But that's not entirely accurate. If you buy a complex product that has the potential to do great damage if it has a defect, it can be nearly impossible to pin the blame on any one person. Ford's supply chain consists of twelve thousand one hundred companies spread out over sixty countries providing over one hundred thirty thousand parts (These are just parts for the vehicles. It does not include parts, supplies, and services that Ford needs to run its operations.) Many times it's just not possible or practical to determine who is at fault. So, ultimately, it's the corporation that needs to own the liability for the error and to potentially provide recompense for any financial or physical harm.

But how could we possibly transfer that responsibility and liability to an autonomous vehicle or intelligent device which doesn't have the ability to own anything, insure itself, or otherwise follow through on a legal liability? The answer is a recently developed technology that provides the mechanism to do just that for any object that has a digital twin or digital-self. It's called the blockchain.

The Building Blocks of Trust

If you just tuned out we're not surprised, that is exactly the reaction most people have to blockchain. They discount its impact because it sounds like techno-speak. After all, if block-chain was important it would be easy to understand its value. At one time the same was said about the internet. The biggest challenge in explaining the impact of blockchain is that it is itself an invisible technology from the standpoint of a user. In the same way that you do not see the databases which store all of the information for a computer application, there's no way to see blockchain. Yet, we are already starting to see the potential it has to shape the future of ownership for both digital and physical assets.

Blockchain is typically associated with Bitcoin and digital cryptocurrency. We'll talk about that more in Chapter 8 because the blockchain and cryptocurrencies have a very specific and unexpected link to how we protect our digital-self, but over the long-term cryptocurrency is only one application of blockchain. For now, we'll look at how it impacts the basic challenge of ownership of digital assets.

A blockchain is a digital file that records a user's public key and a transaction in a block. The block can only be accessed by someone who has the corresponding private key. Public and private keys are simply encrypted codes that identify the owner of a piece of data. The block can record any digital asset or link to a specific physical asset. The blocks are stored on nodes in an extensive network of computers called a P2P (peer to peer) network. The advantage of a P2P network is that it is highly decentralized across thousands or millions of computers. That provides redundancy as well as what's typically referred to as "self-correcting" or "self-heal-ing," which simply means that errors or hardware failures of one or a few nodes in the network won't impact the integrity of the data being stored in the blockchain.

The integrity of the blockchain is also in how it encrypts what's being recorded using what's referred to as a hashing algorithm. That means any information referenced by the blockchain can never change without it being evident that it has been changed. There's a risk here of getting too far into the mechanics of blockchain and that's not our intent. But a basic understanding of hashing is worth having in order to understand a bit of what's going on behind the scenes.

In the case of the blockchain an algorithm called SHA-256 (Secure Hash Algorithm) is used. This just means that whatever the source document or transaction is, it can be represented by a unique fixed length alphanumeric string. In practice here's how it works.

If I take the title of this book, *Revealing The Invisible: How Our Hidden Behaviors Are Becoming The Most Valuable Commodity Of The 21st Century*, and hash it, what I get back is "9be39603a405eabbe8aaaec8f2cf086e."

That string is the hash which identifies the title in a unique way. To show just how unique, if I only add one more space after the colon, *Revealing The Invisible: How Our Behaviors Are Becoming The Most Valuable Commodity Of The 21st Century* my hashed result looks like this "c98fd53e159c5be029dbb1c01411c489."

You'll notice that the two have no remote resemblance to each other. In fact, it doesn't matter how long the text I hash is, it could be this entire book, the same number of characters are used to create a unique hash. For example, if I take the first sentence of the paragraph that follows this one and hash it, I get, "5e6c32cd3f97e37ab098de0207c433f9."

The hash algorithm is not encryption; it's a one-way street, meaning that you can't reverse engineer it to determine the text which created it. But if I were to change just a single punctuation mark in this book, its hashed value would be entirely different.

The technology is fascinating, but how blockchain works is less important than what it does. The blockchain provides a definitive and indestructible digital record of ownership, provenance, and rules for the stake you have in something. This indisputable chain of ownership is why, when talking about blockchain, people usually refer to contracts—these are the agreements to conduct transactions that are supported by blockchain.

To keep this simple, imagine that you are conducting a transaction online—let's say you're buying a product. Typically that transaction would be stored in a database on a server in the cloud. It may get backed up but it has one primary location where it exists. The risk in that centralized approach is that if the record of your transaction is tampered with or somehow altered, destroyed, or otherwise rendered unusable, you've just lost the proof that the transaction ever occurred. Since blockchain stores the transaction across an extensive network of computers, the transaction is only valid if it agrees across that entire network.[75]

By using a combination of incredibly computer intensive algorithms to create a unique identity for a digital transaction and then storing the resulting information in this distributed network (also called a distributed ledger) the transaction is for all intents and purposes immutable. There is a price that's paid for public blockchains since the entire blockchain is stored on every node in a network. This works for applications that involve relatively low volumes of hundreds or thousands of transactions. When hundreds of thousands or millions of transactions are involved enterprise class blockchain frameworks are also available, such as Microsoft's Coco.[76]

There are two primary benefits to using blockchain. One is obvious and one is not. It's the not so obvious one that creates the greatest promise for blockchain.

The first benefit is that you have a virtually bulletproof vault within which to store a transaction or anything that's digitally attached to the transaction. This includes physical items with a digital twin. The second benefit is that blockchain removes any need for intermediaries. Transactions can now occur between totally unrelated parties, who know nothing of each other, with complete trust in the integrity of the transaction. This is also what allows parties who are anonymous to each other to have an ownership stake in something of value without the need for a centralized administrator. To appreciate how radical that last statement is imagine the New York Stock Exchange without the need for an exchange or brokers and traders, or a currency without the need for a treasury or a central bank, or mortgages without the need for bankers. All of these scenarios may seem like ludicrous examples but we'll come back to exactly how this is already being done in Chapter 9.

Notice, by the way, that we said ownership *stake* in, and not just ownership. The blockchain radically alters our very notion of ownership by shifting the focus from hiding, hoarding and protecting ideas to exposing, sharing, and distributing them. Imagine for example that in writing this book every footnote, reference, attributable quote, and case study was a contract in the blockchain. Conceptually that would mean that every time someone buys a copy of this book all of the individuals and entities referenced in it could be entitled to some piece of the proceeds.

Doing this democratizes economic value flow at the most granular level. If you have a stake in one thousand value creating entities you then have a potential revenue flow from each one. Your employer now becomes the blockchain, except that the blockchain isn't an entity, like a corporation. Instead it's an algorithm which enables trust and transactions with an absolute minimum of friction.

The tell-tales of this shift to more collaborative work have been there for some time. A similar mechanism is already used in the music industry where artists share royalties for whatever portion of a work they contribute to. Granted, in that case the contract is a manual one created and agreed to by human beings and stored in a physical or digital file folder.

Another tell-tale is the more generalized trend toward greater distributed collaboration. Consider that, as shown in Illustration 4.1, during the first half of the twentieth century (1901–1949), 70 percent of all Nobel prizes in the physical sciences (Physics/chemistry/medicine) were awarded to individuals. In the second half of the last century (1950–1999) the ratio flipped, with 66 percent awarded to teams. In the first seventeen years of the 21st century, 88 percent of Nobels in the physical sciences were awarded to teams.[77] Further evidence: Delphi Group, conducted a study of six hundred individuals in which 20 percent of respondents indicated that patents no longer served any useful purpose. 74 percent indicated that the current patent system needed a radical overhaul.

By promoting frictionless collaboration, blockchain is likely to accelerate 21st century innovation in the same way that patent law did for the 20th century, but in a way that will allow anyone who contributes to a good idea (man or machine) to protect their stake in it, while also allowing the transparency needed for these ideas to build on each other at a rate and scale unimaginable in the past.

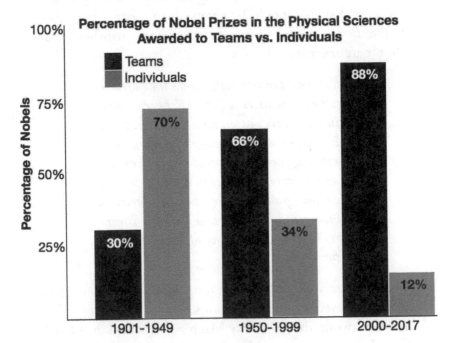

Illustration 4.1
There has been a steady increase in the number of Nobel prizes awarded to teams (multiple individuals) as opposed to individuals, from 30 percent in the period of 1901–1949 to 88 percent in the period from 2000–2016.

We realize, by the way, that there is an added wrinkle to the issue of patent and copyright ownership based on our earlier discussion about these rights only being granted to the products of human authorship. But this is not an immutable obstacle. And there's a mounting sentiment among patent attorneys that this should be changed. In a paper published in the *Boston College Law Review*, patent attorney Ryan Abbott argues that:

> *An innovation revolution is on the horizon. Artificial intelligence ("AI") has been generating inventive output for decades, and now the continued and exponential growth in computing power is poised to take creative machines from novelties to major drivers of economic growth. A creative singularity in which computers overtake human inventors as the primary source of new discoveries is foreseeable.*

Computers are already creating works of art, original music, and even product inventions. A computer using a dual neural network, the Creativity Machine, invented the Oral-B Cross bristle pattern toothbrush. However, the machine does not own the pattern, that still belongs to the machine's inventor, computer scientist Doctor Stephen Thaler.[78]

Why would we even want to grant non-human AI entities ownership rights? For the same reason that corporations can own assets, it provides the ability to create value, enter into binding agreements, accept liability, provide for insurability, allow for the flow of value to and from other human and non-human entities, and optimize the use of resources. In fact, we see blockchain as being one of the most significant contributors to the increased efficiency we will need to responsibly scale the planet to ten billion people.

A Wildly Distributed Future

Let's make this notion of ownership and efficiency even easier to follow using Uber as an example. Today Uber relies on owners of cars to provide ride sharing services to clients. What makes this model work is that there are lots of car owners who have cars that are on average only used 5 percent of the time.[79] That's an enormous waste of value and resources. Which is why Uber's model is a great way to leverage latent assets and people while addressing a fundamental need of a modern urban ecosystem: the need for frictionless mobility. Now let's apply blockchain and autonomous vehicles to that model.

When most people try to adapt the Uber model to an autonomous vehicle the natural inclination is to imagine Uber buying fleets of robotic cars. But that just perpetuates an industrial era ownership model. You can picture row upon row of Uber cars that all look the same; we've just gone back to any color as long as it's black. It would certainly be more efficient from the standpoint of resource utilization since the cars wouldn't be sitting in a garage or a parking lot 95 percent of the time. However, there's still a corporation with employees, management and executives, offices and equipment to factor into the equation. Additionally, the competitive landscape would be limited since enormous initial investment would be required to effectively compete against Uber's scale.

Instead, what if autonomous cars were non-human legal entities in which many people had a stake—not unlike a public corporation, which has many owners? We'd ask that you stop here and think about all of the reasons why that wouldn't work. We're going to guess that your list may include: individual cars would be much more expensive assets since they could not achieve economies of scale; autonomous cars could not maintain themselves; if riders were unhappy there's nobody to complain to. What happens to a car when it's no longer viable? Who's to blame if the car is involved in an accident?

Blockchain addresses every one of these concerns: it allows cars to collaborate with each other and to form coalitions with buying power, clout, and economies of scale; it enables transactions for self-service to be conducted with other human or non-human entities, such as an automotive repair shop. The AV can even sell itself off for parts and distribute the proceeds to its owners when demand for its services dips below a profitable threshold; and, just like a human, it can have insurance and funds to pay for damages or liabilities.

Depending on how profitable any particular AV is, you could move your stake from car to car based on which ones perform best. Pools of cars could join forces to create their own AV corporations and build in redundancy to increase profit margins and return to owners; they could even build a brand image for themselves.

You're starting to see just how foundationally radical and disruptive blockchain is. Simply put, this is the stuff that social and economic revolutions are made of.

After we strip away all of technology jargon that surrounds blockchain, what we are left with is a new way to conduct business that is based on our very simple notion at the outset of this book; that every person, product, organization, and device exists not only in the physical world but also in the digital world. While the real world may be subject to the laws of physics, where friction is part of every movement and action, in the digital world there is no friction. That opens up doors to a new age of frictionless transactions, and that's our next stop in revealing the invisible.

CHAPTER 5

The End of Friction and the Industrial Age: How Behavior is Reshaping Business

*It's not the revolution that
destroys machinery, it's the friction.*
—*Henry Ward Beecher*

Henry Ford's innovation was not mass production, nor the principle of interchangeable parts. Both had been in use for at least one hundred years prior to the invention of the Tin Lizzie. In fact, Ford did not even create the assembly line. Ransom Eli Olds and the Cadillac Motor Co. were already using complex interchangeable parts and assembly lines in their manufacturing processes.

Ford's innovation was so simple as to be overlooked even in most history books. He viewed the complex problem of assembling an automobile as an engineer would have contemplated the workings of a complex machine with thousands of moving parts, and he set out to minimize the one universal impediment to the efficiency of any machine: friction.

The assembly lines in a Ford plant moved like the carcasses he had observed being carried by overhead conveyors in Detroit's meat packing plant lines—work was transported to the worker, not the other way around. Ford perfected the assembly line and reduced its friction to the absolute bare minimum he could. For example, he realized that by manipulating the speed of the line, he could find the maximum rate at which work moved before quality was compromised and errors set in, thereby manipulating the output of his workers.

As the writer E.L. Doctorow noted about Ford: "He'd conceived the idea of breaking down the work operations in the assembly of an automobile to their simplest steps, so that any fool could perform them...Thus, the worker's mental capacity would not be taxed. The man who puts in a bolt does not put on the nut."

From these principles, which today strike us as archaic, Ford established the final proposition of the theory of industrial manufacture—not only that the parts of the finished product be interchangeable, but that the men and women who build the products be themselves interchangeable parts.[80]

Ford's success was self-evident. He began to implement the assembly line system in the spring of 1913. The first component to be manufactured on the line was the magneto coil assembly. Prior to this, a single worker assembled a magneto from start to finish, a process that took twenty minutes. A good employee could produce thirty-five or forty units per day. Ford divided the process into twenty-nine discrete steps, to be performed by twenty-nine different workers, and the time for producing a magneto fell to thirteen minutes.[81]

Ford then extended the concept to the assembly of motors and transmissions. The first moving assembly line was installed in 1914. Where assembly of a car took seven hundred twenty-eight hours of one man's work (forty-three thousand, six-hundred eighty minutes) several years before, the new system allowed a Model T to be assembled in just ninety-three minutes.[82]

The efficiency of Ford's system was undeniable. A worker in the door panel division of Ford's River Rouge factory would have known nothing about the way in which those doors were attached to the chassis; that was the job of another worker "down the line."

Hot on the heels of Ford's early developments, Frederick Winslow Taylor developed scientific management principles for industrial work. He attempted to create near-perfect harmony between workers and their tasks. Soon, the science of "time-motion study" had employers taking motion pictures and stop-action photographs of their workers to determine exactly how many strokes of a hammer it should take to drive a nail, or how many twists of a wrench were needed to join two parts of a widget. Absolute efficiency and minimal friction—not a single wasted moment or movement—was the goal.

So, why are we recapping the evolution of the factory in a book about the next industrial revolution? Because it's easy to forget that there was a very specific reason why the factory model was necessary and replicated across nearly every organizational and social institution of the twentieth century. It's not just that it was a more productive use of human resources, or that it standardized the quality of products, or even that it drove down costs. All of these were critically important to its success, but there was one overriding reason that factory automation flourished.

The single most pressing challenge of the twentieth century was to build an industrial complex that could scale to meet the needs of a burgeoning population in the developed world. Between 1900 and 2000, the increase in world population was three times greater than during the entire previous history of humanity—an increase from 1.5 billion to 6.1 billion inhabitants in just one hundred years.[83]

The one-size-fits-all, any color as long as it's black model of manufacturing was the only way to achieve the scale necessary to deliver products and services to global mass markets that were growing at unprecedented rates. Customization, which had been the hallmark of craftsmanship could never have scaled. There just weren't enough craftsmen and the world could never train enough of them. And this is exactly why most pundits of late nineteenth and early twentieth century got the next one hundred years so wrong.

One apocryphal story has it that Mercedes projected that only as many cars would be in use at any time as there could be chauffeurs trained to drive them. As laughable as that is to us today you can easily imagine how much sense it might have made. In fact, if today you projected the number of cars in use by some future date wouldn't you use the number of eligible drivers between sixteen and eighty as one metric? And yet, as we'll see, that is just as absurd of a rationalization. Didn't the fathers of modern computing do the same thing when IBM's president Thomas Watson said in 1943, "I think there is a world market for maybe five computers," or Ken Olsen, founder of one of the most popular computer companies of the 70s and 80s, Digital Equipment Corporation, who said in 1977: "There is no reason anyone would want a computer in their home."

The problem with that industrial age model is that it's already starting to see the limits of growth. Not because there is anything fundamentally wrong with factories. We need them to be more efficient and productive than ever. Even though the rate of population growth has been dropping for the past five decades, we will still need additional capacity and scale as the developing countries of the world become more active participants in the global economy. The challenge to the industrial model is that we cannot continue scaling it the way we have been.

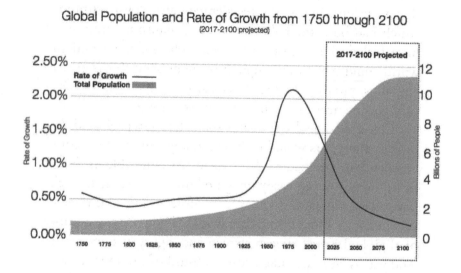

Global Population and Rate of Growth from 1750 through 2100
(2017-2100 projected)

Illustration 5.1[84]

The chart above shows how the annual rate of growth for world population peaked in the late 1970s at 21 percent and then steadily declined, while total world population is projected to slow and peak sometime in the early 2100s at between eleven and twelve billion. Current thinking is that the maximum carrying capacity of the globe is somewhere in that range. However, that is based on the industrial era models of energy and natural resource utilization as well as environmental impact, healthcare, and sanitation. The upper bounds of population projections by the UN reach seventeen billion by 2100.

The industrial model is so much a part of how we view the world that it's not easy for us to see beyond it and appreciate how dramatically different the world will become as we shift from globalization to personalization. This shift doesn't mean that we no longer need to scale products and services, but rather that the way we define scale will have to change from what has been called mass production to what we call mass innovation. (see Illustration 5.4) Not coincidentally, what makes mass innovation feasible is the ability to hyper-personalize at scale, something which is only possible with the concurrent shift to behavioral businesses.

"Hyper-personalizing at scale" means that we can have both enormous scale in how we manufacture and distribute products as well as incredibly personalized experiences at the level of the individual. However, there's one big caveat to achieving personalization at scale it can only be done to the extent that we build businesses that share a common digital ecosystem as their foundation.

Digital Ecosystems

Business ecosystems aren't a new concept. Every industry that relies on partnerships, suppliers, or some form of network of collaborators with a common interest in designing, developing, and distributing a product has to build a set of rules and mechanisms by which they can work together. The problem is that many of these ecosystems have grown organically in a disconnected fashion and not by design.

A prime example is the automobile. At our present rate of production and demand, the number of automobiles worldwide will exceed two billion by 2050 and by some projections as high as two and-a-half billion. The friction in that scenario is not in the factories—we could easily scale production to that level—but rather in the impact it would have on urban congestion, energy use, safety, and pollution.

What makes the automobile an especially interesting player in illustrating the benefit of shifting to an ecosystems model is that it is a vital part of the much larger physical and digital ecosystem within which it operates, and yet, your automobile does not communicate with its local environment in any meaningful way. If you stop to think about what single technology advance has most changed the experience of driving so far, it's undoubtedly the integration of real-time GPS, which provides a way to intelligently connect to the larger ecosystem that the car is part of.

But why stop there? Most of our world, but especially the structure of a city, is built around transportation. The roadways, intersections, traffic lights, roundabouts (rotaries for our Boston readers), shopping and dining, are all part of an organically grown ecosystem that is loosely connected and coordinated. However, each of these components of the city/transportation ecosystem generates friction that detracts from the experience of everyone involved. So, what if we were to remove that friction?

It's amazing how dramatically an industry, and more importantly an ecosystem, changes the moment friction is taken out of the equation. Let's go back to Uber for a minute. Uber hasn't just change the way people move around in cities; it's literally changing and transforming cities. Uber through its app gathers so many behavioral data points in real time that it's able to understand the large behaviors of a city.

Knowledge of our digital habits, needs for mobility, transactions, lifestyle, where and when we shop and eat, and the two billion rides people have taken using Uber, give it the ability to understand how our digital-selves' behaviors contribute to the efficiency of the entire ecosystem and all of its participants. Today Uber provides this data to urban and city planners through a service called Movement, which anonymizes drivers' patterns of behavior. It's a small step to get from there to a future where the same data is used as part of an integrated city-wide mesh that has the intelligence to not only personalize the transportation experience for an individual but to also minimize the overall impact of congestion, energy use, traffic flow, and safety.[85]

This approach is what we refer to as an open-orchestrated digital ecosystem in which the broadest possible range of intelligent devices, infrastructure, and your digital-self all communicate with each other in order to enable the highest possible level of efficiency for the overall ecosystem and hyper-personalization for the individual.

Open

Owned Vehicle
Relatively Inefficient At Any Scale
High Personalization
Minimal Ecosystem Integration

Smart Cities
Efficient At Highest Scale
Personalization Across Diverse Ecosystem
Highest Ecosystem Integration

Orchestrated

Captive

Public Transportation
Very Efficient At High Scale
Virtually No Personalization
Static Ecosystem Integration

Ride Sharing
Efficient At Moderate Scale
High Personalization Within Narrow Ecosystem
High Ecosystem Integration

Closed

Illustration 5.2

A digital ecosystem can be defined by two basic dimensions: how open it is in integrating devices and technologies, and how well diverse players in the ecosystem are organized. This illustration shows various forms of transportation ecosystems as the four basic types that result from this model. The most dynamic and efficient ecosystem at scale is one that is both exceptionally open to the integration of diverse technologies and devices with a well-orchestrated collection of players.

Simply defined, a digital ecosystem is an orchestrated set of capabilities and constantly communicating devices across digitally connected businesses and consumers. The value of a digital ecosystem is four-fold:

1. It reduces inherent friction across its network of partners;

2. It creates a highly personalized experience for customers since it is able to leverage behavioral data collected across the ecosystem;
3. Transparency across this same network of behavioral data enables it to predict and evolve with the markets it serves;
4. Constant intelligent communication and awareness of each component in the ecosystem enables it to learn and evolve.

The third and fourth aspects of the digital ecosystem are arguably the most important and what differentiates it from ecosystems that grow organically and without the benefit of connected intelligence that can observe, learn, and decide. We know that may seem like a stretch, but later in this chapter we will actually show you an example of how this is already being done today.

Ultimately, Digital ecosystems provide an alternative to the more traditional industrial era value chain on which to scale a business, but that only works if you can plug into that platform. Take Apple's App Store. If you can work within the digital ecosystem of the App store, then you have the potential to realize tremendous value, not just initially but through in-app purchases which are nearly frictionless for customers. While this isn't an open-orchestrated but instead a closed-orchestrated ecosystem—because of Apple's control over the apps it allows into its store—it is still a very effective digital ecosystem.

The digital ecosystem business model is to the behavioral business what telecommunications was to globalization. Both create a universal foundation on which you can build new value and competitive differentiation.

The difference is that digital ecosystems involve much more than just superficial communications; they require high transparency and trust since they cut deeply into nearly every aspect of how a business builds products, services, and customer experiences—to the point where the business has to reconfigure itself entirely around the customer experience, and more specifically, for our topic, to the personalized needs of each customer. Which is why the notion of a digital-self, which bridges the physical and digital, is so critical in enabling communication between the many entities that make up the ecosystem.

Digital ecosystems are an essential part of any behavioral business model because the fundamental principle behind them is that individuals have personalized needs that a commoditized offering will always fall short of. In other words, observing and understanding customer behaviors is worthless to a business and meaningless to the customer if the ecosystem cannot respond to those behaviors.

There's also a significant benefit to ecosystems when it comes to mitigating risk. industrial era business models focus enormous energy on managing risk because there is no way to understand the degree of risk in each in each transaction. Risk was not personalized—it was aggregated. The only option in that case is to spread risk across all transactions.

For example, let's construct a hypothetical scenario around car insurance and risk. Today your insurance will vary based on your car's value, where your car is garaged, the annual mileage, and your age and incidents in your driving history. You pay X each year and the insurance company calculates your risk at some factor of X that projects a profit based on the aggregated risk and premiums across everyone it insures.

This means that even within any single category of risk, some drivers are still going to be a higher risk than others.

So, what if drivers could be insured each time they drive based on the risks of the route they take? And what if the car could also present the driver (or owner in the case of an AV) with a choice based on the road conditions, prior incidents, and the capabilities of the car? Route A is twenty minutes at five dollars, route B is two dollars and fifty cents at twenty-five minutes, and route C is twenty-five cents at forty-five minutes. By the way, it could be the case that a shorter route costs more than a longer route or that the same route costs different amounts for different drivers. The point is that the risk is now hyper-personalized to the situation in the moment. The insurance company still determines risk in order to meet the goal of its profit margins, but the owner has the choice to pay for the level of service they require. Nobody loses here since even a high-risk driver can now choose the lower risk routes. This can only be achieved at scale with the digital ecosystem model that we are describing in this chapter.

The fact is that risk is always best measured on an individualized basis, but an industrial era model built for scale doesn't have the behavioral information or the capacity or the resources to do that.

Given the increasing complexity of all industries, we are convinced that one of the greatest contributors to economic growth for the remainder of the 21st century will be in rebuilding them with entirely new frictionless digital platforms that have the ability to use a hyper-personalized model.

However, there's one wrinkle in the ecosystem fabric. If you noticed. we said "rebuild," not "incrementally improve" or "reengineer." That's because every indication is that the economics and the speed of rebuilding far outweigh those of reengineering. The fundamental reason for this is not, as some would claim, a lack of vision or ambition to innovate. As we'll see, its roots go back to the issues we began to introduce in Chapter 1 about the necessary shift from an industrial economy of scale business model to one that can respond to markets at the level of the individual consumer. In the same way that an old house with a cracked foundation, worn out plumbing and electrical systems, and wood rot from a leaking roof may take much longer and cost much more to renovate than to rebuild, many of the systems that today shore up these tired old industries are likely to suffer the same fate.

As industries undergo the transformation to digital ecosystems an entirely new set of opportunities begins to emerge. Not only because friction is reduced and the rate of innovation increases, but also because digital ecosystems provide the opportunity to capture behaviors throughout a product's lifecycle and then build new services that are uniquely suited to each customer with relatively little effort. The result is that moving to a digital ecosystem redefines and significantly expands a company's potential market space, while it also simplifies and reduces the effort expended to achieve a particular goal, whether it be getting you from point A to point B in the fastest or most pleasant (to you) way possible, or minimizing the carbon footprint of transportation within a city.

The ecosystem concept is by no means limited to just vehicles. For example take Nike, Lego, and Philips. Each took simple physical objects (shoes and apparel in case of Nike, bricks in case of Lego, and light bulbs in case of Philips) as the foundation for the creation of complex multi-layered platforms of very complex digital business ecosystems.

What's especially important to understand in each of these cases is that the potential market for these companies was historically very compartmentalized. Their ecosystems were limited by their brand, the way in which customers experienced their products, and their partner and distribution channels.

The way traditional ecosystems operate limits the breadth and engagement of companies and brands. It would be like having an automobile that only operated in one of the fifty states in the USA. You could not cross a border into another state because every state had its own set of roadways and infrastructure, special fuel that only worked for cars in that state, mechanics that didn't have a clue as to how any other state's cars operated. It sounds ludicrous but it's pretty close to the way companies have been limited in their ability to build across industry boundaries. It actually gets even worse because companies become so steeped in their own industry's best practices that they often ignore the ways in which another industry might be addressing similar challenges in a novel way.

There's nothing new in the idea of looking to other industries for best practices that can be applied in a novel way. One of our favorite examples is that of the Maclaren Baby Buggy (yes, a baby carriage) which was made by Owen Maclaren in 1965. Maclaren was an aviation engineer and a test pilot who had worked on one of World War II's iconic fighters, the Spitfire. Maclaren had noticed his daughter dealing with the use of cumbersome baby carriages and so he created the first collapsible, portable, stowable baby buggy, which today is commonplace. The connection? The spitfire was one of the first fighters to have retractable landing gear which folded neatly up into the plane's wings.

Of course, these types of stories make for wonderful anecdotes but they are purely the result of serendipitous encounters and connections that seem to have no rhyme or reason. And you'd never rely on these sorts of chance encounters to build a business, right?

In a digital ecosystem however, you can extend the reach with which these types of connections can be made with far greater ease, leveraging capabilities across nearly infinite spectrums of opportunity. The business you're in doesn't have to carry a label that confines it to a historical set of opportunities for innovation. This is especially true of organizations as they become more data driven and start to use what we will call the five stages of digitalization in the next chapter.

If you're Nike, you're not in the shoe business; you're in the sports, personal fitness, and health business. Nike took something basic, a pair of shoes which are hardly high-tech, and made them the core of a data-driven, experience-led ecosystem dominated by services that allow its customers to experience a better, healthier, more active and engaging life. Similarly, Lego isn't supplying plastic bricks; it's in the learning and entertainment business. Philips is not simply providing light bulbs; it's in the business of creating a home experience.

Let's look specifically at the case of Philips to describe the five distinct layers of value that can be created with a digital ecosystem. We'll call these five layers the value-creation chain.[86]

Layer 1: The Physical Object

The physical object, which in this case is the LED lightbulb, forms the first layer of the value-creation chain. It supplies the first direct, physical benefit to the user in the form of the function supplied by a light bulb. Because the light bulb is a physical object it, is always tethered to a location and can supply benefits at this layer only in its immediate environment—for example an office, a kitchen, or a bedroom.

Layer 2: The Sensor

In layer 2, the physical object is equipped with computational skills provided by sensor technology and actuating elements. The sensors measure location data, while the actuating elements deliver services and thus generate insights and rewards for the user.

For example, a microwave sensor embedded in the LED light bulb continuously measures whether people are present in the space—reliably and at a low cost. The actuator turns the light on automatically when human presence is detected and off again when not, thereby supplying local benefits. Because the smart LED light bulb functions without a separate wired motion detector to discern presence the value of the bulb just increased dramatically without any additional effort on the part of the user. The bulb is now also able to capture behavior but in an invisible way since the user has added nothing new to the experience of screwing in a light bulb. However, the light bulb is still far from intelligent.

Layer 3: Connectivity

This is where the digital ecosystem starts to get interesting. The sensor technology and actuator elements in layer 2 are connected to the internet so that they become globally accessible. The light bulb can be addressed through an embedded radio module in order to transmit its status to authorized subscribers anywhere in the world at negligible marginal costs. In layer 3 we have the shift from something local and small, to a global data driven and context relevant service that can connect with any other digital service or product.

Layer 4: Analytics

Capturing data and connectivity per se do not deliver any added value by themselves. In layer 4, the data collected is stored, checked for plausibility, and classified. Then the findings of other web services are integrated with this data to arrive at consequences for the actuator elements—typically in a Cloud-based backend system. In layer 4 the on-and-off times in a household are collected, motion patterns are discerned, and the operating hours of individual light bulbs are recorded as well. Now the light bulb is not only an instrument for collecting data but also for exhibiting behaviors that apply this data to add value for the user.

Layer 5: Digital Service/Behavioral

At this, the final layer, the options provided by the previous layers are structured into digital services and packaged in a form suitable for an entirely new product experience. Since the light bulb now "knows" some aspect of your behavior it can combine this knowledge with other smart devices, also at level 4 or 5, to make decisions. For example, if your bedroom light bulb went on at 3 a.m. and your kitchen light bulb went on at 3:03 a.m., followed by the refrigerator light going on at 3:04 a.m. we could begin to make some determinations about what you might be doing. But when you couple this with the sensors and actuators in your bed, refrigerator, and microwave a much clearer picture starts to emerge.

Today we are somewhere between layers 2 and 4. Companies are attempting to use the data being collected to determine behavioral characteristics or patterns through algorithms and AI, but much of what's being done involves teams of what are called Data Scientists pondering over the statistical patterns created by these massive collections of data. While this Big Data approach has merit, it is not a personalized approach to understanding the data. It is still using an old and very limited model of understanding behavior and delivering individualized value. That's not to say that Big Data initiatives are fruitless. They are a quantum leap beyond focus groups and customer surveys, but they are just as far removed from the sort of individualized value creation that we are describing.

In our five-layer model, the physical objects, products, and devices are just the elementary particles used to form and build massive complicated data-rich ecosystems, which are constantly creating value by enhancing and adjusting products and services in real time.

As you read this we're sure that some of the earlier questions we raised about privacy are starting to resurface. Can we ever be comfortable with products and services that know us this well? Is the value worth it?

In an August 2017 article in *The New York Times*, Pamela Paul summed up the way many people feel about this degree of overwhelming change and disruption:

> *Disruption can be a positive force in the office, but at home it feels the way disruption has always felt: intrusive and annoying. At home, at least, we have the power to pace the change, to choose the old over the new. These incremental lifestyle downgrades help calibrate a rate of technological change that might otherwise produce a resting state of whiplash.*[87]

While Paul's comment is understandable it also feels to us like it's throwing pebbles into a raging river hoping to stop the water from flowing. Disruption is destructive; there's no way around it—it needs to be in order to dislodge the status quo.

The twentieth century economist Joseph A. Schumpeter who coined the term Creative Destruction in his 1942 book *Capitalism, Socialism, and Democracy,* said of disruptive competition, "[What counts is] competition from the new commodity, the new technology, the new source of supply, the new type of organization...competition which...strikes not at the margins of the profits and the outputs of the existing firms but at their foundations and their very lives."

That's exactly to sort of wholesale disruption we're talking about in this chapter, digital disruption that threatens nearly ever incumbent in every industry.

Digital Disruption

The most opportune markets for this sort of digital disruption are those that have the greatest organic friction. Think of healthcare, education, insurance and banking, shipping and supply chains—they have all evolved organically over time in highly regulated industries, they involve innumerable hand-offs from person to person, system to system, and silo to silo; worst of all, none were ever really architected—they just sort of incrementally and haphazardly grew. The risk that digital disruption presents to these industries is what we call "uberization" or the re-creation of these industries as entirely new frictionless platforms that are built for a digital architecture and leverage behavioral data to deliver personalized products and services.

Uberization, of course, refers to how Uber disrupted the industry for taxi cabs. Uber did not attempt to reengineer cabs. It didn't purchase a fleet of cars (at least not as part of its initial business model). It did not hire employees or retrain existing cab drivers. And it did not attempt to change the way the industry is regulated, nor did it choose to work within those regulations. What Uber did was to leverage both technology and behavior to create an experience for drivers and users that wasn't incrementally better but instead rebuilt the industry from the ground up. By doing this Uber eliminated much of the intractable friction that had been baked into the cab industry as the result of a century long legacy.

However, there is one part to the Uber story that is never talked about. A recent study, "Drivers of Disruption? The Uber Effect," looked at Uber's effect on the cab industry. While you'd expect that Uber would have decimated cabs, something remarkable has happened. According to the study's authors:

> *Our analysis exploits the staggered rollout of Uber across U.S. cities, showing that employment of payroll taxi services if anything expanded after the introduction of the Uber platform, accompanied by a marked relative shift toward self-employment.*[88]

Two things are worth noting here. The first is that throughout the course of the industrial and information revolution we've heard about how every disruptive technology will displace workers and create a jobless future. There is truth to the first part of that argument, that jobs will be eliminated and people displaced. But the second part of the argument, a jobless future, has been disproved regularly on a very large scale. As we pointed out in the Introduction, the US agricultural workforce dropped from 83 percent in 1800 to 2 percent today. The number of jobs in agriculture has dropped precipitously, but the number of people to feed has increased seven-fold globally. The same will happen to cabs, and eventually ride sharing, but the need to transport people will only increase. (Although this will only partly be due to an increase in population and more so due to migration toward more developed economies and a broadening of access to AVs by demographic groups that do not have access to transportation today.)

In any case, we do not hold out much hope for the cab industry's survival for more than another five to ten years at most. In cities where medallions are needed to operate a cab the turnover may take longer; the medallions are owned predominantly by investors whose interest and ability to lobby will undoubtedly have an effect on measures to protect their investment. In fact, in just about every US city with a medallion program, the number of medallions issued has barely increased since 1930!

In many ways, the artificial supply-demand that this creates speaks directly to the sort of inefficiency and friction created by industrial era models that use unnecessary intermediaries to enable ownership. However, the slow inevitable decline of the cab industry does not mean that cab drivers will suddenly be walking the streets en masse. The transition will be fairly gradual for the next three to five years. We'd expect that the approximately 80 percent of drivers who are not already independent operators will transition to being independent. But let's not limit ourselves to passenger cars. According to a study there are three million truck drivers in America.[89] However, that industry is also about to change for good for various reasons. One of them is that Uber has entered the market with its acquisition of Otto, a company focused exclusively on autonomous trucks.[90] At the same time, Tesla introduced an electric truck with AV capabilities in 2017.[91]

There will no doubt be much displacement, but it will not come from ride sharing services but rather AI. In order to minimize social disruption and future turbulence, we need to reconsider how social norms will be adapted to this. According to a *Wall Street Journal* story in September 2017:

> *We need to update the New Deal for the 21st century and establish a trainee program for the new jobs artificial intelligence will create. We need to retrain truck drivers and office assistants to create data analysts, trip optimizers and other professionals we don't yet know we need. It would have been impossible for an antebellum farmer to imagine his son becoming an electrician, and it's impossible to say what new jobs AI will create. But it's clear that drastic measures are necessary if we want to transition from an industrial society to an age of intelligent machines.*[92]

The specter of a future in which AI and robots will displace workers is not new. And each time this threat resurfaces we're told that this time it's different. While there's no argument that disruption brings temporary unemployment and displacement, history has shown that we always find new, more valuable uses of our human capabilities.

A United Nations official once approached Tom at a conference in Geneva asking, "Isn't there a technology that will reduce productivity?"[93] This wasn't meant to be funny. His point, which was received with curious looks from members of the audience, was oddly valid. The countries of the developing world, in which unemployment is rampant, do not need greater productivity; they simply need to employ people—for both economic and social reasons.

Was his question that absurd? We seek perpetual productivity increases yet, when we realize them, unemployment invariably follows suit. Are we creating what Jeremy Rifkin, in *The End of Work*, called "The Cult of Efficiency"? We don't subscribe to the point of view that increased efficiency or job destruction in one part of the economy is any indication of long-term unemployment across an economy. In fact, if anything, history has proven that the greater the near-term job destruction, the greater the long-term potential for job growth.

Our era is certainly not the first to be confronted with the issue of technology that threatens to displace workers. From 1912 until 1913, Ford's Model T production doubled and so did its workforce. However, in the next model year, as production again doubled, Ford cut one thousand five hundred jobs, the result of enormous productivity increases brought on by the moving assembly line.[94] Did the century-long evolution of manufacturing and robotics that followed create a permanent class of unemployed? Absolutely not!

The percentage of unemployment in the developed nations of the world has certainly experienced oscillations throughout the twentieth century, but there is no long-term upward trend. The US experienced five percent unemployment in 1920 and 6.2 percent in 2014. The UK entered and exited the twentieth century with five percent unemployment.[95]

It seems that we're outstanding at describing how technology will replace humans, but we consistently fail to predict how it will create new jobs. That's because we fail to appreciate the scale of the new prosperity that it will enable. For instance, the tremendous success of the automobile, and the industries it spawned, created far more jobs than it ever eliminated by replacing the carriage and horse.

If Uber shows us nothing else it is that although traditional employment may be eroded by the evolution of a new digital ecosystem, overall employment increases, as individuals are able to more fully participate in the economy as free agents—another benefit of reduced friction.

The End of Friction

Simply defined, friction is the result of any unnecessary work that adds time, cost, transaction layers, or complexity to a product or service. Friction exists in every industry; there is no immunity, only relative degrees of friction. The problem with identifying friction is that aside from slight incremental reductions it is nearly impossible to eliminate it from inside of a company, or from the inside of an industry. Even customers become accustomed to it and accept it. It's seen as the natural and necessary way that things work. What's even more perverse is that any attempts to drive out friction are perceived as a threat to the people and processes that own it! As a result, friction is almost always eliminated by some sort of existential threat.

The classic example is Apple's shake up of the music industry. The initial threat to record labels was the music sharing service Napster, which had about eighty million users when it was finally shut down by the music industry for copyright infringement. Napster created a nearly frictionless ability for consumers to download songs to their MP3 players. It was one of the first successful examples of the sharing economy that over a decade later spurred companies such as Uber, Lyft, and Airbnb.

However, in 2003 the music industry was very comfortable with its established model. The artists, the media, the pricing model, the distribution channels all worked well, but it didn't scale. That was evidenced in the lengths people would go to in order to get around the system. The market was not just voicing its displeasure—it was screaming out loud while also giving the finger to copyright law.

If you are the incumbent you can look at this in one of several ways:[96]

1. Protect your current business model at all costs by going after the innovators—the route major record labels took initially by suing Napster, Morpheus, Grokster, LimeWire, and a host of other file sharing services;

2. Protect your business model by going after the marketplace—the music industry indiscriminately sued thousands of individuals from grandmothers to college students;[97]

3. Educate the market on how amazing your business model is and why they would be really stupid to try and undermine it—yes, the major labels tried this as well by appealing to college students (the same ones they were suing).

Steve Jobs, Apple's Iconic CEO, saw it differently. Jobs contacted the senior execs at each major record label and convinced them that they had two choices: continue to fight an unwinnable and very expensive war against file sharing services that would only spawn two more for every one the record industry shut down; or become part of a new model that would provide music lovers with an experience which they were willing to pay for.[98] (Later in Chapter 6 we look closer at how the iTunes model evolved to use behavioral data.)

By driving out the friction of physical media, distribution, and payments to artists, Apple was able to build an industry that was far more focused on the provider and the consumer. Suddenly anyone could publish their works to the iTunes store, customers could download only the songs that they wanted, and iTunes organized and protected all of their music in one easy and intuitive interface. While overall revenues from music sales fell, it could be argued that without iTunes the music industry would have suffered a much worse fate.

Although Napster and a cadre of other music sharing services flourished and later disappeared, piracy has not gone away.[99] In fact, according to a report by MUSO, an independent research firm that tracks piracy statistics globally, there were over fifty-eight billion visits to pirate sites where music can be downloaded illegally in 2016.[100] The risk increased but so did the value created.

Without Apple's iTunes game-changing model, someone else would eventually have come along to offer a similar solution. The transformation of businesses to a digital ecosystem is a necessary evolution in order to continue scaling and creating value.

Driving much of the friction out of the music industry also gave Apple another advantage. Because Apple's model was so much more efficient at music distribution than retail stores, such as Tower and Virgin, its margins were much greater, allowing Apple to charge less for music and still make more overall than retailers.

While we could argue that the pressure to change came from Napster and the greater threat of piracy, we see that only as the instigator of the change. Piracy of digital assets will always be a threat. However, a digital business ecosystem delivers a new type of value that is designed to allow an industry to continue scaling with minimal friction. To put it another way, iTunes made it easier to buy than to steal.

Of course, there are many other areas where the friction of over regulated and incredibly complex industrial model ecosystems has become its own worst enemy when it comes to any sort of substantial improvement. Education, healthcare, and financial services are all encumbered by enormous legacies of processes that create unnecessary friction and ultimately erode and stress the relationship between a brand and its customers.

The real threat for companies in these industries is not an existing competitor but rather one which is not playing by the same rules nor limited by the same constraints. As a result, they can build an entirely new relationship with the consumer without the friction of the current marketplace. For example, Google could conceivably disrupt the insurance industry by using its vast warehouse of behavioral insights to determine the risk for life, property, or even health insurance. While it may not have the sophistication of actuarial processes and experts to model life expectancies and risk, it doesn't have to be as precise since it will have a much higher profit margin to work with if it attacks the areas of friction in the current model used to sell insurance.

Another example of how friction can be driven out of an existing industry is what's called usage-based insurance. We briefly mentioned this earlier in the chapter when we used the hypothetical model of risk-based insurance that would provide drivers with costs and options for each use of their automobile. When you purchase insurance today it's done on a monthly, semi-annual, or annual period. However, we've already said that the typical car remains idle 95 percent of the time. Usage-based insurance takes into consideration circumstantial data about the driver's age, location, history, and miles driven yearly coupled with the driver's real-time behavior and specific environmental factors to create what's called a contextual score. That score can then be used to purchase insurance on-demand for a single trip. For example, startups such as Metromile charge customers based on actual miles driven. [101]

Friction is also embedded in most administrative processes. A study conducted by Boston Consulting Group showed that the actual work time for an insurance application was typically 1 to 5 percent of overall process time. For example, an automobile policy that takes six days to process consists of only twenty minutes of work time, which is how Geico was able to radically streamline automobile insurance. A property and casualty application takes just as long to process but has only eight minutes of work time. [102] The rest of the process is idle time, handoffs, and transit.

Illustration 5.3 – Contextual Insurance
A contextual insurance model eliminates a great deal of friction by creating an insurance marketplace and policy that would charge drivers a per-ride rate based on a variety of factors that determine the actual risk for any given set of contextual circumstances.

To be clear, we're not just saying that digital ecosystem alternatives are an interesting option for insurance. They are necessary for the survival of the industry. A McKinsey study, "Time for Insurance Companies to Face Digital Reality," found that:

US auto insurers have already lost on average $4.2 billion in underwriting profit a year over the past five, with expenses and losses consistently outweighing premiums. They should expect further annual profit declines of between 0.5 and 1 percent if they fail to use digital technology to improve efficiency and effectiveness.[103]

What's at stake in so many of these cases is the fundamental sustainability of existing industrial era business models that we typically take for granted as immutable.

These are not new issues. When Michael Hammer and Jim Champy wrote *Reengineering the Corporation* in 1993, one of their central messages was that non-work time bloats transactions, frustrates customers, and is simply accepted as normal because that is the way the process has always been run. However, reengineering industrial era organizations only goes so far, and often not far enough. As was the case in our example earlier of Uber and the cab industry, building an entirely new digital ecosystem begins without the burden of legacy processes, business models, and entrenched interests. This also affords the opportunity to build the ecosystem entirely around the behaviors of the customer.

What's especially interesting about the impact that these new technologies and business models are having is that the value they create for customers is directly erosive to the entrenched interests of existing business models. Inevitably what this means is that many existing companies in well-established industries, such as insurance, will either have to make some significant and painful changes in the way they do business or become casualties of friction.

All of this requires a new way of looking at how we will re-orchestrate our businesses to meet the demands, scale, and expectations of a marketplace where hyper-personalization, rapid innovation, and infinite selection are the measures of success—a marketplace where behavior drives innovation.

Held Hostage by the Past

Perhaps one of the best examples of how an industrial era company can be held hostage by an industrial era ecosystem that is inflexible and unable to respond to the behavioral cues of a marketplace is that of Kodak, the iconic twentieth century company which invented both modern film emulsion photography and digital photography, and yet still found itself unable to move into the future.

George Eastman, the founder and former CEO of Kodak, identified one of his company's guiding principles as "mass production at low cost." This is precisely the mindset that has driven every company of scale for the past two hundred years, because it worked. By 1976, Kodak had an incredible 90 percent share of the film market.

Eastman's vision was to make photography "as convenient as a pencil." The problem with achieving production at scale when it came to film was the complicated and messy process of wet plate photography. To get around that, Eastman invented a process for using dry plates that could be "exposed and developed and at the photographer's convenience."

In 1879 he "invented an emulsion-coating machine that made it possible for him to mass produce photographic dry plates." In 1880 he started commercially producing the dry plates in a loft he rented in Rochester, N.Y. as the Eastman Dry Plate company. Then in 1883 Eastman invented a roll film adapter for plate cameras, and shortly thereafter the first transparent photographic roll film that would be the hall-mark of photography for the next century.[104]

Eastman's invention revolutionized the film industry. If there was ever a disruptive technology, this was it. It's supremely ironic that the company which introduced such a disruptive technology was unable to take advantage of the switch to digital photography—especially given that Kodak invented digital photography in its own labs.

Steve Sasson, the engineer who built the first digital camera in 1975, and who went on to receive the National Medal of Technology and Innovation, the highest honour awarded by the US government to scientists, engineers, and inventors, recalled Kodak management's reaction in a *New York Times* 2008 interview: [105]

> *My prototype was big as a toaster, but the technical people loved it. But it was filmless photography, so management's reaction was, "that's cute—but don't tell anyone about it..."*[106]

As the story is most often told, that lack of support from leadership was the reason for Kodak's ultimate failure. But there's much more to the story that goes well beyond that simple and naïve explanation and which cuts to the core of the transformation every industrial age company will need to make from mass production to mass innovation. (Illustration 5.4)

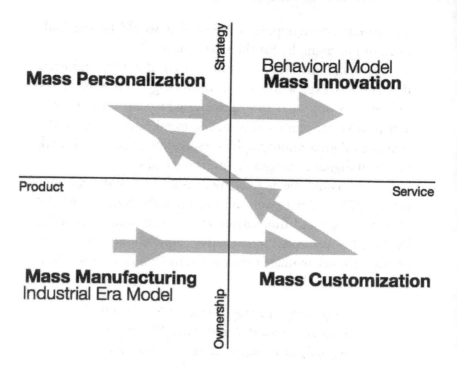

Illustration 5.4

Every ecosystem consists of a demand chain (buyers) and a supply chain (suppliers). Each of these can be known or unknown. For example, mass production relies on a well define product and marketplace with no variability. Whereas, mass innovation involves a constantly changing set of buyer behaviors and suppliers. Kodak was well equipped to address the lower left quadrant of this chart, but it was unable to move into the upper right hand quadrant to rebuild its supply chain to meet the needs of buyers who Kodak did not understand. Kodak did make significant headway into mass customization and even personalization through its in-store film development labs and eventually personal kiosks for digital photography. However, the final move into mass innovation is only now beginning to take place and on an entirely different platform than digital cameras, apps on smartphones.

Kodak's failure was not one of vision. The direction of photography was clearly understood by the company's executives.

In a 2016 issue of the *MIT Sloan Management Review*, Willy Shih, who served as president of the Kodak's consumer digital business from 1997 to 2003, wrote about how Kodak's enormous investment in plant and equipment along with an industrial era ecosystem that did not allow the company to move with the market was a significant contributor to Kodak's downfall.

It can certainly be argued that Kodak could have done more to better position itself to take advantage of digital photography. However, we would challenge the merit of that argument. We don't think Kodak had any good long-term options in photography—only short-term options to prolong its eventual exit from the market.

Perhaps the most striking evidence, and example of how companies cling to the culture of industrialization, is that even after Kodak emerged from Chapter 11 bankruptcy it still held fast to its position in the photography market, though by then smartphones had dealt the final deadly blow to everything but the high end professional segment of the camera industry. The one piece of Kodak that it spun off in 1994 and then sold off after bankruptcy was Eastman Chemical, which no longer has any affiliation with photography and is doing exceptionally well as a business.

The culprit in Kodak's case, and in many others, wasn't the lack of ambition or even vision. The culprit was an industrial model whose ecosystems ultimately made it nearly impossible to respond to the market and to transition into mass innovation. The same investments and strategies that support economies of scale make agility extraordinarily difficult, if at all possible.

Kodak's plight is hardly unique. The industrial model of the last two centuries is dying. You only need to look at the consistent reduction in the average time on the list of the *Fortune* 500 to see that this is not a near term phenomenon. The seven-year trailing average falloff in 1977 was 38 percent. It's projected to be 15 percent by 2027 (it's at 27 percent today).[107] An earlier study of one thousand three hundred companies across thirty-five industries, published in the *Harvard Business Review*, showed that the topple rate (the rate at which a company in the top 20 percent of revenues in its industry will lose that position in the next five years) doubled between 1972 and 2002.[108] All indicators are that sustaining success has become —and will continue to be— increasingly more difficult.

You can look at this and say, "It's as it should be. Greater churn means more innovation." We agree! We're not saying that the topple rate is a bad thing any more than we'd say that Kodak could have somehow transformed itself into a provider of smartphones. Industries change and there will be casualties. And when technology moves fast, the long-term incumbents are the most susceptible to obsolescence. We are, however, saying that if you want to survive and scale in a sustained way, you cannot follow the same industrial era model that the majority of companies have followed so far.

Blurring the Boundaries of Business

Ecosystem business models reflect an increased recognition that few companies can 'go it alone' in making the transition from globalization to personalization. Instead, they need to figure out how to work with—and orchestrate—capabilities and assets, products and services from a wide range of firms both to increase their likelihood of capturing new sources of value and to decrease their risks of doing so alone.

At the same time there is a blurring of the traditional boundaries among companies and industries as well as the boundaries between customers and producers. What is Tesla, after all? Is it a car or an energy storage company? What about GE? Is it a manufacturer or—as CEO Jeff Immelt is aspiring to transform it into—a new platform for the industrial economy?

Immelt's thinking also applies to purely digital companies. The central premise of this book is that you are—we all are—becoming the product. So, where, precisely, do we draw the boundary between the business and the partner, the producer and consumer? Better yet, are these boundaries even meaningful in anything other than a financial reporting perspective? Not only do we believe that the answer is an emphatic *no*, but drawing these hard boundaries actually creates impediments to growth and even survival.

In the same way that you can't separate and isolate the players in a biological ecosystem without creating risk for the entire ecosystem, you can't simply isolate one company in a business ecosystem without creating enormous risk in the viability of an entire industry and its ability to innovate.

In fact, we'd go so far as to suggest that some of the biggest failures over the last decade—the example of Kodak we just described, Borders and Blockbuster—were not just the result of poor product strategy, or an inability to innovate, because each of these companies had innovated new products and services that recognized the future. Still, despite Kodak's invention of digital photography, Blockbuster having on-demand streaming before Netflix, and Borders being one of the first online booksellers, they could not squeeze the enormity of their industrial legacy through the doorway to the future.

The problem in each case was an inability to rebuild and repurpose their ecosystem to respond to new behaviors. Each one built what was effectively a fortress of vertical integration in the closed-captive quadrant of our ecosystem model, rather than move into the open-orchestrated quadrant, by building platforms for partners and customers that could evolve as the market, technology, and expectations changed. (see Illustration 5.2)

So, how might a digital ecosystem leverage the behavioral knowledge of your digital-self? Imagine that the behavioral profile of your digital-self, which represents all the ways in which you live your life, was able to communicate with a digital ecosystem. We don't need to go too far down the path of how human-like that communication needs to be. For our purposes, a basic ability to share information about your behaviors is adequate. And to keep things simple, we'll even limit the information to your sleep habits.

A European mattress manufacturer is doing just that. By embedding sensors into its mattresses, it can identify the exact sleep patterns, ambient noises, snoring, apnea, how many times you get up during the night, which side you sleep on and in which position, your weight, heart rhythm, and breathing patterns. Or it may be that your mattress has outlived its useful life, or if it has an unsafe level of dust mites or allergens. That information can now be used not only by the mattress manufacturer but also in an orchestrated manner with other parts of an overall health information and well-being ecosystem. Perhaps there are aspects of your behavior that signal a health condition which needs further diagnosis or therapy. If the digital business ecosystem communicates with your blood pressure cuff, then it can monitor correlations between the quality of sleep and elevated BP readings.

So, what business is the mattress company in? The traditional answer would have been bedding. But in a digital ecosystem it plays an important role in your health and well-being. But let's not stop the value proposition there. How do you pay for the mattress? In the past you would have paid for a mattress when you purchased it. If it was an expensive mattress it may have come with a guarantee of performance. For example, a US-based mattress startup, Casper, lets you try out their mattress for one hundred days. So you could conceivably keep playing Goldilocks and trying mattresses until you found one that works. However, there's another way that's based on behavioral outcomes rather than promises.

Since the mattress provider knows so much about the quality of your sleep, why not pay based on that? If the ecosystem has a stake in your quality of sleep, do you think it may be that you'll actually end up with a better mattress than one that comes with a time-limited guarantee of satisfaction? If a typical mattress costs one thousand dollars and has a lifespan of five to ten years, then its daily cost is fifty-four cents per day. What if you paid from twenty-five to seventy-five cents a night based on how well you slept? And what if other players in the digital ecosystem also participated in that? We know that this raises questions about how quality would be measured but that's only because we've never had the ability to do it in the past.

This shift toward purchasing products as a service is a significant departure from what we are accustomed to. But it's a much more equitable relationship between a supplier and the customer. Amazingly, the idea is one that we had discussed with Peter Drucker in 1998 when we asked him what he felt was the greatest shift that he had seen in business during the twentieth century. Drucker believed it was the combination of the shift from product to service and ownership to strategy.

This isn't a sudden phenomenon brought about in just the last decade through the digitization of business. It's actually been evolving over the past century as a slow but steady shift from the notion of standardized products and clearly delineated organizational boundaries (think of the Ford Model T where the product was "any color as long as it's black" and where every supplier was owned or controlled by Ford) to networks held together by strategy where nearly every product is sold with a service or experiential component. Digital ecosystems are just the latest evolution of this trend.

Owning the Ecosystems Touch Points

Ecosystems can vary in their size, number of partners, and geographic scope, however one thing they all have in common is the ability to provide a unified product, service, or experience.

In the absence of a digital business ecosystem these three touchpoints—product, service, and experience—are typically disjointed since they rarely share information in real time and do not have access to a unified view of a product's lifecycle or the customer's experience. For any digital ecosystem to deliver significant added value, there has to be coordinated ownership of these three critical touchpoints. How that's done will differ depending on the ecosystem, but it can never be absent.

Let's use the example of Tesla. Product, experience, and service are all owned by Tesla. There are no distributors, dealers, or third-party service centers. This might seem like the furthest thing from a digital ecosystem since it implies a model much like the highly integrated supply chain of Henry

Ford's original factory village, where everything from the rubber tree plantations to the dealerships were under Ford's control. This is the industrial era closed-captive ecosystem model we described earlier in Illustration 5.2. However, there is a distinct difference between the Ford and Tesla ecosystem models.

Illustration 5.5

In a digital business ecosystem the three touch points of product, service, and experience each provide ongoing insight into how customer and market behaviors change over time. In most industrial era businesses these three touchpoints are disjointed and owned by separate organizations that are each responsible for only one touch point. Behaviors, and the digital-self, are therefore never understood in a coordinated manner.[109]

Tesla realizes that ownership is critical at the periphery where these three touch points meet the market. For example, it owns its stores and controls the entire lifecycle of the experience from purchase to buy back at a guaranteed price point. Additionally, Tesla owns the product despite an extensive supply chain. Its Gigfactory in Nevada even goes so far as to integrate some of these suppliers, such as battery providers, as an independent but intimately connected part of its ecosystem. Lastly, Tesla captures data about the customer, service, product, and experience to create a unified understanding of the customer's digital self.

How is this different from just buying the batteries and having them shipped via a traditional just in time method? On the surface the difference isn't apparent; it appears to be a way to better coordinate external activities by bringing them in-house. However, by having an ecosystem were the most critical partners are intimately involved in the manufacturing process the rate of innovation is accelerated significantly. Tesla controls the three product touch points. This is not vertical integration, instead it's what we call ecosystem orchestration—a relationship in which strategy, not just ownership, contributes to the rate of innovation.

From a service standpoint, Tesla orchestrates the ability to service by using onboard diagnostics and real-time updates and downloads to modify the platform while also capturing real-time data of the user experience, which can then be used to personalize the customer experience. An excellent example of this is how Tesla responded to customers who were trying to evacuate Florida during the devastation of hurricane Irma in 2017.

Tesla used to offer its Model S with seventy-five kWh batteries that were locked by software to limit battery access just sixty kWh. This limited the effective range of the car to two hundred miles, about a thirty-to-forty mile lower range than the seventy-five kWh option. A Model S owner trying to evacuate called Tesla to ask if they would unlock his extra fifteen kWh to provide the added range for his evacuation. Tesla not only unlocked his battery's capacity but also did the same for every Tesla owner whose battery was similarly limited. This is only possible with a digital ecosystem that integrates the three touchpoints into one view of the customer's digital self, as shown in Illustration 5.6.

Illustration 5.6
In a coordinated digital business ecosystem the three touch points of product, service, and experience are integrated in order to provide a single view of the customer's digital-self.

Can you imagine how that same scenario would play out with a traditional automobile manufacturer where the product, service, and experience touch points are orchestrated by different disconnected players, the manufacturer, the dealer's service, and sales? What about a used car where there is no attachment whatsoever to any of those three parties?

A traditional automobile manufacturer's organic ecosystem is not only fragmented and disconnected but, as we saw with Kodak and as we will see with Sears in the next chapter, it actually insulates the company from the customer. In industrial era ecosystem the manufacturer, at best, only orchestrates the product touch point and purposefully distances itself from the customer since the product provides no option through which to meaningfully connect with the customer. While an organization can establish general guidelines for the experience and the service, neither is tightly integrated with the other two ecosystem touch points. The bottom line is that you cannot create a digital business ecosystem if each of the touch points does not allow for the ability to digitally integrate it with the ecosystem, which is why the role of a digital-self is so critically important. (Illustration 5.6)

The Walled Garden

You may have also noticed that Tesla's digital ecosystem is much like Apple's. They both fall into the category of what's often called a walled garden ecosystem, because each flourishes but is tightly controlled, allowing only well vetted partners in and owning each of the three touchpoints. Since both of these companies are admired as market innovators, they create a tempting role model to emulate. Be careful. Creating this particular sort of ecosystem comes with great risk. Walled gardens work well in situations where one or more of the following are present:

1. The company's survival is predicated on positioning or maintaining the product as the market's innovation leader.
2. Sudden spikes in demand for the product can stress the supply chain and create significant production delays.
3. The product's rate of innovation creates the need for very quick product changes that exceed the ability of third party retooling times.
4. Understanding customer experience with the product across third party components is critical to the product's success.
5. The product has created a new category. (Sony's Walkman, Apple's iPod, Tesla)
6. The product requires unusually high degrees of personalization that demand constant significant reconfiguration of the supply chain.

Not every one of these cases requires a walled garden under one roof, as is the case with Tesla's batteries. Apple has built a walled garden that expands across a network of global partners. McDonald's restaurants are independently owned but tightly controlled, Starbucks locations in bookstores, convention centers, and hotels are owned and operated by the local venue. In each of these cases, and many more, the ecosystems extend well outside of the four walls of the organization and yet are still under the tight control of the anchor brand. The apparent purpose of a walled garden is to maintain control and quality. However, the larger value is in being able to continue collecting behavioral data across all parts of the ecosystem, and most importantly to respond quickly in bringing new innovations to market. While this type of ecosystem works well at scale, when one or more of the six situations we described are present, it is also the most costly way to innovate. In some cases that cost is necessary and can still support a thriving business.

However, there is another approach to the walled garden which is increasingly altering the way supply chains are managed. This is the idea behind creating a business ecosystem that allows organizations to manage not only their own resources but the resources across an entire value chain. Without this capability, you can't reengineer a supply chain quickly enough to respond to changing behaviors in the market. Similarly, the market doesn't have a single voice to tell you what it wants or how its demand for a particular product or service might change. The result can be a product that stays in inventory much longer than it should. One of the reasons that Apple is considered a global leader in supply chain is that it turns over its inventory in less than five days whereas a competitor such as Samsung takes up to two weeks.

The benefit of this can seem relatively small in some cases. For example, if a market suddenly starts to demand a product with a specific set of features, you would typically not know it until well after the demand has occurred. The alternative is to attempt to forecast demand through derivative indicators and adjust the supply chain so that everyone from the commodity providers and suppliers to the manufacturer can adjust their forecasts.

A derivative indicator is the tell-tale of a market but not an actual measurement of market interest. For example, a seasonal adjustment based on weather forecasts, broad demographic shifts, or even sociopolitical factors (i.e. an election forecast or an act of terrorism). Using derivative indicators has been the model that has been used and is still being used in the vast majority of supply chains, and it's the furthest thing from a digital ecosystem.

The problem with these sorts of derivative-based forecasting approaches is that they create what's referred to as a bullwhip effect throughout the supply chain.[110] For example, if a manufacturer of foul weather apparel forecasts a mild winter that will reduce their sales by 10 percent, they will reduce orders from suppliers by 10 percent. However, the suppliers may then hedge their bets and reduce orders from textile suppliers by 15 percent. The textile suppliers may then do the same and reduce orders from commodity and raw material providers by 25 percent. Each level of the supply chain, moving upstream toward the source materials, is reducing the likelihood of being overexposed and left with excess inventory. (Illustration 5.7)

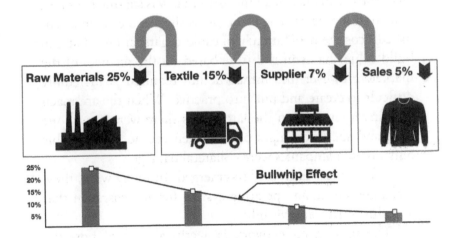

Illustration 5.7
Derivative-based forecasting can have a bullwhip effect through the supply chain by amplifying perceived risk from retailer to suppliers to raw materials providers.

An ecosystem doesn't rely on market estimates based on derivatives but rather actual behaviors of a market at the level of the individuals who make up that market. The ecosystem provides transparency across the entire supply chain so that simulations and models can be developed for all possible scenarios. It then moves in lock step with the market as demand changes. This might seem like a flight of fancy. After all, how could any supply chain possibly react this fast? Yet it is being done through sensing technology that measures and communicates every change in the market throughout the ecosystem. And the example exists today.

One of the best examples of how this can be done is E2open. E2open was founded in 2000 by a group of high-tech companies—including IBM, Lucent, Hitachi, Seagate, and Solectron—which saw the need for an exchange among all of the companies in an industry that was sharing suppliers and common parts. The principle is simple: create an established ecosystem of interchangeable organizations that can build value chains in real time based on the nuances of the market. However, the infrastructure required is incredibly difficult to create and put into practice. When the approach was first attempted in the late 1990s there were nearly one thousand such exchanges built. When the dot-com bubble burst, these companies were collateral damage.

Fifteen years later they re-emerged. In many ways, these exchanges create an operating system for an ecosystem that introduces trust and visibility.

The underlying network is a critical part of how the cloud enables this level of service. There are more than forty thousand suppliers established in the E2open network; when supplier A suddenly comes up short, a company can instantly switch to supplier B or C. Not only can a company get connected to the supplier, it can have real-time visibility into the supplier's inventory, shoot a message out to an alternate supplier saying, "I need another one hundred thousand components; what can you give me?" and instantly get a commitment. This is not just getting someone on the phone, it's an electronic commitment that happens faster than a person could read an email.

Every supplier and customer in the E2open ecosystem is always looking at the same dashboard with the same information about supply and demand levels, allowing companies to respond to variances in a way they couldn't before. This is what E2open calls "a single version of the truth." That concept has profound implications in practice, because it takes the guesswork and potential errors inherent in any complex ecosystem out of the equation, increasing reliability and confidence in making changes to the product, service, or experience.

But there is another benefit that goes well beyond the near-term visibility we've described. The next generation of ecosystems will focus on being truly demand-driven, so that the forecasting and innovation is based on real-time demand signals rather than just past performance and demand. Using real-time data, through market behavior and making real-time decisions about the entirety of an ecosystem provides the ability to increase the rate and speed of bringing new innovations to market. This is, once again, the behavioral aspect of what we've been describing.

Ecosystem Fuel for the Economy

There's one final aspect of the ecosystem model that we want to look at before we close this chapter and move on to hyper-personalization; it's the critical role of ecosystems in fueling startup innovation.

Silicon Valley is littered with thousands of hi-tech companies, including forty of the *Fortune* 500. With over a third of all venture capital being invested in Silicon Valley startups, you'd think that this would inherently create an organic ecosystem rich with opportunity for new ideas. You'd be right, but it's still a relatively inefficient ecosystem that relies on serendipity and chance encounters. In our parlance, it's a system with a great deal of friction. It's also a model of innovation that limits growth opportunities to startups in a particular geographical region. Clearly, innovation knows no geographical boundaries.

To facilitate the creation of an ecosystem-based approach to promoting the growth and success of startups, businesses known as accelerators have stepped in to help. By our estimates there are at least one hundred fifty accelerators in the US and two to three times that many worldwide. Many of these are fairly well known, such as Plug and Play, AngelPad, Y Combinator, Alchemist, MuckerLab, and StartX. An accelerator usually provides at a minimum: a collaborative sandbox; some basic resources; and access to investors. That may include office space, the ability to brainstorm with like-minded entrepreneurs, help in creating a business plan or a pitch deck to present to investors, and introductions venture capital or angel investors.

To understand the value of this think back Drucker's model of an ecosystem held together by strategy and service. One of the hardest aspects of creating organizations that can thrive in that upper right-hand quadrant of innovation is aligning the interests among all of the players that need to be part of the ecosystem. That's relatively easy to do with established players through vast partner networks with an anchor player that acts as the center of gravity and the coordinator of the ecosystem. For instance, Ford, Walmart, and Apple all have a high degree of control over their suppliers. However, this is the classic industrial era model of an ecosystem built for scale. The suppliers are most often established players with products and services ready to add value and plug into that digital ecosystem.

So, what happens to the much larger community of startups and early stage companies still trying to get to that point? The answer is usually that they need to somehow raise capital, establish relationships with corporate buyers, prove that their products work, and cultivate a host of other competencies in order to grow. That's a five to ten year proposition.

The risk in that journey is shown in the numbers. Fifty percent of all startups will fail within five years. Twenty-five percent after just one year. And these are the startups that get to invest several months to several years in building a product and a business. For each of these there are hundreds that never have a chance to see their idea get beyond the whiteboard for lack of funding and resources. That is one of the greatest sources of friction for any startup and it may be one of the greatest untapped potentials of the global innovation economy; it stifles innovation and creates severe economic impediments to growth. A 2015 Report from MIT, The Future Postponed, looked at the increasing Innovation Deficit being caused by a reduction in US funded R&D from ten percent of the federal budget in 1968 to two percent today.

If we go back to one of the core themes of this book, the increasing velocity of a post-industrial era economy, the model for innovation in place today is not adequate for an economy that relies on innovation more than it ever has.

Once again, we are being held hostage by the friction of an industrial era model for innovation.

Enter Silicon Valley investor Amid Saeed.

In 2006 Saeed founded Plug and Play, which calls itself "Silicon Valley In A Box." Saeed had been a successful technology investor for over fifteen years through his fund, Amidzad, which had worked with over seventy technology companies. Having seen the challenge of funding and growing a company, his idea for Plug and Play was a simple one, create a rich ecosystem for companies with a good idea who need capital, resources, and mentoring. To date Plug and Play has invested in more than five hundred fifty companies which have raised nearly five billion dollars. Some of it's more notable successes are PayPal, Danger, DropBox, and Lending Club.

Unlike many other accelerators (which provide the training, access to venture capital, and the physical space to collaborate) the key to what Plug and Play does is its obsessive focus on the entire ecosystem, including a long list of nearly two hundred corporates such as DHL, Intuit, Deutsche Bank, Bosch, Aflac, Travelers, Phillips, Goodyear, and TJX. The corporates have the ability to either present specific areas where they would like to see innovation or to work directly with Plug and Play's companies as collaborators or investors. Even Saeed, who had originally envisioned Plug and Play as a just a physical space for startups, says, "I never imagined the positive energy it has created."

While there has always been an informal mechanism by which startups can bootstrap and raise capital, the inherent inefficiency of the process has undoubtedly stifled and slowed many innovations as they struggle to find the resources needed to commercialize ideas. The accelerator ecosystem is a critical part of the post-industrial era economy because it both reduces the friction of growing new companies, and fuels the rate of innovation with a more predictable and sustainable model of growth.

It's this last piece, quickly bringing new innovations to market, that is often the most challenging because only part of the innovation is in the product and increasingly more of it is in how the customer experiences the product as something which has been built to address his or her specific needs, desires, and behaviors. That's what we'll look at next.

CHAPTER 6:
Hyper-personalization: Creating Ten Billion Futures

"Personalization is the automatic tailoring of sites and messages to the individuals viewing them, so that we can feel that somewhere there's a piece of software that loves us for who we are."
—David Weinberger

It was the summer of 2004. Netflix CEO Reed Hastings and his CFO Barry McCarthy were on an earnings call in the conference room of their Los Gatos headquarter overlooking the picnic tables outside. On this particular call they mentioned their chief competitor Blockbuster no less than twenty-two times. One thousand, six hundred and eighty-nine miles away in Dallas, Blockbuster executives were listening to the call on speaker phones when Hastings told analysts, "In the last six months, Blockbuster has thrown everything but the kitchen sink at us." The next day an overnight shipment arrived at Hastings' office addressed from Dallas; it was a kitchen sink.

In 2000 Blockbuster was the leader in DVD rentals. Only four years prior it had been acquired by Viacom for 8.4 billion dollars. At about the same time Blockbuster passed on the opportunity to buy the fledgling two-year-old Netflix, founded by a disgruntled Hastings—supposedly, after he was charged a forty dollar late fee for his Blockbuster DVD rental of *Apollo 13*.[111]

Hastings had approached Blockbuster CEO John Antioco with the idea that through a Netflix/Blockbuster partnership, detailed data about online subscribers' viewing habits could be used to intelligently target changing interests and behaviors. The price was fifty million dollars. Hastings was quickly shown to the door. At the time, Blockbuster had already approached Enron to use their bandwidth for on-demand videos. It would take Netflix another six years to introduce its streaming service. Hastings had also already approached Amazon CEO Jeff Bezos in 1998, but balked at Bezos' twelve million dollar offer.

Over the next four years, Blockbuster and Netflix would both attempt to redefine the market for video rentals. This was not an asymmetrical competition in which the companies were offering two separate products, Blockbuster with DVD and Netflix with on-demand video, as it's often been portrayed. Both companies were investing in both DVD and streaming. Even Blockbuster's CEO, Jim Keyes, said in 2008, "I've been frankly confused by this fascination that everybody has with Netflix...Netflix doesn't really have or do anything that we can't or don't already do ourselves."[112]

But the underlying business models of the two companies couldn't have been more different.

Blockbuster used an industrial era business model that relied heavily on mass distribution, storefronts, economies of scale, and lack of transparency. And it all seemed to work out pretty well. In 2004 Blockbuster had stores in nine thousand one hundred locations. However, there was a dirty little secret that created enormous friction in the customer experience. Approximately 15 percent of Blockbuster's revenues came not from DVD rentals, streaming, or the assorted candies and snacks it had packed its stores with, but instead from late fees. Blockbuster was punishing its own customers.[113] Even though Blockbuster had in-store personnel who could have built a personal relationship with the customer, anyone who ever walked out of a Blockbuster store after being hit with late fees could tell that the last thing they felt was that this was a brand which they had a relationship with.

Netflix, on the other hand, had no late fees, no storefronts, and a brand that was almost cult-like among its customers.

Within five years, Blockbuster would file for bankruptcy and Netflix would claim the title of the world's largest provider of DVD rentals and streaming content.

What happened with Blockbuster is a classic story of how any company can fall into an industrial era mindset which prevents them for innovating, even when they can see the innovation happening all around them.

Innovation is not an inalienable right. No single company has a perpetual license to innovate. Netflix learned that the hard way during the summer of 2011 when they announced the splitting of its business in two groups: Qwikster, a DVD rental company, and Netflix, the online streaming company. That and a near revolt on the part of its members, more than eight hundred thousand of whom canceled their membership within a few weeks of the announcement brought on an apology from Hastings and taught Netflix an invaluable lesson: intuition is risky business. That's nothing new for

Hollywood, where trying to predict a blockbuster has historically always been a gamble. But that's changing radically.

Today Netflix is perhaps one of the best examples of what we call fourth stage digitalization later in this chapter—the use of behavioral data as the governing model in creating new products and services. By analyzing the individual viewing habits of its one hundred million members, the company is able to understand behaviors at an unprecedented level of detail. As Joris Evers, Netflix's former Director of Global Communications, once quipped, "There are 33 million different versions of Netflix."

Not only does Netflix use individualized behavioral data to make recommendations to members, but it also uses this data to produce its own original content. For example, when Netflix dished out one hundred million dollars to purchase the rights to produce *House of Cards*, it was betting on a trove of data which, among other things, indicated that Director David Fincher, Actor Kevin Spacey, and the British version of *House of Cards* formed a sort of perfect storm for the interests of its members (at the time, at least).

Netflix goes to what might appear to be absurd lengths to understand and cater to its members at a very fine degree of resolution. It has seventy-six thousand, eight hundred and ninety-seven microgenres of movies.[114] When it develops the identity for a new movie it will analyze the specific color content of promotional images for other successful movies and series. It even has a thirty-six-page manual that is used to train specialized movie "viewers," who are tasked with watching movies and using metatagging to indicate everything from how sexually explicit or violent a movie is to the moral character of the actors.[115]

When you view a trailer for a new Netflix movie or series, you will see one that is optimized for your behavioral style.[116] As with so much of what we've talked about, this too isn't universally applauded. John Landgraf, President of FX Networks, doesn't buy into the ability to predict success. "Data can only tell you what people have liked before, not what they don't know they are going to like in the future. A good high-end programmer's job is to find the white spaces in our collective psyche that aren't filled by an existing television show. [Those are choices made] "in a black box that data can never penetrate."[117]

While we understand and agree with the sentiment that breaking new ground often requires a totally counterintuitive move, that decision is simply a matter of the degree of risk that you're willing to take. In that respect it's no different than any business today where the incumbents may rely on more conservative and predictable bets and new upstarts will purposefully place a risky bet that sometimes pays off.

If we really do believe in the dynamic of a free market, why would we not want to raise the bar as high as possible? If Netflix wants to rely on algorithms and AI to determine its next best blockbuster, that does not obviate the opportunity for an independent studio to go in an entirely different direction. In fact, we'd argue that this sort of dynamic, which is merit-based, creates much more value than large studios making decisions based entirely on intuition (which in many ways is just a front for bias and personal preference.)

In other words, we'd much rather tell Hollywood what we like and have that be what comes out of a studio than having Hollywood tell us what we *should* like!

The phenomenon we're describing by using Netflix as an example is not in any way limited to Hollywood or entertainment. It is a much deeper trend that we see shaping the way in which companies innovate. It's an evolution that has been following a definite trajectory from the earliest days of industrialization through to the present. It's what has come to be called digitalization.

Let's be clear from the outset that digitalization is not the same as digitization. The latter has been achieved by every organization competing effectively using digital technologies to run its internal systems, work with partners, market and sell to customers, and support customers.

Digitalization is the act of creating a product, service, or organization which uses digital technology at its core to fundamentally change the user experience. At its pinnacle, the ultimate purpose of digitalization is the creation of hyper-personalized products that understand and evolve with market and customer behaviors.

Hyper-personalization is also not simply a means of creating a product that has variability or a selection of options. Whether it's something as simple as a monogrammed watch or an automobile ordered from the factory with a customized set of options, these are examples of mass customization in which a customer selects from a series of preconfigured options which are determined by the manufacturer based on prior market research or customer preferences. We're not saying that mass customization is no longer required, but rather that it alone is not enough.

My Coke

One of the most popular but extraordinarily simple examples of personalization, as opposed to hyper-personalization, is Coca-Cola's Share a Coke campaign, which started in Australia before achieving massive success and being rolled out to seventy countries. The campaign was brilliantly simple in concept. Choose one hundred fifty of the most popular names in Australia and print them in bold letters on the face of Coke bottles and cans. According to Jay Moye, Editor-in-Chief, *Coca-Cola Journey*:

> *The moment Lucie Austin saw her name on a Coke bottle, she knew her team had a hit on its hands.*
>
> *"My reaction was childlike," she recalls. "I knew many others would have the same reaction."*
>
> *Austin, who at the time was director of marketing for Coca-Cola South Pacific, was huddled with her colleagues inside a Sydney conference room in 2011, listening to five agencies pitch concepts for Coke's next summer campaign. A couple of weeks prior, they'd received a 151-word creative brief that gave them free reign to deliver a truly disruptive idea that would make headlines and capture the country's attention.*
>
> *The resulting campaign, known internally as "Project Connect" based on its ambition to both strengthen the brand's bond with Australia's young adults—and inspire shared moments of happiness in the real and virtual worlds—became known as "Share a Coke." The first-of-its-kind campaign celebrated the power of the first name in a playful, social way by swapping out Coke branding on bottles and cans with the 150 most popular monikers in Australia.*

And it worked.

That summer, Coke sold more than 250 million named bottles and cans in a nation of just under 23 million people. The campaign has since made its way around the world, reaching more than 70 countries, to date. Coca-Cola teams from Great Britain, to Turkey to China—and, most recently, the United States—have put their own creative spin on the concept, while preserving the simple invitation to "Share a Coke with (insert name).[118]

Why would something so utterly simple be so powerful? Personalization is an acknowledgement on the part of brand that the consumer has an individual identity and that he or she is worth recognizing. In many ways, what Coca-Cola proved is that even a large multinational company can create the sort of relationship with customers that would only be possible through a local retailer.

Another example is Nike, which in 2017 opened a studio in New York where people are able to create a hyper-personalized shoes. According to Mark Smith, VP of Innovation Special Projects at Nike, "The intention of the project is to bring to life the collaborative design experience that we offer our athletes…[they] love products that tell their story, so we wanted to combine that idea with a new process of live design and manufacturing that allows our guests to come into the space, work collaboratively with us and leave with a special product in less time than ever before."

Prior to this Nike did provide consumers with the ability to design their own shoes and have them delivered within a few weeks. However, now the whole value chain is redesigned and customers can walk out of the Nike store with their own personal pair of sneakers. This is clearly a far cry from mass production, but it only addresses known needs and expectations with bespoke or tailor-made requirements.[119]

Bridget Fahrland, SVP Client Strategy at Fluid, an agency that works with dozens of name brands including Estee Lauder, the North Face, Puma, and Vans, to build highly personalized and custom customer experiences and products, talked to us about the changing role of the customer-brand relationship. She used the example of Fender, the legendary seventy-year-old USA guitar manufacturer, and their Fender Mod Shop, an immersive digital studio experience providing consumers with the ability to design their dream guitar by choosing from a wide variety of customizable options.

> *Shoppers don't just want to be consumers; they want to be co-creators of unique products.*
>
> *Customization is a way to differentiate and to offer products that [most retailers] simply can't offer. I think it also shows a deeper engagement with that customer. The customer who's doing a Mod Shop guitar with Fender is a higher price point. They've been playing guitar more. Now you're starting to build a more personal deep relationship with that customer [that] connects them to brand a little bit more intimately with a longer-term relationship that will carry through.*
>
> *One aspect of this which applies to both mass customization and mass personalization, because we're talking about doing this*

at scale, is that it's being done for hundreds of thousands or millions of people.

To some degree, you never get away from the mass market model. You are still marketing to a large group of people. But if you attempt to personalize a product you will get insights that you otherwise wouldn't get [from] a focus group of your traditional mass market behavioral profiles of large groups or large demographics. You're really understanding what the market wants at a very intimate or a very low level of granularity. And it would seem to me that part of the benefit of going that route is to satisfy certain customers who want a highly personalized product, but also getting insights into where the marketplace is going or trends that might otherwise not be obvious to you.

While each of these companies—Coke, Nike, and Fender—provide examples of product variability and the move toward mass personalization, they do not use the ongoing behaviors of any particular customer—while they are using the product—as a means of understanding individualized preferences. However, it is worth noting that capturing personalized preferences for how a product is configured (for example, Fender's Mod Shop Guitars) can lead to insights for new variations of the product for a mass market.

The typical impediment to hyper-personalization is that most manufacturing processes cannot allow for real-time changes to a product which requires retooling of the assembly process. Even in the case of Coca-Cola's Share a Coke, with bare minimal personalization, the amount of effort required to select the names, make sure they did not infringe on trademarks, insure that each name did not have the potential of offending someone or worse yet be a profanity in another language, and selecting a digital printing process that would replicate the red Coke color took months of effort.

In Fender's case, it was much easier since the assembly line was already configured in a way that allowed for customization, which could be scaled with relative ease.

Thomas Hischerman, CEO of Braingraph, a UK based data strategy and advisory firm, shared with us a much more radical view of where the hyper-personalization of manufacturing might go:

> [A] radical way of thinking would be to not just move product design but product manufacturing completely into the hands of the consumer. I see consumers technically becoming manufacturers with the power of AI and 3D printing allowing them to come up with new patents and new ideas which [they can] translate into finalized products based on shared schematics and shared blueprints. Building onto existing design guidelines and existing patents, the consumer should technically be able to set up his own manufacturing process and his own production site at scale and things like blockchain will even allow him to sell products himself. Technically, the differentiation between consumer and producer should become meaningless.

Hischerman's view is a tantalizing one in which the manufacturer becomes the provider of "manufacturing as a service." However, the physical product is only one dimension of the customer experience. The greater the degree of digital technology integrated into the product the easier it is to personalize the product experience while the product or device remains fundamentally the same. The example we used earlier was that of a smartphone which is primarily customized by virtue of the apps that it uses. In Nike's case, the shoe itself would be outfitted with connected sensors that would track the use of the shoe, the ways in which it was used, the conditions that it was used in, and the lifecycle of the shoe. While all of this is being done, the shoe could be transformed into a digitalized version by using connected diagnostics, usage recommendations, and reminders—"Hey, you, we haven't gone running in a while." This doesn't mean that the shoe will talk to us directly, but that it can communicate through its integration with a larger ecosystem, which may include a health and wellness app on your smartphone.

The same principle applies to much more complex devices such as automobiles. Tesla has a platform which allows for both the ability to capture a driver's behaviors and to then configure the performance, user interface, and behavior of the car to align with them.

Faurecia one of the world's largest automotive equipment suppliers with twenty-three billion dollars in global sales and a venture fund which invests in startups in the AV industry is looking closely at how it can recreate the interior cabin of AVs to conform to the moods, context, and emotions of the inhabitants. The experience in this case may include lighting, music, video, seating configuration, even the driving behavior of the car. This doesn't require a different manufacturing process for each AV, but it provides a level of adaptation that could not be achieved otherwise.

The Role of Digitalization

The only way we can possibly approach a business model that achieves hyper-personalization is through the digitalization of a product. Simply put, digitalization is the ability to innovate based on direct sensing of behaviors through the use of digital technology. This means the product has to have the ability to collect behavioral data, connectivity to a digital-twin where that data can be analyzed and understood, and the ability to make modifications of its behavior in real-time in order to continuously innovate itself and the customer experience.

Digitalization is a unique way to think of a product because it now not only provides value to its users but it's also the only category of product that gathers value *from* its users. This symbiotic relationship occurs in real-time, it's not the result of market research, focus groups, surveys, or the derivative approach we described earlier in this chapter. Instead it's provided directly through the use of the product. To make it easier to understand digitalization let's break it down into five stages.

These five stages are not limited to just pure digital products. Since nearly every product has a digital component, or a digital-twin, we can apply the concept of digitalization to products across nearly every industry.

Table 6.1 shows some examples of the five stages of digitalization in several industry categories of products.

Table 6.1

	First Stage	Second Stage	Third Stage	Fourth Stage	Fifth Stage
Music	MP3 Players	iPod	iTunes	Genius Mix	Individualized
Vehicles	Manual	Assisted	Connected	Autonomous L3/4	Autonomous L5
Telecom	Landlines	Wireless/ Cell Phone	Smartphone/ Apps	Wearable	Augmented
Electricity	Local Generators	Regional Generators	Utility Providers	Grid	Smart Homes
Computers	Centralized Terminal	Desktop Local	Networked PCs LAN	Mobile	Neuralink
Software	Mechanical Automation	Digital Automation	User Interface Focused	Apps	AI

Stage of Digitalization	Characteristics
First Stage	Device-based, high risk, no behavioral tracking, first to market, rarely makes it to Stage 2, new technology with no analog for comparison, widespread market adoption is exceptionally rare.
Second Stage	Still device-based, but disruptive potential starts to appear. Combines multiple Stage 1 innovations, introduces new business model, not yet perceived as threatening to incumbents, number of players rises significantly to form a product category, some basic ability to capture behavioral data.
Third Stage	Behavioral data becomes competitive differentiator, slight or no departure from Stage 2 device (almost unnoticed change in device other than incremental innovation), exploits new business model fully, creates copycat innovators, becomes competitive threat to old business models and devices, standards are selected by the market, competition among players of Stage 3 peaks, market reaches tipping point.

Fourth Stage	Behavior-based differentiation is now key, a market leader, pulls ahead of a crowded field, changes user experience in a dramatic way through a rich ecosystem that allows for advanced personalization, competition begins to thin as incumbents from Stage 3 begin to dwindle and die off.
Fifth Stage	Builds on the Stage 4 behavioral model but also adds intelligence and/or the ability to predict future behaviors and anticipate needs and preferences in a hyper-personalized manner, at scale. Hyper-personalization creates high levels of intimacy with the technology. Moving into Stage 5 requires significant resources from a trusted provider because the market is so well entrenched in Stage 4 that users and consumers are very reluctant to make an uncertain bet on the future. For that same reason, it has to make much more economic sense than any of the prior stages in order to justify the transition from what is perceived as "good enough."

The key benefit of a digitalized approach is that it can challenge and displace existing products that are well-understood, and widely adopted in markets that are considered saturated. A well-known example, which illustrates a product that has done this, as it has progressed through all five stages, is Apple's journey from iPod to iPhone.

The iPod and the iPhone were relatively late entrants into crowded markets toward the end of Stage 1 digitalization. Devices such as Creative's Nomad and Diamond's Rio had built a near-monopoly in the MP3 portable media player marketplace. The advantage that Apple leveraged from the outset was that customer behaviors were captured and analyzed as part of an overall ecosystem that Apple developed with iTunes.

It's easy to forget that even after the iPhone was first introduced it was not at all clear who the breakthrough innovators were. Just before the iPhone was introduced, Nokia had nearly a 50 percent share of the smartphone market.

Two years after the iPhone was introduced Apple only had 4.2 percent market share. RIM, manufacturer of the popular Blackberry, had a 3.6 percent market share and was growing. Samsung had a 26 percent share. A 2011 *Forbes* article noted that, "Judging by the number of younger buyers who have chosen BlackBerrys over iPhones, I am not worried about RIM's staying power or growth."[120] In less than two years RIM would report its first quarterly loss and within five years it would shut down production of the Blackberry. Nokia would fall to 3.1 percent by 2013.

iPhone's introduction is even more amazing when you consider the sort of lukewarm welcome that the iPhone received in 2007 from competitors who universally derided it. Ed Coligan, CEO of Palm—which succeeded wildly in the PDA market where Apple had failed miserably with the Newton in the early 1990s—saw Apple as the outsider, "We've learned and struggled for a few years here figuring out how to make a decent phone. PC guys are not going to just figure this out. They're not going to just walk in." Mike Lazaridis, CEO of RIM, was no less complimentary, "Apple's approach produced devices that inevitably sacrificed advanced features for aesthetics." And Steve Ballmer, former CEO of Apple's longtime rival Microsoft, didn't hold back when he quipped that "[Apple would] have the most expensive phone, by far, in the marketplace. There's no chance that the iPhone is going to get any significant market share. No chance." These sorts of reactions are typical of incumbents who already have a stake in the current market.

Apple's ability to rise to a position of dominance in the smartphone market is in no small part due to the digitalization of its entire ecosystem and the resulting ability to respond to customer behaviors in a nearly instantaneous manner. This is not because Apple itself is especially ingenious in how it innovates the device (although we'd argue it has been) but in how the entirety of its digital ecosystem continuously adapts to customer needs.

The same holds true for Samsung and Google's Android operating system which competes with Apple and its proprietary OSX operating system. The competition now is between digital experiences, and while the device is clearly still front and center, the greater value is all about the experience. Which is why companies that try to replicate the device alone are rarely rewarded, but instead seen as laggards. This was precisely the case with Microsoft's efforts to introduce its Windows Smartphone. Despite enormous investment (7.6 billion dollars just for its acquisition of Nokia and subsequent write off) Microsoft has less than 1 percent US market share compared to Apple's 40 percent. The remaining market share belongs to Android (a miniscule .02 percent is for other proprietary OS).[121]

During Stage 2 and 3, Apple had done little outside of ongoing incremental innovation for the iPhone. The device, standards, and the App store have not changed radically but the way in which consumers experienced them has. The majority of innovation has come from Apple's digital ecosystem, which allows users to build a device uniquely suited to their needs.

At this point in time we'd say that Apple (and Samsung) are well into Stage Four digitalization, which provides an abundance of insight into the actual use of the device and its entire ecosystem. AI is also starting to find its way into the device through Apple's A11 Bionic chip and Apple's "neural engine," a pair of processors dedicated to performing machine learning tasks for face recognition, animated emojis, and augmented reality.

However, there is a school of thought that Stage 4 digitalization can actually limit innovation. The reason being that Stage 4 creates a cognitive bias. By now customers have become accustomed to the experience and have invested heavily in understanding it and integrating it with their lives. Manufacturers then use this data about use to reinforce and better meet these needs. As that cycle repeats at a large scale, it reinforces and buttresses the past.

However, there is another way to look at this which we believe is a foundational benefit of digitalization. Historically, by the time a market evolves to the point where it has become well-established and widely adopted, breakthrough innovations make little sense to a market researcher or a focus group. The reason is simply that people only know what they have experienced. This becomes the framework for how they measure the value of any new product. The late management guru Peter Drucker was a strong disbeliever in this sort of "ask the market" approach to innovation, as was Steve Jobs. Both believed that while markets could express dissatisfaction with a product, they could not envision solutions that stepped sufficiently outside of the existing product's frame of reference. As Marshall McLuhan said in 1955, "It is the framework which changes with each new technology and not just the picture within the frame."[122]

The bottom line is that if you ask a market what it wants, the answer will be, "What we have now, but faster and cheaper." The promise of digitalization is that the market does not need to speak for itself. Instead, it's the otherwise invisible behaviors of the individuals in the market that drive the innovation.

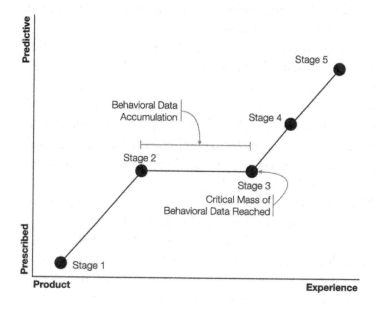

Illustration 6.1 – Stages of Digitalization

The five stages of digitalization progress from Stage 1, tightly prescribed products with no connectivity or ability to collect behavioral data, to Stage 2, products with basic connectivity and a greater experiential component. The Stage 2 to 3 transition focuses primarily on greater connectivity that increases the experience, although it does not yet increase the predictive capability of the product since the amount of data needed to do this hasn't yet been gathered. Once a critical mass of data has been collected, the product progresses to Stages 4 and 5 where the behavioral data now informs predictive and experiential innovation.

That's pretty much where we are right now when it comes to smartphones. We have become so accustomed to the incremental innovation of what we have that it gives the illusion of a product that will always stay fundamentally the same.

Whether it's automobiles or smartphones, it's exceedingly difficult to imagine what could possible replace what we are now using. Historically at this point the ecosystems and the business models are also set in stone. This was the Kodak challenge we described earlier. While Kodak was stuck to an industrial ecosystem model, the same could apply to a digital ecosystem.

The power of digitalization is that it creates a direct link between the product and the user's digital-self. Rather than rely on broad demographic trends and self-reported behaviors to identify areas for innovation, the innovation now happens as a direct result of the actual behaviors of the user or customer.

You're Not Who You Thought You Were

Generally speaking, our actual behaviors are often vastly different from our perceived behaviors because the image we have of ourselves is a necessarily biased one. If you don't believe that, just ask someone you know well who has subscribed to an online dating site how often the pictures they see of the person online differ significantly from the person who they met in person. Research done on this shows that while there may sometimes be deception involved, in the overwhelming number of instances it's simply because we have biased view of ourselves.[123]

A wonderful example of this is an online video run by Dove as part of its Real Beauty campaign in 2013. The video starts with a forensic artist, whose job is drawing pictures of a criminal from an eyewitness description. The forensic artist is on the right side of a large draped partition. On the other side of the partition, a woman is asked to be seated and to describe herself to the artist so that he can draw her. Neither the artist nor the woman can see each other at any point.[124]

Once the woman is done, she is escorted out and several of her friends are asked to sit down, one at a time, and describe the woman to the artist. At the end the artist pins up the original picture as the woman described herself next to each of the pictures drawn from her friends' descriptions of her. The woman is brought back in to view the drawings and drawn to tears by the stark contrast between her version, which inevitably appears much more haggard, worn, and tired than that of her friends. The point of the ad is that our self-image is rarely accurate and always influenced by our complex emotional state.[125]

This phenomenon spills over into much of how we understand our behaviors as well. How often have you had a conversation with someone about something they did within the last twenty-four hours, which they claim they didn't do or have no recollection of? What about idiosyncratic behaviors that a close friend, relative, or even spouse is totally unaware of, but which drive you crazy?

This is one of the hardest things for us to accept when it comes to the topic of hyper-personalization. We want desperately to believe that we are consciously aware of our every behavior, that we know what appeals to us and what does not, and that we can recall perfectly our actions and thoughts. According to research it's not true.

Since the 1980s we've had a fairly large and convincing body of evidence that we are consciously aware of very little of what we do—perhaps only five percent! Doctor Anthony Marcel, a Cambridge University psychologist, conducted many experiments in the '80s that were fascinating examples of this. In one he worked with patients who had a form of blindness called "blindsight" in which the eye and the optic nerve are undamaged and function perfectly. However, lesions in the brain effectively render the patient blind. It would be like hooking up a camera to the internet and not being able to find its IP address.

Doctor Marcel would place objects in front of the patients within arm's reach. Then he would ask them to reach for the object while recording their movements with high-speed cameras. According to a *Time* magazine article about the research, "The film showed that the patient did not grope; instead he reached directly for the object—his preparatory motions fine-tuned to its specific location, shape and size. 'They thought I was mad, at first, because they couldn't see a thing,' [said] Dr. Marcel. 'But when they finally tried it, they reached for the object perfectly. It turns out their vision is, in a sense, superb, but they don't know they can see.'"

The same phenomenon is now widely recognized as part of the reason why marketers have such a hard time trying to gauge the success of a new product through the use of focus groups, which is why companies have been steadily moving away from that sort of highly biased approach to understanding behavior. In fact, the founder of the modern focus group, psychoanalyst Ernst Dichter, who immigrated to the US in 1938 from Vienna, once said, "You would be amazed to find how we mislead ourselves, when we attempt to explain why we behave the way we do."

For the last one hundred years, companies have been attempting to understand mass markets as though every person who made up a market was subject to the same motivations, needs and desires. We've so bought into this notion of a "marketplace" that we simply accept that if a product or service doesn't meet our individualized needs then clearly it is we, the consumer, who should adjust our needs. After all, a brand cannot be all things to all people.

The flaw in the mass-market model is only clear when you are able to contrast it with the ability to truly understand each consumer. That sort of understanding was simply not possible to scale. You could either be a small business that worked with each customer or a large business that worked with large stereotypes of customers.

The other problem that mass marketing creates is that one-size-fits-all products are often so misaligned with the needs, attributes, or behaviors of the customer that the product is returned, rarely used, or soon finds its way to the trash bin. This is especially peculiar behavior when you stop to consider that if a product isn't suitable you'd expect it to be returned 100 percent of the time. The reason that's not true is that we hold on to the product because we want to believe that it is right for us, that we are defective rather than the product. Those skinny jeans that looked so wonderful when worn by an online model can really look that good on you if you just try hard enough to fit into them.

According to a report on returns in the retail industry, "Total merchandise returns account for over $260.5 billion in lost sales for US retailers. that number is so large that if merchandise returns were a corporation it would rank #3 on the *Fortune* 500 list."[126]

This is becoming an unsustainable problem. A *Wall Street Journal* article summed it up well, "You still haven't worn that item of clothing that seemed perfect in the shop but at home seems so wrong. You can't bring yourself to get rid of it, though. It's in a corner of the closet that could be labeled 'regret.'"[127] We can chalk this up to rampant consumerism, but that offers no solution. Chastising a market is a fool's journey. The key in addressing this is to find a way to create additional value for customers. That won't stop anyone addicted to retail therapy; however, it will appeal to the larger mass of consumers who would prefer to look good in what they do buy rather than to have an impressive closet filled with regrets.

Hyper-personalization changes that drastically by allowing a company to scale while maintaining intimacy with each customer and an understanding of their behaviors. And this creates a virtuous cycle. Since the customer experience improves dramatically, the customer is much more engaged, allowing the brand to learn more about the customer, and the cycle repeats. With each iteration of this cycle, the bond of loyalty between brand and the customer grows stronger and harder to break by a competitor. In our clothing example, this might mean that a retailer has the behavioral data to predict the styles, sizes, tailoring, durability, and anything else that may determine what items will work best for you. That's the value of hyper-personalization, a highly individualized relationship with each customer that reinforces trust in the brand.

The ultimate goal for hyper-personalization is to address a customer's needs without requiring him or her to spend any time or effort thinking about what their needs are. This may sound odd but it's the principle at the heart of how much of the world already works. The ABS (anti-lock braking systems) in our cars is a prime example. It's there, we never learn how to use it, most of us don't even know what it is or how it works, but it's always ready to help and protect us. Again, in the parlance of this book, it's invisible. With advances in AI, cars are already at the point where they can sense danger, predict accidents, and avoid them before they even happen. This is the sort of trusted relationship hyper-personalization enables, one that until now a human has only been able to have with another human.

The key to hyper-personalization is constructing every aspect of your business around the customer experience. In his book *Innovative State*, Aneesh Chopra, former Chief Technology Officer for the USA under President Obama describes how Aetna created a hyper-personalized approach to working with customers by putting them at the center of the healthcare ecosystem:

> ...customers calling in to [Aetna's] nurse call center, designed an IT cockpit. When a customer called a nurse, a series of applications opened on his or her screen, providing location-specific government data related to everything from environmental factors to quality measures—in order to guide advice. In this way, a patient discharged from a hospital in Georgia could get tailored assistance from a nurse in Ohio, from the booking of appointments at the best place to seek treatment, to the latest evidence from the National Institutes of Health on managing their condition.[128]

The cockpit-based approach that Aetna uses relies on the intersection of three vectors that define the customer's specific circumstances: their medical history; their current physiological state; and their location. If you stop to consider your own experiences with healthcare in situations where continuity of care is critical (an emergency or a handoff from one clinician to another) these three cover 90 percent of all decisions that need to be made in order to deliver an adequate level of care: what is your health history; what are your current symptoms; where do you need to be to get the right care. With nearly forty billion dollars spent in the USA yearly on unnecessary ER visits, the economic payback, as well as the overall efficacy of healthcare, both increase dramatically as the result of a hyper-personalized approach to medicine.

David Park, the Founder and CEO at VirtuSense, shared with us another situation where hyper-personalization can have an enormous impact on healthcare for an aging population.

> *In the US alone, one in three seniors reported falling each year. Our mission, simply put, is to reduce falls so seniors can age well. We're doing that by deploying predictive and preventive solutions for homes and senior living facilities. We're also planning to deploy these fall prediction and prevention solutions for hospitals. We do it using machine vision, artificial intelligence, and data analytics. The big goal is trying to provide successful aging through innovative technologies and data analytics. This has tremendous implications for the health industry because the mega trend that we're all riding is the aging of our population globally; it's going to impact our society, healthcare, and government for decades to come. And every study I've seen says life expectancy is projected to increase across all industrialized countries.*
>
> *So, for example, we're working with an executive of a senior living community with*

independent living apartments, an assisted living facility, and a skilled nursing facility. So he's got the whole continuum of care. He said, "I want to know if the seniors living here are eating, taking their medication, or if there's any significant change in their gate, so that we can schedule an appointment with a physician to avoid a more expensive procedure down the line."

Clearly this sort of intimate knowledge of each resident brings us back to the issue of privacy. We asked David to address how VirtuSense is dealing with that aspect of monitoring.

We don't record anything. We actually provide the option for our clients to either turn the recording on or off. If it's turned off, then we just convert the image into an avatar, essentially a stick figure where you can't tell if it's a male or a female or if the person is overweight or skinny so it's completely private. We can even turn that feature off and instead only send an alert in case of a certain event occurring. Of course it's natural that people are apprehensive, but the practical side of this is that most seniors want to stay in their homes as long as possible. Using that technology will allow them to do that. By the same token, if you go into an assisted living facility this level of protective monitoring keeps you out of the next level of care, a nursing home.

For example, Albert Einstein College of Medicine studied 300 to 400 seniors over more than the three-year time period, and they've determined that if a senior has a gait speed of .7 meters per second or slower, then they are 54 percent more likely to fall over the next 12 months. So, we build gait analysis that observes you during the course of your day. If you're moving slower than that then a warning is triggered. We have over a hundred systems deployed at the Mayo Clinic and the Cleveland Clinic, as well some very large skilled nursing facility.

However, the bigger opportunity is reducing the approximately one million falls that occur in US hospitals alone. Typically, these happen when the patient is in bed and they try to get up by themselves and go to the bathroom or try to reach for something and fall.

One specific patient I can recall, over a course of two days, tried to get up three times unaccompanied by a nurse, and the hospital's bed alarm caught one out of the three times. Worse yet, it sent 24 false alarms to the nurses' station! During that same time our system only sent three alarms, with zero false alarms. However, more importantly, we sent the alarm to the nurse about 40 seconds before the bed alarm went off.

The VirtuSense approach provides one way that behavioral observations can help us deal with aging demographics, but why stop there? One of the greatest impacts we see of a digital-self is in addressing the larger healthcare challenge by extending the notion of a digital-self to that of a personal advocate which is able to act on our behalf even when we can't.

Personal Advocates

The ultimate form of the digital-self is as an autonomous entity that has the ability to advocate for the human it represents. Although this stretches our imagination, nearly every component of the digital-self as an advocate already exists. Think back to our description in Chapter 3 of the digital-self as an entity that's able do far more in any given period of time than its human counterpart. A prime example of how this would work is in healthcare.

One of the most serious flaws in the healthcare system is the lack of coordinated care for someone who does not have an advocate who can provide critical information about him or her if they are unable to do so because they are physically, emotionally, or cognitively impaired. This ranges from being there with the patient at meetings with doctors, monitoring compliance with prescribed medications and therapies, scheduling appointments, and navigating insurance coverage and billings.

A typical scenario is that a patient finds himself or herself in an emergency room without a list of their current medications, no medical history, is unable to describe the context of what was happening to them prior to arriving at the ER, and because of their medical condition or cognitive impairment is unable to adequately communicate to coordinate his or her care.

Even if a family member or friend is present, it's unlikely that they will have all this information at hand, and an even greater likelihood that they will make mistakes in accurately relaying it to a clinician. The complexity of today's healthcare system has created an exceptionally difficult maze to navigate even for the most aware and involved patients. However, for someone who is not able to do this for himself or herself, and has nobody to act as an advocate, it's nearly impossible. Errors are common in clinical settings due to this complexity. As a result, every party in the system suffers.

The role of a personal advocate in this capacity would be threefold: to access and use all of the patient's historical and current healthcare information in order to communicate and coordinate care with clinical staff and the patient's healthcare provider (PCP); to provide early warnings of potential health problems based on changes in behavior and habits that could be indicative of an underlying condition; and to ensure the patient's compliance with prescribed pharmaceuticals, therapies, and other treatments.

The other aspect of healthcare that can be devastating is navigating insurance companies. This can be hard enough to do when you are healthy and have the mental, emotional, and physical capacity to do the work involved, but it's typically the last thing someone battling an illness can afford. And the irony is that the worse the illness, the lower the capacity on all three fronts, and the greater the costs and complexity that need to be managed.

There are already companies doing this as a service. For example, Patient Navigator provides specialists in healthcare and insurance who will act as a patient's personal advocate. In one example the company was engaged by a client [we'll call her Maria] "to remedy a four-year logjam of unpaid medical claims totaling $80,000 in provider billings. The situation required discussions with Medicare, the Social Security Administration, a state civil service commission, and two group health plans for retirees that did not coordinate efforts to provide Maria with the coverage she should have received. First, Patient Navigator assisted Maria in enrolling in Medicare Part B and terminating one of her retiree health plans. Then, [they] worked with her other health plan to have all outstanding claims processed correctly. Finally, [they] negotiated settlements with many of Maria's healthcare providers and had her removed from collection agency dunning. The result was that the insurer claims gridlock was resolved, and Maria's total provider obligations were reduced to $175."[129]

In another case the company was "contacted by the adult daughter of an elderly man who was a patient at a top cancer hospital. She requested that [Patient Navigator advocate] Doctor Zorrilla accompany him to his oncologist appointments in order to relay information accurately between the oncology team, her father, and his family. Serving as a liaison proved to be instrumental in optimizing this gentleman's care during an unexpected hospitalization. He was unable to advocate for himself due to the nature of his condition. His adult children were unable to be at the bedside because they resided out-of-town. At their request, Doctor Zorrilla stepped in and was able to request an appropriate second opinion consult within the hospital which served to clearly identify the underlying problem and allow the patient to be discharged to home to be reunited with his wife."

With one of every three dollars spent in the US by 2040 being on healthcare, it's easy to see how this sort of advocacy will become essential. [130] We'd suggest that the advocacy role can be played, at least in part, by your digital-self. With access to your healthcare and insurance records, the ability to monitor your health 24/7, and integration within a larger healthcare ecosystem it's possible to now use digitalization as a means of not only hyper-personalizing healthcare but also navigating it.

The final area where a digital advocate could make a dramatic difference in healthcare is with what may be the ultimate form of hyper-personalization: creating diet, pharmaceuticals, and other therapies that map to the genome of each individual. Called personalized medicine, genomic medicine, precision medicine, and nutrigenomics, this approach is revolutionizing the effectiveness of healthcare. Consider a two-year European study of one thousand obese people. The participants were split into two groups and each group's diet was reduced by six hundred calories/day. However, the participants of one group (the nutrigenetic group) also had their genome mapped and had a genetically tailored diet developed that factored known markers that indicated sensitivity to or an inability to metabolize certain foods. Over a two-year period, the nutrigenetic group lost 33 percent more weight than the control group. The nutrigenetic group also lost as much weight at the end of one year as the control group did in two years.

Much of this is being driven by the amazing drop in the cost of sequencing the human genome, which has dropped from three hundred million dollars in 2000 (the cost of the original genome sequencing) to under ten million dollars in 2007, to one million in dollars 2008, to under one thousand dollars today. The expectation is that the cost will have dropped to under one hundred dollars within the next five to ten years. The rate of decrease in the cost exceeds even that which is predicted by Moore's law when projecting the advance of semiconductor technology.

Because of this the ability to explore how various therapies and treatments affect an individual based on their personal genome has created a sea change in the future of medicine from the "standard of care" approach which used a one-size-fits-all model of medicine to a hyper-personalized model where each patient is unique in how their genetic profile defines the treatment best for them.

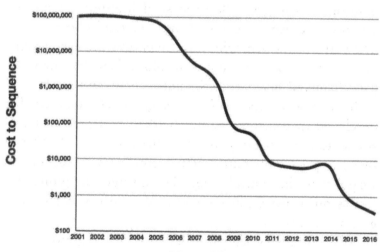

Decrease in Cost Per Genome Sequenced 2001 - 2016

Illustration 6.2 –
Drop in cost of sequencing Human Genome[131]

Cancer treatments have been among some of the most promising that are following this approach using genetic markers to indicate the type of pharmaceuticals and therapies that particular cancers in specific patients respond to. To date there are over one thousand eight hundred genes that have been identified as markers of specific diseases, there are two thousand genetic tests, and more than three hundred fifty clinical trials for genome specific biotechnology therapies.[132]

We can anticipate the many obstacles that will arise from a concern that so much sensitive data is being entrusted to various entities in order to create this level of hyper-personalization. But the disjointed access to all this information today (if it's available at all) creates far greater risk for the data as well as all of the parties in the healthcare system. And that's not factoring in the increasing economic and social burden of inefficient disease treatment on a rapidly aging population. Today 15.5 percent of the US population is over sixty-five but accounts for approximately 35 percent of healthcare costs. By 2050 the percentage of population over sixty-five will climb to 23.5 percent. If we use the same ratio of contribution to healthcare costs by 2050 the over sixty-five age group will account for over 50 percent of total healthcare costs.[133] And that number will only climb as the rate of growth for the over sixty-five age group increases at a faster rate than that of the working age population.

The digital advocate will clearly provide benefits across the entire population. However, the simple fact is that we have an incredibly inefficient and unsustainable situation as it stands now from the standpoint of both the cost of care and its efficacy. Having a digital advocate that can hyper-personalization healthcare, from the administration of insurance claims, to providing continuity of care across various providers, to the alignment of your genome with personalized-medicine, isn't just a nice-to-have; it's an imperative if we are to deliver healthcare to a growing and aging global demographic.

Granted that digital advocates may not resemble the kinds of all-purpose mechanical robots that we had once envisioned, but our opinion is that the future is much more likely to follow the same sort of trajectory that AI is taking toward the evolution of special purpose "bots" that will have narrow and finite applications with clear value in very specific areas. These collaborator robots (let's call them "collabots") aren't anywhere near as sexy as R2D2 or C3PO, but they deliver an immediate benefit by reducing the friction in our businesses and our lives.

The Bots

Few things have captured our image of the future better that the twentieth century icon of innovation, the robot. Czechoslovakian playwright Karel Capek first introduced the word robot in his play *Rossum's Universal Robots*. But it was Isaac Asimov who popularized the term in his book *Runaround*, where he first defined the three laws of robotics, something we'll come back to later in this chapter.

Since then the robot has been idealized in thousands of books, movies and television shows, from the *Jetsons* to *Lost In Space* and R2D2 to Wall-e. The robot has become a constant companion of the future, promising to make our lives easier by performing household chores and serving us tirelessly.

For those of us who grew up with this image of the mechanical servant, there was never any doubt that at some point robots would be commonplace. But we also came to the conclusion that the robotic future was farther out than anyone expected. For most of us, robots would never be more than a gadget novelty. And a litany of consumer robots, including Sony's AIBO robotic dog, Honda's Asimo, Lego's MindStorms, and the once popular RoboSapian humanoid toy robots, conditioned us to expect very little from consumer robots beyond an expensive toy that even the most ardent enthusiasts quickly tired of.

At the same time that man's mechanical friend was being popularized in early media, Marvin Minsky was establishing the first AI lab at the Massachusetts Institute of Technology. Minskey's early work set the stage for fifty years of robotics leading to a tremendous surge of investment and application of robots in manufacturing. Yet robots in the home were still an elusive dream. That is until the company iRobot came along with what is arguably the first useful and commercially successful home robot.

iRobot made a mark for itself by building robots for extraterrestrial exploration, military use on battlefields, clearing mine fields, and in 2001, searching the rubble of the World Trade Center in the aftermath of the terrorist attack on the US. The company grew steadily but the consumer market was still an elusive target. In 2000, Colin Angle, iRobot co-founder and CEO, thought it was time to take a crack at the consumer once again, but this time without all of the hyperbole and promise of the Jetsons, but with a much more practical approach.

Colin's idea was to revolutionize a one hundred fifty-year-old industry where extensive innovation had already occurred. But it was also an industry stuck in incremental innovation. While much of the tedium of housework has been automated to operate in the background—in other words, your dishwasher, washing machine, and oven all work without your constant attention—one aspect of keeping a house clean had barely progressed since the early part of the last century: cleaning floors. Vacuuming and mopping have experienced countless incremental innovations but still require someone to do the work.

If you're building vacuum cleaners, how do you innovate? Well, of course, you make the vacuum faster, more powerful, and lighter, because that's what your market research and your focus group tell you to do.

So, consider that your company sells vacuum cleaners and someone comes along to suggest that the problem is that the task should be eliminated altogether. It wouldn't take long to show them the door.

Which is why when iRobot introduced the Roomba, a vacuuming robot that looked like anything but the proto-typical sci-fi robot, in 2002, nobody paid much attention. There was nothing especially inventive about the idea of a robotic vacuum cleaner. The basic sensors, components, and software had all been developed by iRobot or were already in use in the robotics industry in some form. According to Colin, for iRobot's thirteen-year history, prior to its intro-duction of the Roomba, friends and associates would consis-tently ask if iRobot could create a robot to help clean their homes. So, what stopped iRobot and so many other potential manufacturers, especially the classic incumbent players such as Electrolux, Hoover, and Oreck, from introducing a robot vacuum?[134] Like so many innovations, the idea had been set aside as unlikely given the history of consumer robots. Remember our description of Stage 1 or Stage 4 innovation as being especially difficult to break out of? There were plenty of people who would buy a traditional vacuum cleaner; it was what they were used to.

However, Angle and his colleagues had several things going for them: they were not afraid to experiment, they had a deep core competency in small, compact, low cost robots, from years of experience in practical solutions for space and military use, and most importantly, they were not tied to the old notion of a home robot and they certainly were not tied to the notion of "traditional" vacuum cleaners. Angle had learned from his days at MIT that the key was not the notion of what a robot was but rather in what it could do. The intent was to keep it simple, practical, and useful. This is precisely what we were referring to when we described the notion of a collabot, which works with a human in a very narrow way to address a specific task.

iRobot didn't expect the Roomba to sell more than fifteen thousand units in its first year. They were right; it didn't. It sold over ninety thousand units. From the outset it was clear that the Roomba had hit an exposed nerve in the market. Since that time, its Roomba and Scuba have been market leaders for robotic vacuums and hard floor mops.

iRobot is one of the few companies to make the journey from Stage 1 digitalization all the way to Stage 3 (and soon to Stage 4). While this is a rare exception, iRobot had the ability to be patient as the market transitioned to Stage 2 and 3. As iRobot's footprint in the home increased, it also started to collect behavioral data, first locally within the device and then remotely through connected devices using Amazon's cloud for data storage and also introducing a partnership and integration with Amazon's Alexa home assistant, which allows the two to work together. The transition to Stage 4 digitalization comes with the most advanced Roombas which capture and relay information about the floor map of a home and its contents.

While your robotic vacuum is sucking up all the day-to-day dirt that accumulates on your floors, it's also vacuuming up a different kind of dirt: digital dirt, the myriad details about the layout of your home and your day-to-day habits. Its onboard sensors and camera are developing an intelligence about you that has enormous value to other retailers and service providers.

No wonder Angle calls their home robots the "connective tissue for the smart home."

Big pet stain on your carpet? Surprise, suddenly ads start to appear in your browser for carpet cleaning and pet deodorizer. Better yet, Amazon will just take it upon itself to send you everything you need to take care of that nasty stain without your even asking for it. Don't like it? Just send it back, although Amazon is betting you won't.

While iRobot has stated explicitly that the data will not be sold to third parties, it has said that the data would be shared at no cost with user consent. iRobot stressed the same, and elaborated in a *New York Times* story in which the company said that they were, "committed to the absolute privacy of our customer-related data." Consumers can use a Roomba without connecting it to the internet, or "opt out of sending map data to the cloud through a switch in the mobile app. No data is sold to third parties," the statement added. "No data will be shared with third parties without the informed consent of our customers."

But here's the piece of the story that's not being talked about as often and which we believe signals just how inevitable the trend toward making our homes, cars, and our every behavior utterly naked is becoming.

Ultimately economics drives every innovation. Follow the money and you'll find the future. The same is true for the evolution of robots.

After the announcement of iRobot's behavioral capability the company's stock jumped about 17 percent from eighty-seven dollars and ninety cents on July 24th to one hundred six dollars and forty-nine cents on July 25th. As of the writing of this book, that's the second-largest single day gain for iRobot over the last decade. It's also nearly three times the stock's price in 2016, one year prior. The point is that investors are putting a huge premium on a company's ability to not only capture, but to be able to share, integrate, and monetize behavioral data about you as part of the new digital ecosystem that we inhabit.

While iRobot provides one narrow glimpse of how a robot could adapt to our physical world, the basic principles it uses to capture and use behavioral data is applicable to virtually every consumer industry. So, why haven't we seen more applications of robots in the home?

The challenge goes back to our example of Air France flight 447. Recall how the robotic stall warning was continuously sounded on the flight deck and yet how both pilots repeatedly ignored it. We are still at a stage where AI is considered more of an annoyance or a curiosity than a necessary collaborator. Getting over this is partly a function of the actual utility that the robotic device provides. That's the reason iRobot has done as well as it has, and it's likely that will be the case with other narrow purpose robots in the home. But we'd like to stretch your imagination a bit further.

Bad Dog

The super glue Angle talks about is the overall intelligence of the home. But why should any one special purpose robot be the center of intelligence for a home? The robotic vacuum doesn't live in a, well, vacuum. It interacts with myriad other intelligent devices, including the home itself. The intelligence does not reside in one of these devices but rather as a meta-intelligence that hovers above all of them—in fact, it hovers above all of your neighbors' houses as well. In that way, the behavioral clues aren't limited to when you last moved your ottoman but rather the overall experience of living in your home. Anything less than that will, by definition, be a partial and incomplete understanding of behaviors leading to a rather inept robot that still does very dumb things, which in turn gives us pause to trust its ability to truly understand and comprehend.

It's our opinion that trust (or a lack of it) is at the center of the reluctance to move toward the use of robots. Trust is a human emotion which requires three basic elements: an expectation of performance, a track record of performance, and transparency about lack of performance.

Think about this first in terms of human interactions. When we place our trust in someone, we are doing so based on prior performance. Perhaps the person was recommended by an already trusted friend or they are someone who we've known for enough time to notice a track record that imbues trust. At the same time, we are constantly keeping a mental register of how well that person continues to perform. If that trust is compromised, we want to know it through that person not through another channel. For instance, if you have a housekeeper or cleaning person who you trust to leave in your house alone and they inadvertently knock over an heirloom vase, you'd expect them to admit to it. If they didn't and you found the vase, knowing it was intact when you left the house, it's highly unlikely you would trust them again.

However, if a Roomba did the same thing you wouldn't expect much of a confession. You will be just as heartbroken over the vase but you wouldn't take it out on the Roomba and you wouldn't be upset by the broken trust, because there wasn't any trust to begin with. If anything, you're more likely to call iRobot and express your displeasure to a human. But once we cross the line into a hyper-personalized experience, something interesting happens.

Let's replace the Roomba with a very smart family dog. We're specifically using a dog since it can be trained (apologies to our cat-loving readers). And let's assume that since you have various precious fragile items throughout your house you've taught your dog to stay out of certain rooms to avoid accidental damage. If your dog did go into one of those rooms and knocked over the same vase, what would your reaction be? It's almost certain that you would reprimand your dog. Why? Think about this for a minute, because the answer is very relevant to our discussion about trusting robots.

The reason you reprimand the pet is because it has a capacity to learn. If you didn't reprimand your pet but instead installed a gate or closed off that same room in the future it would be because you felt your pet was untrainable. In either case your action is based on the fundamental concept of learned behavior and a certain transference of values. By that we mean that you want the pet to learn that certain behaviors or their absence constitutes a value with an associated reward or punishment.

What we've just described is a well-understood mental model that defines how we view our interactions with domesticated animals. It may not be as sophisticated as the mental model we would use when interacting with humans, which is rich in verbal communication, but it is still well understood and it enables a bond of trust to form. The extreme case of this, by the way, is a service dog which develops an extraordinary bond of trust with its owner.

There are some important lesson to be learned from the human-animal framework.[135] Historically, service animals replace, multiply, or augment our human abilities. Think about what that means in terms of trust. We place our trust in them because of one basic reason, they understand us. The better they do, the more we trust them. Whether it's a workhorse pulling a plow or a hunting dog hot on the trail of a fox, they are extensions of ourselves and our expectation is that they will not only do our work for us but that they will do it better than we ever could. That is the essential framework behind all trust, which is why there is a direct link between how much of ourselves we reveal and the commensurate trust we expect.

This similar sort of framework does yet apply to our robots, at least not in a way that creates a true bond of trust. You're likely thinking that it never could. After all, these are machines not sentient living creatures.

Enter Alan Turning who set the benchmark for what it means to be a machine that might as well be human. Turing is credited with building the computer that broke the German's Enigma code during World War II; the outcome of which may have been completely different otherwise. In fact Churchill called Turing and his team "the geese that laid the golden eggs," citing their work as the single biggest contribution to Allied victory.

Turning established the most basic architecture of computing, the Turing Machine, which has defined how software has worked for nearly a century; namely, that computers are programmed to follow a predetermined set of rules, or code.

The computers don't come up with the rules; they just execute them much faster.

If a computer made a mistake, it was due to a human incorrectly coding the computer's response. It was all very linear and predictable. Think of the classic "if this, then that" logic that every set of pre-programmed interactions is built on.

But Turing postulated that there is a point at which computers would no longer follow a rigid set of prescribed rules, the point at which, "A computer would deserve to be called intelligent if it could deceive a human into believing that it was human."

We give our pets and animals names to humanize them, as you would your Tesla. The significance of that is in how we introduce very human constructs such as trust and loyalty into our interactions with non-human collaborators. We'd suggest that this is the single most important and absent piece of the human-machine relationship that's still missing. And this leads to one of the most dramatic shifts in how we build the relationship between a brand and its customers. Hyper-personalization requires a level of humanizing AI in a way that encourages us to reveals our behaviors at a level far beyond anything we've become accustomed to.

What do we expect back from that intimate connection? In a word, loyalty.

CHAPTER 7:

Loyal Brands, the Death of Anytown, USA

*"An organization's ability to learn,
and translate that learning into action rapidly,
is the ultimate competitive advantage"*
—Jack Welch

From a very young age, Richard had to work to help support his family. His father, once very wealthy, had gambled the family fortune on a failed farm venture and Richard had to pick up the slack. He was committed and driven to creating financial stability for himself. Which is likely why the resourceful young man worked his way up to the position of railroad agent by the time he was only twenty-one.

It was an enviable job.

In the late 1800s, the railroads were the country's lifeblood, transporting goods at a rate that fueled a booming economy—the equivalent of the internet today. Richard had learned Morse code and was an adept telegrapher. It was a secure position in a growing industry. But he was always looking for ways to make a little extra income.

When a local jeweler refused a large shipment of watches, the enterprising Richard suggest to the shop owner that he let him have a try at selling them. It's not clear exactly how Richard got the word out—perhaps it was by using the telegraph he was so adept at and with which he'd connected to so many colleagues—whatever it was, he soon had railroad agents at stations across the country ordering the watches.

Richard ended up with a five thousand dollar profit, about one hundred ten thousand in today's dollars. It was enough to start his own mail-order watch and jewelry business along with a local watchmaker, Alvah C. Roebuck. After three years, Richard Sears sold his fledgling business for one hundred thousand dollars, the equivalent of just under two million dollars today.

Flush with cash, Richard headed to Iowa for the next two years to be a banker. That could well have been the end of the story. It wasn't. Mail-order was all the twenty-seven-year-old could think about. If he'd so easily achieved initial success, what more could he do if he went back. So, back he went to Minnesota and set off on a trajectory that would revolutionize the way America bought and sold goods for the next hundred years when he produced his first catalog for Sears Roebuck and Co.

According to Sears, "By the time Sears was started, farmers in rural America were selling their crops for cash and buying what they needed from rural general stores. But when they laid their money on the line for goods, farmers saw red. In 1891 the wholesale price of a barrel of flour was reported to be $3.47. Price at retail was at least $7, a 100 percent increase. Farmers formed protest movements, such as the Grange, to do battle against high prices and the middleman."

It is worth noting that the infrastructure that made the Sears' catalog possible was the burgeoning railroad system. And while the catalog is what's most often regarded as Sears' great innovation, it was really something else. His principle innovation was using his catalog and the railroad to eliminate the friction created by the storekeeper middleman.

Everything from headwear to headstones could be purchased through the Sears catalog at what was promised to be the "price your storekeeper at home pays for everything...and will prevent him from overcharging you."

Sears grew dramatically as did consumerism. And, despite the apparent threat to the general store, the retail industry also flourished.

The Sears catalog was a mechanism by which to increase market efficiency in an era of increasingly greater complexity of transportation systems, product alternatives, and a more widely distributed populous outside of the city.

But Richard Sears did one more thing that's often lost in the telling of his story. While the catalog was bursting with variety and choice there was little in the way of personalization. The general store had the upper hand when it came to understanding the needs of customers who would share much more than just a transaction with the store-keeper. The general store was not only a place to buy and sell; it was a place to share information about yourself, your family, and your community.

What Sears did was brilliant and became a role model for twentieth century retail and marketing. One of his earliest mailings was a handwritten postcard to prospective buyers. Sears understood the value of building a trusted relationship; in 1903 it was the first retailer to make the incredibly bold move of promising customers that if a purchased item didn't meet their standards, they could simply return it. So committed was Sears to developing that personal bond with customers that during the early years of the Sears catalog's distribution, Richard Sears wrote almost every word that went into it.

Sears did much more than make products easy to buy:

- It pioneered the idea of product promise. If you weren't satisfied, you had a right to return merchandise.
- It created a trusted relationship with customers at scale by using customer-centered copy in its catalog and by processing seventy-five thousand customer letters a day—in 1906![136]
- It introduced the notion of having a permanent connection with a customer through the permanence of its catalog, which in 1927 was in over half of all US households.

In 1931, while the country was in the midst of the Great Depression, Sears made the equivalent of 2.5 billion dollars in profits. Over the next ten years it contributed an astounding one percent of US GDP.[137]

Sears made perfect sense at a time when scale could only be achieved by mastering the science of mass production, mass markets, and mass distribution. So, here's a question: what if we were to rebuild Sears today from the ground up, what would that company look like? The first company that comes to mind is obviously Amazon. What's interesting however, is that the three differentiators we just listed—product promise, a trusted relationship, and permanence—are just as relevant to Amazon, but with one very important difference. Sears never had the ability to know the needs of each customer. So, why can't Sears, which has been descending into the same seemingly inevitable fate as Kodak, Blockbuster, and so many other industrial era dinosaurs, do that now?

We'd like to take you back to the earlier discussion we had about Kodak. Recall that Kodak not only invented the technology that put it out of business, but that its executives realized the threat that digital posed to the film business, even if they didn't appreciate its magnitude. Still, Kodak was shackled by the industrial era investments that they had made in plant, equipment, and an ecosystem that was dedicated to film. That created a period of denial at a point when Kodak may have been able to do something to recreate itself. Although, we would still argue that it's nearly impossible for an industrial era company to react quickly enough due to the intractability of its supply chain. It's like trying to turn a naval flotilla with hundreds of ships; it requires a clear and apparent threat and it still takes a lot of time.

However, there's something else that held Kodak back, much more than its factories and supply chain, and it's the same thing that holds virtually every industrial era company from moving into the future. It's what made Sears an icon— its brand, or more specifically, the loyalty customers had to its brand. Sears had built brand loyalty that spanned a century and five generations. If you're a boomer, you undoubtedly have fond memories of the Sears catalog, which often occupied a place of reverence as the largest and most in-demand book in most homes.

Ultimately that loyalty turned into an immutable set of expectations about what Sears was. And that brand loyalty held Sears hostage to its legacy. It insulated Sears from threats that should have been obvious. It cocooned it in the past.

LOYAL BRANDS, THE DEATH OF ANYTOWN, USA

In a *Fortune* 2016 article, "Why Sears Failed," journalist Geoff Colvin talks about how an article he wrote in 1991 about Walmart's potential to pull ahead of Sears triggered an indignant response from Sears executives who called his article irresponsible and misleading.[138]

This sort of denial has its roots directly in brand loyalty. When a company starts to sense its market potential slow, it instinctively attempts to hold onto its best customers. In many ways the company will start doing what any good company should do: develop a closer bond with its most loyal customers. Sears did this by putting in place a loyalty program called Shop Your Way. The program provides point incentives for what Sears CEO Eddie Lampert calls "members" and not customers or consumers. It's also intended to give Sears a better understanding of members' behaviors.

In a 2013 *Ad Age* article, a spokesman for Sears said, "Shop Your Way is at the core of everything we're doing. We're focused on our most loyal customers, and building relationships with them is something that will drive our company to profitability."[139]

According to another Sears' spokesperson, "Shop Your Way is more than a loyalty program...It transforms customer transactions into relationships and allows us to know our members better and to serve them better."[140]

Today, Shop Your Way accounts for over 75 percent of Sears' sales.[141]

This all sounds great and it would seem that Sears is doing everything right. So why are things still going wrong with revenues declining steadily for the past decade and a market cap that's down to one billion dollars from seventeen billion dollars during the same period? It's a trajectory, which will likely see Sears filing for bankruptcy by the time this book is published. As with every large brand that slowly loses ground over time, there is no single reason at fault. The complete answer to that question is well outside of the scope of this book. Yet, at the core of Sears' problems lies an undeniable inability to capture new market share. Loyalty programs can be a powerful draw, but they can also further isolate a company from new opportunities. Providing only what your existing customers, or members, want, while your business is failing, is like offering cabin upgrades, instead of lifeboats, to passengers aboard the *Titanic*.

The challenge for Sears, and for any large brand, is moving with a changing market and letting go rather than holding onto the past. You can't do that with loyalty programs which inevitably reinforce relationships with customers who are the most brand loyal. The reason is simply because you are only building a confirmation bias loop in which customer behavior reinforces the current business model which then reinforces the customer behavior. Congratulations, you've not only further strengthened your brand's legacy image in the eyes of "members," but you've also done a great job of convincing the rest of the marketplace that you really are stuck in time.

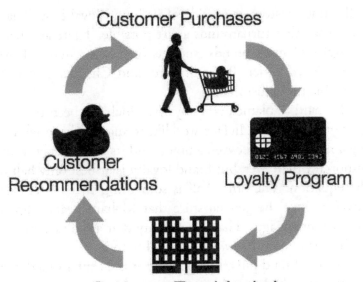

Customer Purchases

Customer Recommendations

Loyalty Program

Customer Trend Analysis

Illustration 7.1 – The Brand Confirmation Bias Loop
Loyalty programs can be a valuable asset in understanding customer behaviors, but they do not provide insight on customer behaviors when they are not being your customer. What ends up happening in company's whose brand is stuck in a shrinking demographic is that its most loyal customers will reinforce the experience they have always had with the brand. The brand uses that reinforcement to further isolate itself from external trends and behaviors that it has no access to or simply chooses to ignore.

As we saw with Kodak, the initial period during which an industrial era company needs to take action in order to address this sort of threat is typically occupied by denial because the business is thriving. Yet, this is the most opportune time to make the transition, when a company has the resources to build a parallel new era business model that will attract customers outside of its brand loyal base. That's not to say that turnarounds aren't possible. There are many examples of great brands, such as Starbucks, Xerox, IBM, Caterpillar, Hewlett Packard, Ford, and Chrysler that have been able to do just that.

It's hard to blame brand loyalty, which has been the holy grail of every brand. In fact, we'd like to suggest that establishing a relationship between a brand and its customers is more important than ever, but brand loyalty is at best only half of the equation. The other half is something that hasn't been possible since the general store that Richard Sears eclipsed over a century ago. That's the loyalty that a brand expresses to the customer, what we call a loyal brand.

A loyal brand puts the customer at the center of a digital ecosystem, which can be reconstituted on demand to suit the needs of each customer based on his or her behaviors. By developing an understanding of the customer that provides visibility into otherwise invisible behaviors, leveraging a digital ecosystem that allows the entire value chain to evolve, and building a brand that is uniquely suited to the needs of each customer, a relationship is formed that is based on deep value and virtually impossible to compete against.

Turn the Brand Around

At its most basic, brand loyalty is the attachment to a brand based on a feeling of trust and loyalty to it because of familiarity. Although the company behind the brand never really knew the individuals who made up their market, and their many personal preferences and habits, brands still evoked a broad sense of community that tied people to them. You were part of the youthful Pepsi generation, Nike's motivated Just Do It! crowd, DeBeers' Diamonds Are Forever romantics. Each of these slogans spoke to something that drew us to the brand and helped us align our values with it, or at least with our perception of it.

Although we were loyal to certain brands, the brands could not be personalized to each of us. Brands were designed so that they had the broadest possible appeal to the largest number of people. Companies made enormous investments in understanding these large markets through focus groups, demographics, sales analytics, surveys, and myriad metrics that provided a broad-based understanding of what consumers wanted. This average customer, from an average family, living in an average home became known as "Anytown, USA" since it reflected the values of Main Street America.

Companies were doing the best they could, given what they had for tools, to gain insight into their market's behaviors. But trying to understand the needs of any single individual was like trying to pick out someone's height and weight from a Google maps satellite image.

Simply put, *a loyal brand is one that understands your behaviors and their context well enough to be able to anticipate and respond to your preferences and build meaningful and personalized experiences.* Most importantly, loyal brands can act proactively to serve new needs and expectations before they've been expressed. This goes beyond just making the promise that a product or service will meet your known expectations. For example, in the last chapter we introduced the idea, which Amazon has explored, of predictive sales where a product arrives at your doorstep without your having ordered it. At first blush this may sound outlandishly creepy.

But stop and think about what's actually going on. Let's set up a hypothetical scenario. If you had a personal shopper on monthly retainer who knew your tastes and behaviors intimately and you happened to be going on vacation to a warm weather climate in the middle of winter, what might she or he do? Look at what you had for warm weather clothing, what still fits, the particulars of styles worn at your destination, and then, naturally, buy you what you needed. Nothing creepy about that, right? Why not? Because it's a human. And if your personal shopper decided to leave and move to another state, we'd guess that you'd be pretty upset at losing the value of someone who knew you so well. That's exactly the value of a loyal brand; it understands you well enough to deliver value you may not have asked for, which in turn encourages you to disclose more of your behavior to the brand.

Anticipation of unexpressed needs is the hallmark of every great brand, company, or person. We value most those companies and people who invest the time and energy to think ahead and deliver product or service before we ask for it. Ultimately nothing creates a greater bond of loyalty.

Clearly, even the companies best positioned to understand your digital behaviors and to build experiences that understand and respect them are just starting down that path. However, the gap is growing by the minute between companies who are utterly in the dark when it comes to the power of a loyal brand and those who understand its value.

For instance, see if this sounds familiar. You have a problem with a product you have been using for years and call customer support. The call is placed from your mobile or house phone, on which you've had same phone number for the last two decades. An automated attendant asks you to enter your account number before transferring you to a live rep. You are then asked a series of questions through the company's IVR (Interactive Voice Response) to determine what your problem is. By the way, you were just on this same company's website using their FAQs and talking via chat to another representative who was unable to help. When you're finally transferred to a live representative, what's the first thing that he or she will ask you? "What's your account number?" of course! It's nothing less than dumbfounding that a company you've been loyal to for so long hardly knows you.

In today's world a digital journey with most companies includes numerous online, web, mobile, and in-store interactions. This provides an incredible amount of information through which to understand a customer's behaviors and preferences, but, more importantly, with which to predict that same customer's future behaviors, or, at the very least, to know who they are when answering an incoming call.

Identity is the very first step toward the creation of a loyal brand. Simply knowing who the customer is, acknowledging that, and having some basic context for the journey that the customer has taken so far is table stakes.

The next step in developing a loyal brand is what we call contextual knowledge. This applies to online experiences, but it can also apply offline. For example, if you own a BMW, your key fob will uniquely identify you once you drive into your dealership to have your car serviced. Not only are you greeted by name, no matter who is welcoming you, but your car history and current maintenance due are immediately available.

The third level of becoming a loyal brand is anticipatory knowledge. For example, GM's OnStar, which we talked about briefly in Chapter 1, has enough information today, through onboard sensors, real time weather and traffic conditions, and prior accidents at any specific address, to determine with uncanny accuracy how likely an accident is to occur. This information can be used to warn you of an especially risky situation ahead, or, in the case of an AV, to route around it.

The fourth level is predictive knowledge. Using our OnStar example, if an accident does occur, OnStar has enough information to predict the likely injuries based on real-time data about the incident from the automobile, which can then be passed on to first responders so that they are prepared before they even arrive at the scene.

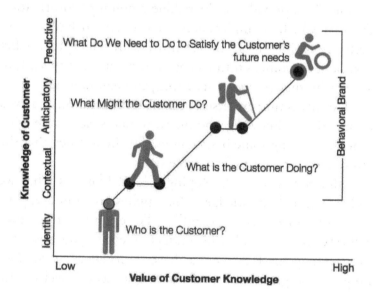

Illustration 7.2 – The Four Levels of a Loyal Brand
A loyal brand begins with knowing who the customer is, then understanding the context of the customer's behaviors, anticipating them, and finally delivering goods and services that predict future needs.

It doesn't take much to see how these three levels build increasing trust and reliance on a loyal brand.

A caution here, when we talk about loyal brands, we're not referring to the kind of Big Data analytics that are used by retailers today to create algorithms that can predict broad-based trends and overall market behaviors. For example, Target was held out as a poster child for how not to personalize a customer relationship when Charles Duhig wrote a widely circulated *New York Times* article about how Target used data analytics to determine if a shopper was pregnant. Pregnant mothers are one of the most lucrative markets for retailers since they are the least likely to scrimp on purchases for their baby's health and well-being. If Target knew who those shoppers were early enough, then they could use their loyalty program to reward the shopper with promotions intended for the products they are most likely to buy. This sounds like a brilliant marketing strategy, but, Target became the example of Big Data gone wrong when it sent promotional collateral to an underage mother who was still living at home. As Duhig tells it, the girl's father went to his local Target store "clutching coupons sent to his daughter" with offers for a variety of products such as cribs and baby clothes.[142] As it turns out, his daughter was pregnant, but the fallout for Target was anything but flattering.

What Target did wrong was that it focused exclusively on the Big Data and not the Small Data, the detailed information about each of us as an individual, which we mentioned in Chapter 1. This is why customer identity is the first step in creating a loyal brand. Without basic identifying information such as age, it's unlikely that you will be able to demonstrate any real degree of loyalty. The key to developing a loyal brand is demonstrating respect and creating individualized value for the customer on his or her terms.

So, who owns the loyal brand in a very complex ecosystem? The most likely candidate would appear to be whoever or whatever best integrates the overall digital ecosystem since they will have ownership of all three customer touch points and the most detailed understanding of your behaviors. But that doesn't necessarily hold true. We believe the loyal brand will go to whichever organization creates the most value from the ecosystem.

And this brings us back to an earlier conversation we had about creating digital ecosystems and walled gardens. Both Apple and Amazon are working toward building walled gardens around your healthcare, but in very different ways. Apple's strategy is to use Apple Watch to monitor your health through sensors and apps that can provide notifications of issues that need your attention. What that means, for now, is gathering data on your activities, heart rate/rhythm/trends/anomalies, and using prompts that remind you to take action. Amazon isn't relying on wearable sensors but instead using a combination of its home companion Alexa, shopping patterns and searches, and in-store experiences to make inferences from these behaviors. They are each building two very different digital ecosystems to sense your behaviors and both of these players, and many more, will be competing to gain the broadest possible access to your behavioral history—what you buy, how you use it, and how all of that changes over time.

The obvious question then seems to be, "Ultimately who will own the largest digital ecosystem?" While we've talked at length about the usual list of suspects, we'd like to suggest that there's another way to look at this—the scale and scope of digital ecosystems are not as important as the value created from them. That changes the competitive landscape significantly. What we anticipate is that the obvious candidates for the largest digital ecosystems, Apple, Amazon, Google, Facebook, which today are vying for the enviable position of being your loyal brand, will end up being the platforms on which loyal brands are built. There are three reasons for this.

First, an omnipotent loyal brand which holds you captive to a single company would reek of monopolistic intent and quickly encounter numerous antitrust issues. Because of this, growing through acquisitions, in the way that Amazon has and intends to, will soon start to pose much more of an obstacle to Amazon's growth. It will also start to create mounting antipathy on the part of customers who will see the behemoth as Big Brother. There are claims that the fear of monopolies is also an industrial era artifact. PayPal co-founder Peter Theil has argued that, "Creative monopolies aren't just good for the rest of society; they're powerful engines for making it better." [143] While there may be cause to revisit the way in which antitrust is defined and applied, we do not see this changing the fundamental premise that the value of a digital ecosystem, as with a biological ecosystem, is in the innovation that results from variety and diversity of the flora that it supports.

Second, picking up on that last point, the value of creating a platform which acts as the foundation for an ecosystem is greater than that of developing each of the loyal brands that are built on top of it. The temptation to monetize your digital-self is going to be hard to ignore for any of the ecosystem platform players. However, if we look at the model Apple has used in building its current digital ecosystem, it becomes clear that the greater value is in creating a thriving ecosystem that becomes its own free market.

Apple does not invest in the R&D for the 90 percent of apps that fail but it does collect approximately ten billion dollars billion for those that do succeed. Consider that by the time this book is published Apple will be getting one hundred thousand submissions per month for new apps to include in its app store. If the average cost to develop an app is five thousand dollars, then that represents an annual R&D expense of six billion dollars, effectively eliminating the majority of Apple's gains from the apps that do survive. Of course, that's not the case since Apple pays nothing for third party R&D.

Third, the ability to create the level of detail needed to deliver on the promise of a loyal brand (recall our personal shopper analogy) will be much harder for a large brand which is attempting to do this across a multitude of products and a much more diverse community of customers. While having detailed knowledge of an individual's behaviors creates the opportunity to translate that into value, it doesn't guarantee it.

The good news is that these platforms will create opportunities for loyal brands in areas where we would never have expected them to. To list all of them here would be both tedious and highly suspect. We don't claim to be able to predict every one, but there is one that might be easily overlooked and which, although rarely considered to be a loyal brand, will most shape our perception of the value that a loyal brand can have.

You should be able to guess where we're going with this based on what we've already said is likely to be the product capturing so much of our behavior. That's right, the autonomous vehicle.

Driving Behavior

On average American's spend seventeen thousand, six hundred minutes driving each year.[144] That's the equivalent of seven forty-hour weeks of full-time employment. And that does not include the amount of time we are also passengers. With 86 percent of households owning at least one car, we'd claim that this is the single most pervasive and consistent device-based activity that we are involved in which cuts across every demographic boundary. Wait, what about mobile phones and computers, aren't they the most pervasive digital devices? There's no argument that our many online activities are a significant window into our behaviors, however they differ from the experience of the car in one critical way.

Devices that give us the ability to work online still draw a fairly hard line between the digital world and the physical world. Even with coming advances in augmented reality—the ability to use your mobile phone to overlay virtual reality on top of a physical image—they are still primarily online experiences that are delivered through a digital interface.

I (Tom) often tell the story of going to the launch of the last space shuttle in 2011. It was the first rocket launch I'd ever witnessed in person and the last flight of the space shuttle. I was lucky enough to be there on a press pass which gave me access to the closest viewing location next to the outdoor countdown clock. During the launch I used my iPhone to capture the shuttle launch from the magnificent launch pad plume of smoke and fire, to the crackle of breaking the sound barrier, and eventually up through the clouds. When I'd finally lost sight of the shuttle the realization of what I'd just done dawned on me as I looked around and saw hundreds of people all viewing this awe-inspiring, historic, once-in-a-lifetime, never to be repeated event...on the three-inch screens that stood between them and the real world.

Smartphones will no doubt play a critical role in capturing behavioral data, but they are an interface to the digital world, not the physical world. However, a car is, by definition, a physical/digital experience. Chris Nicholson, CEO of SkyMind, a company which develops software for autonomous vehicles, put it to us this way:

> *A lot of people don't realize autonomous vehicles are basically going to be a smartphone that we live in for hours every day. We're literally inside of it. It's an app we can't escape.*
>
> *We're entrusting our lives to it.*
>
> *When we get into that smartphone and it starts rolling, we're sending it the highest and most powerful signal of intent that any human can. It's much more powerful than going on a website when you're browsing. That's what anybody building a recommendation system wants. They want a signal of intent. When you say, 'I'm getting into a car now and I'm going in this direction and at this time of day, [that's a] huge signal [of] intent."*
>
> *There's a possibility here to make much better recommendations and surface alternatives for people in their lives. At the same time, because it's a smartphone we live inside, the sensors will be able to collect much more data about us. There could be webcams trained on our faces. Microphones*

> *trained on our voices. Rather than just*
> *clicking on a website, we're giving the sig-*
> *nal of intent with our direction and we're*
> *also showing it our whole analog expression,*
> *"Is your face angry or content? What is your*
> *voice saying? Who else is in the car?" We're*
> *actually digitizing much more of reality*
> *and by doing so, we'll be able to read more*
> *subtle signals which gets into the collection*
> *of behavioral data. The cars are going to be*
> *data gathering mechanisms par excellence.*

We love Chris's description of an AV as a smartphone you step into. With this sort of "phygital" (a mashup of physical and digital behaviors) insight into our behaviors the AV is uniquely positioned to be a central player in leveraging a vast digital ecosystem to become a loyal brand. But it also does something else which has been an ongoing debate in our transition to a digital world. Namely, it counters the increasing trend toward the sci-fi vision of a Wall-e-like culture were humanity is relegated to a chair-bound existence where all their needs are met by robots who replace their need for mobility. Granted, you could spend all of your time sitting in your car as easily as you could on a La-Z-Boy in your living room, but your La-Z-Boy doesn't take you anyplace.

A Car with Personality

We're accustomed to thinking of cars as having an image which speaks to the kinds of people who buy them. A BMW is typically the car of choice for people who love the experience of driving a bit on the aggressive side. Mercedes owners are considered a bit more refined, appreciating comfort over raw power. Volvo appeals to safety-conscious drivers. Subaru to practical and conservative drivers. Manufacturers will both equip their cars with features that speak to these identities and market them in a way that reinforces the image. In some cases, the cars can also adapt to very generic categories of a driver's behavior. Having a "sport" mode that decreases fuel efficiency and increases power and responsiveness is typical for many high-end cars. However, the car cannot exhibit behavior beyond its tightly controlled range of options.

AVs are not similarly constrained. An AV can adapt to a set of deeper behaviors, intentions, and even the emotions of the driver (or passenger). Michael Flemming, the CEO at Torc Robotics which develops AVs, shared with us a glimpse of what this sort of behavior looks like in today's prototype AVs.

> *I was on a demo ride a few weeks ago and we were autonomously driving—stop signs, traffic lights and so forth. [At one point] we go autonomously down this ramp and we're getting ready to merge onto an interstate... there's this small window for us to merge but we have to speed up. There are several cars behind the car that we're getting ready to move in front of and one of the cars is a police officer. So in that situation, we sped up and we [merged] in front of a police officer. I remember one of the engineers made a comment. He said, 'Michael, do you think that was too aggressive?' I said, 'Absolutely not, because that's exactly what I would have done. If we would have slowed down,*

the other traffic wouldn't have created a space for us and we would have become a safety hazard.

When the behavior takes place, you are in awe... but then afterwards you look back at it and you say, "That made a tremendous amount of sense."

Michael's experience is just a small indication of what it will be like to drive in an AV, but it does lead to a much larger conversation about the role behavior will play in creating AVs that express what we're calling the loyalty of a brand. To understand that, let's go back to a conversation we had earlier about the digital-self at the very outset of this book. If you recall, we said that devices would also have a digital-self that over time captured the experiences and behaviors of the device. That may have seemed a bit outlandish at the time but by now you probably have a better sense for why this might be the case.

As an AV learns, it adapts to a set of constantly changing contextual variables. In the same way that you would never drive in Columbus, Ohio the same way you drive in Athens, Greece, the AV adapts to the nuances of its surroundings. Yet, that same principle applies to nearly all behavior. The way you talk to a child will vary from the way you talk to a parent or the way you talk to a colleague. The sum total of all these nuanced behaviors becomes who you are. It's a learned process that enables us to adapt. But there's also something else about that process that is essential to human interaction. You are likely to be drawn to a person who has a similar behavioral profile. You will choose to be surrounded by people in your personal life who share your demeanor. Let's take that and apply it to the relationship with an AV.

It's entirely feasible to have your AV sense and respond to your behaviors in how you drive. For example, if the AV senses that you are stressed, late for a meeting, and had a fitful night of sleep it may set the cabin lights, entertainment, speed of the car, its maneuvering and how aggressively it drives to correspond with a combination of factors that are most likely to calm you. With connectivity to wearable health devices, it's also possible to adjust the AV's parameters to respond directly to your physiology and emotional state.

Two points we want to make before continuing. The first is that the cabin setting that we described may make no sense for your personality. If you're stressed, dim lighting and Mozart may be the last thing that you want to experience. But that's exactly why the nuanced behavior of the AV will be based on *your* behaviors, patterns, and stimuli, not generic mass-customized settings for "stressed out" drivers. The second is that it's much too easy at this stage to take the path of a *Westworld* analogy and come up with scenarios which include killer cars that translate their passenger's stressed and frustrated behavior into road rage.

The greater danger of AI is not the evolution of a new species of killer AVs which start to view humans as friction that needs to be removed in order to advance their own causes, but AVs which make small mistakes with big consequences.

With the attention being paid to the potential for AI gone wild, we are going to see enormous public interest in incidents where an AV is involved in any sort of harm, injury, or death to a human. We can do the math and prove that an AV is one hundred or even one thousand times safer than a human-driven car, but that's like trying to convince someone who's terrified of flying that they should get on a transatlantic flight because it's one hundred times safer than a car.[145]

What we're most likely to see is a very compartmental-ized progression toward full autonomy over the period of five to ten years. And some of the easiest ways to go down that path are in adopting changes that adapt the car to the driver, developing a bond of trust and predictability in how an AV behaves. For instance, consider the peculiar lane changing behavior of a Tesla as Mike Nelson described it earlier in the book (Mike was the lawyer we talked about in Chapter 4 who drove coast to coast). For Mike, a big part of the getting comfortable with the technology was getting used to the way his Tesla changed lanes.[146]

As you think about how these nuanced behaviors will adapt over time to the driver, it's not difficult to foresee a time when a large part of the buying decision is based on the actual behavior of the AV. In the same way that you might today buy a BMW for its handling and responsiveness, you will buy an AV for the behaviors it exhibits. But why stop there?

If your digital-self can also integrate with the AV's behav-iors, it's entirely plausible that when you get into an AV it will immediately reconfigure itself to your preferences in how it handles, the cabin ambiance, your alerts and notifica-tions, and even the route it takes—based on your interests. It's hardly a stretch to imagine the AV saying, "Tom, we're going to drive by a vegan market in .05 miles. You have your daughter's birthday tomorrow. Do you want to stop in and get a vegan chocolate cake? They have three on hand. It will add 17 minutes to your drive."

Keep in mind that all of this will be happening in a cabin not a cockpit. Matt Benson, a key player in the develop-ment of AV experiences and focuses on what this cabin of the future will look like. Matt mentors startup companies in the AV industry with Faurecia Ventures, the investment and innovation arm of Faurecia, one of the world's largest automotive equipment suppliers with twenty-three billion dollars in global sales.

According to Matt:

> *The thing we're thinking about is how does the [AV] both physically and digitally anticipate and adapt to a person's status and then serve things up that they might want?*
>
> *There are three personalization approaches that I think are important.*
>
> *The first level is providing options for the driver or occupant to personalize for his or her preference. The second is having a vehicle that can optimize these options knowing about these preferences. The third is when the vehicle can personalize for what the occupant hasn't even expressed.*
>
> *So the physical space may need to change. That could mean being able to take on new positions, more relaxing positions. We see people wanting to work out—maybe not a full-blown workout, but being able to give yourself a little bit more flexibility so you can do some stretching, something akin to a Pilates or a yoga kind of situation.*
>
> *Active Wellness is our system for sensing and adapting the environment around the seat and other areas of the interior based on an assessment of what's going on with the human, their biological data, vital signs, as well as where they're looking and*

what they're doing. Are they stressed? Are they fatigued? Are they distracted? Are they uncomfortable? What have they been doing before they got on the vehicle? Where are they going? All those things then help us take actions or countermeasures to address the situation, or even some of those things we may actually be able to predict based on some signatures we see and what's going on.

Matt's focus on creating an experience which respects the driver or the passenger, shows an understanding of their needs and behavioral context, and which provides them with value that they don't even know to ask for is the ultimate objective of a loyal brand. Implicit in that loyalty is a foundation of trust. In the same way that I'd expect my financial advisor to fully understand my financial goals and objectives, and to manage my portfolio with a fiduciary responsibility in achieving those goals, a loyal brand is much more than a casual relationship; it is built on an expectation that the brand has my best interests at heart.

This isn't the way we're accustomed to thinking about how we experience products. We've happily accepted that we are anonymous customers who have little, if any, ability to demand that a manufacturer recognize our individual needs. Unless we're willing to hire a tailor to custom fit our bespoke clothing, a personal chef to cook our meals, a concierge doctor to care for our health, a chauffeur to drive us, our kids, and parents, and a manservant or lady in waiting to attend to our unspoken needs, we accept that the world does not revolve around us—it couldn't. But what if it could?

The differentiator of a loyal brand is that it anticipates your needs and in doing so it over delivers in comparison to any brand that merely meets expressed and well-defined needs.

But there's still one monumental challenge. Your digital-self, this sum total of all the things that make you who you are, physiologically, emotionally, financially, behaviorally, is not only valuable to you but to anyone who wants to profit from it.

The question we still haven't answered is how will you protect what's likely to be the single most valuable asset in your life?

CHAPTER 8:

Digital Dilemma: Guarding the Future

"Impossible is just a word thrown around
by small men who find it easier to live in the world
they've been given than to explore the power they have to change
it. Impossible is not a fact. It's an opinion.
Impossible is potential. Impossible is temporary.
Impossible is nothing."
—Muhammad Ali

We've covered a lot of ground so far in discussing all the ways in which the behaviors of our digital-selves and those of our devices will create a new category of behavioral assets. We've talked about how these assets will bring new opportunities that promise to disrupt so many of the frameworks that we've come to accept as a standard part of how the world operates. But what we've yet to look at are an entirely new set of challenges in how we will protect and secure these assets. That's the topic of this last chapter.

However, rather than just look at ways that we can better secure what we regard today as our digital-self, we'd like to take the next step, which is to look at how the same innovations that we've already discussed, the digital-self, hyper-personalization, digital ecosystems, and loyal brands will lead into entirely new entities that we need to protect.

That's always the challenge with disruptive innovation; it not only changes how we will do what we've always done, but it also introduces entirely new ways of experiencing the world which are driven not just by the technology of new devices but by entirely new behaviors.

Trying to paint this picture of the future is always risky business. Our palette consists only of the colors we already know, so we end up describing the future using the vocabulary of the past. Going back to the AT&T commercials we talked about early in the book, in one of the commercials where a tablet computer was being used by someone sitting by the ocean's edge, the voice over says "Sending a fax from the beach…" We are certainly using tablets and mobile devices in similar settings, but the way in which we are using them so exceeds the very limiting notion of sending a fax.

Still, there are some areas where we know that a digital-self has enormous potential value to solve many foreseeable problems that are on the visible horizon. What lies beyond that horizon is fair game for any of us to guess at. And that's always the fun part of predicting the distant future, as long as we accept that, however expansive we may believe our thinking to be, history has a nearly perfect record of proving us wrong.

Yet, the tell-tales of the future are always apparent when we look back at where we've been.

Nearly twenty years ago, one of us happened to be sponsoring a large event in San Diego on the future of technology. Speakers included the late Peter Drucker, economist Paul Romer, and management guru Tom Peters. All were talking about the future of the organization.

Of all these, one session stands out. Two technologists from the Stanford Research Institute (SRI) were describing their view of the future of the internet. This at a time when just as many people were wondering if the internet was a fad as were claiming it was a revolution—actually there were many more of the former than the latter.

The image the two technologists used to illustrate the internet of tomorrow was a large cloud. In this cloud, they claimed, would exist a nearly infinite number of possible connections, resources, capabilities, skills, and ideas. It was, as they described it, the ultimate free market, where people could instantly access, purchase, and apply the resources of the world to solve almost any problem. They asked the audience to think of it as an infinitely scalable computer with no centralized place of control, authority, or ownership.

They described a scenario where objects that represented digital or physical assets and resources would float around in this cloud, available to anyone who needed them. Many objects would have no owners, belonging to everyone and free to use, while others would be complex objects that could be purchased or rented for single use. But what was most spectacular about their vision was that this cloud would not have any geographical center. It would not be housed on any one machine, server, or desktop, and would not be the property of a single company or even a coalition or cartel. The cloud belonged to everyone and no one.

To call this far-fetched in 1999 is a severe understatement. It was pure science fiction, and the term *lunatics* would have been a more fitting descriptor than *visionaries* for the two presenters. Yet the session drew people to it like bugs to halogen.

For some reason, that utopian view of the future never left me. I tried to apply it to the internet as it evolved and kept looking for ways to use it to describe how technology and behavior was changing. But the fit always seemed forced, contrived, and stretched beyond the boundaries of believability—at least until very recently when we started working on the ideas and concepts in this book.

We are now at the threshold of that wild-eyed future. And it's a future that is going to evolve much faster than we expect it to, which means you can't start soon enough to prepare for it. So far, this book has put in place the foundation for understanding the magnitude of that change and the many ways it will create new opportunities, behaviors, and value. But we've also been up front about the magnitude of the challenges in building a future that continues to protect the privacy, freedom, and liberty that we cherish so dearly as a cornerstone of a free society.

In this chapter we'll push the envelope even further by introducing ways in which we believe we will have to rethink some of the most basic tenets of computing and how we use the power of behavior to secure that future.

Our first stop on that journey is delving further into the radical implications of blockchain and cryptocurrencies in creating a new paradigm for how we build the future of our business, economies, and society.

The Cryptocurrency Link

In Chapter 4 we introduced the concept of blockchain and cryptocurrencies. In this chapter we'll expand on how to create a new platform for computing that is infinitely more secure and scalable than the models we have in place today. Let's start by looking closer at how cryptocurrencies work.

A cryptocurrency is a unit of value that can be used for online transactions. There are well over one hundred cryptocurrencies in circulation today. Among the more popular are Bitcoin, Ethereum, and Litecoin. The total value of cryptocurrencies in circulation is about seventy-five billion dollars as of the date that this manuscript was finalized. That may be a rounding error in comparison to the 1.5 trillion dollars of US currency estimated to be in circulation, but it's nothing to turn a blind eye to.[147]

It's called a "crypto" currency because blockchain encryption is used to assure its validity, ownership, and value. The last of these, value, is actually determined by both demand and an algorithm that caps the number of units that can be issued. In the case of Bitcoin, the number is twenty-one million.

The algorithm gets increasingly more complex as the number of units approaches the maximum that can be issued. Computers called miners are used to apply the extraordinary computing power required to mine or record new Bitcoin transactions. To give you an idea of just how much horsepower is required, even the most powerful laptop with a graphics card would require over five hundred years to mine a single Bitcoin. By the way I'm using the term "mining" as it applies to a Bitcoin, but in fact the Bitcoin is just a reward for creating a block in the blockchain.

The real interesting part of blockchain is not the math but rather the impact cryptocurrency will have on so many aspects of how we use and manage money.

For example, a few years back, one of us was invited to speak at a Federal Reserve meeting in Chicago. At the time Bitcoin and a small cadre of cryptocurrencies had already caught the attention of many in the financial industry. But the Fed had a specific concern about the future of currency as it entered the cyber realm, namely that as it stands now there is no way to use monetary policy to manage cryptocurrency.

If Bitcoins are only worth what people who buy and sell them say they're worth, then are they worth anything at all? After all, although the dollar is a fiat currency the US government still stands behind it.[148] But if a cryptocurrency is used by enough people, then won't it also have value because of all the people who stand behind it? Well, only as long as they all agree it has value. Granted, you can make a case that because it is scarce, transferrable, and backed by a global network of nodes that secure the blockchain, it has some inherent value. But ultimately the value will hinge on how widely used and accepted the currency is. And that only seems to be accelerating. For example, you can get a VISA card that is funded by a cryptocurrency, which you can then use to buy just about anything you could with any traditional currency.[149]

Until now currencies have only been issued by governments. Although you can store that value in digital form or even as gold bullion in a safe, you have to ultimately convert this value into currency through a regulated bank of some sort in order to conduct a transaction. That means you are subject to the inherent friction of the bank's processes, fees, and access. The reason is that since your money is recorded digitally, someone or something with acknowledged integrity has to keep track of what's yours.

From what we've described so far it seems that blockchain and cryptocurrencies are primarily a niche approach to flying under the radar of more conventional banking, business, and economic models. But there's another aspect of blockchain that we haven't covered which takes our discussion well outside of this niche and places it directly in the crosshairs of nearly every major incumbent who is today vying for ownership of the computing ecosystem that controls the many devices you own and your digital-self, and that's its ability to act as a distributed platform for nearly every type of business where intermediaries create friction.

That's exactly what a number of new companies are doing by using blockchain to develop ways that literally circumvent existing industrial era economic constructs and business models. The premise here is simple yet revolutionary. industrial era models of computing and financial transactions (buying, selling, transferring funds) are designed with centralized administration. They rely on a hierarchical model where control is closely guarded. This made perfect sense in an era when every communication was linear and point-to-point.

The game of telephone that kids in the last century were so fond of was a wonderful illustration of how steeped in this model we had become. When you played telephone and passed a message from one person to another, the message would eventually lose all resemblance to the original message. The challenge of point-to-point communication is that there is no way to maintain the integrity of anything, be it ownership, an idea, a request, or a transaction as it made its way through the linear network without an extensive paper trail.

However, if you were to play that same game with children today it's a fair bet that they would email the message to each other thereby making sure it was intact and unaltered. After the email had been sent to each one in the chain, they could then look at each other's emails and see that it hadn't changed. Suddenly there's no longer any single point of failure. Of course, we all know that email doesn't work that way and neither do most other communications or transactions that are subject to alteration, intentional or not. So, to insure the integrity of data we put in place intermediaries who have the responsibility for making sure that the data is intact and trustworthy.

One of these is a company called Golem which has set out to create a global supercomputer by using idle or unused computer resources.[150] They refer to themselves as an Airbnb of computing because you can buy and sell unused time on a computer to anyone else on the Golem peer to peer network.

The concept and practice of pooling computer resources across a network is not new. A variety of distributed computing projects have been around since the late '90s. Some of these are called "volunteer" computing, where anyone can download a small application to their personal computer and volunteer to provide some centralized authority with the use of their computer when it is idle. Some of the better known are seti@home and folding@home. The first is a Berkeley-sponsored project that searches for signals in the background noise of the cosmos in order to discover intelligent life. The second is sponsored by Stanford and does the same but for disease research.

However, the network of computers is still controlled by centralized servers. Think of this in terms of a bank. While we can all exchange currency to pay bills, buy products and services, withdraw cash from an ATM, or otherwise conduct transactions, the money always comes from and goes back to a bank. Unless your employer pays you in gold bullion or you run a cash-only food cart, it's unlikely that you have more than enough cash in your possession to last for longer than a few days. The reason is that you trust the bank to keep your money safe more so that you do yourself.

But what if there was a way to have a debit card that withdrew funds from value that existed throughout a network of other people, organizations, or devices for which you had provided services? Your "balance" wouldn't exist in any one node of that network but on all nodes of the network. That's a tough thing to wrap our brains around but it's something that we all do regularly in another context.

When you ask a friend to do you a favor, perhaps to run an errand, introduce you to someone they know, or help you solve a problem, where does that relationship capital reside? Nowhere except between the two of you. But now let's expand the scope of that scenario. Say you need to gather two hundred people to help you with something significant, perhaps a community effort to erect a new playground. Each person needs to be reasonably qualified in various aspects of building, from wielding a hammer to digging a hole. You don't know two hundred people well enough to do that, but it's likely that you have friends who have friend who have friends and somehow you'd collectively be able to gather up enough qualified people. A lot of relationship capital was just used up in the process. But a great deal was also created because anytime one of those same people need a favor you can rest assured they will turn to someone else in that same group. Again, where does all of that relationship capital reside? Everywhere and nowhere.

Now, if you're sharp, you'll jump to the next question, which is, "But isn't that relationship capital only as good as the integrity and reliability of the people who stand behind it?"

In a peer-to-peer, or P2P, network enabled by blockchain, the same thing is happening but on a scale of thousands or millions of people and with one hundred percent assurance that the capital is being attributed correctly.

That's exactly what Golem is doing. The Golem Network is a decentralized sharing economy of computing power, where anyone can make money 'renting' out their computing power or developing and selling software.[151]

But wait, isn't Golem the centralized administrator in this case? No, and the role that they play and the way they came into being is as fascinating as what they are doing. Golem, raised 8.6 million dollars in funding, but it wasn't from angels or venture capital or any other conventional means of raising cash. It was through an ICO, or an Initial Coin Offering.

An ICO is much like an IPO (initial public offering) except that it is not regulated by any government body, such as the SEC, and it is open to anyone who wants to participate in the offering. But there's much more to an ICO than just raising capital. The entire Golem network will now use its own currency, called GTN. Currently a GTN is worth forty-two cents. However, all cryptocurrencies are capped at a total number that can be issued. For Bitcoin the number is twenty-one million. The total number of GTNs is capped at one billion tokens, which means that over time the value of a token will increase. Of course, none of that is guaranteed in any way. And while we are bullish on the opportunities created by ICOs there is no doubt that there is also rampant speculation going on.

For example, as of the publication of this book, the total funding raised through approximately two hundred ICOs has exceeded two billion dollars, with a single ICO raising nearly three hundred million dollars within fifteen minutes.

Whatever trajectory ICOs take in the near term in disrupting the way capital is raised, the larger promise is in the underlying blockchain technology to create digital ecosystems that are nearly frictionless in how they operate—having removed the transaction intermediaries. What might this mean in real terms? According to Ethereum founder Vitalik Buterin, "Now it takes you several weeks to sell a house, whereas it can take just 3 minutes."[152] (Recall the data we talked about in Chapter 5 on work time versus process time.) That sort of improvement could never be accomplished with organic change and incremental innovation efforts.

If we begin to project that sort of potential increase in efficiency, along with the ability to irrefutably record every step of a transaction, analyze it, and then integrate it with the digital-self, we can imagine a model where friction is close to eliminated across the board. If that seems hyperbolic, consider again that in many administrative processes the actual transaction time is from one to five percent of overall process time. We have been running our economy, government, healthcare, insurance and finance, supply chains, at only five percent of their actual capacity, or, to put it in a more dramatic way, we waste 95 percent of the effort we put into running many industries. And if ever there was an invisible force that drags us down, stifles innovation, and impedes our ability to solve the greatest challenges to productivity, this is it.

So, stop and think about what it would mean to you personally, to your organization, to social institutions if we could recapture even five percent of the time now spent in

existing processes or transactions? We'd effectively be doubling the capacity of the corresponding process. So, let's do
some math. How many times greater would our capacity be
if we started with a process that consists of only five percent
actual work? Simple, twenty times greater. Clearly there are
areas where this math does not apply because of physical constraints or a lack of market demand, but the point is that the
capacity is there for significant improvement.

To be clear, cryptocurrency is not without its risks. At
the writing of this book, the Chinese government has closed
down all cryptocurrency exchanges doing business within
mainland China and further mandated that exchanges hand
over the names of all participants in the exchange. Keep in
mind that there is a subtle but profound irony in Bitcoin, and
pretty much any current cryptocurrency. While you can conduct anonymous transactions you also have an indisputable
audit trail of all your transactions stored in the blockchain.
And there are ways to trace transactions back to buyers and
sellers. This is how thirty-one-year-old Ross Ulbricht, creator
of the now infamous illicit Bitcoin marketplace Silk Road,
which was reported to have resulted in over one billion dollars of illegal drug traffic, was caught and sentenced to life in
prison. Interestingly enough, while the US government does
not have a cryptocurrency, as of yet, in 2014 it did auction
off the Bitcoins it seized from Silk Road for approximately
twenty billion dollars.

The likely scenarios for the future of cryptocurrency are
any and all of these:

- It all goes bust because of speculation and irrational
  exuberance before it comes back in a decade or so
  with more substantial prospects for the future, which

may be Bitcoin or any other existing or yet to be created cryptocurrency.

- Regulators step in and start to, or at least attempt to, impose restrictions on cyber currency and its use. China has already banned cryptocurrencies ICOs, stating that they are a disruptive and destabilizing technology.
- Breaches occur (either architected by nation states or by nefarious criminal interests) which undermine trust in cryptocurrency. Again, leading to the downfall of one, some, or all the current players before a more trusted alternative is created.
- The US government and other governments begin issuing cryptocurrencies.

Note, however, that in each of the above scenarios, and pretty much any other scenario that we can come up with, cryptocurrencies are not going away. That doesn't mean Bitcoin or Ethereum or any of the other one hundred ninety-eight currently existing cryptocurrencies will be here ten or even five years from now, but the idea of a new form of currency that redefines the notion of monetary value is something that is clearly here to stay.

But what about using blockchain to also protect our digital-self?

Do You Know Who I Am?

There's a country where identity is immutable and the birthright of every citizen. Before we tell you where it is, let's describe what they do.

Using blockchain, this country has developed a secure citizen identification system that creates a unique identity once a baby is born. Unlike an SSN, the identity is stored in a blockchain. It's indelible and unalterable. The secure ID enrolls a newborn into the healthcare system and is used to identify and store all medical, school, and any other legal records. When the child turns fifteen, she or he is issued an ID card which is used for virtually every service that requires proof of identity—from banks and ATMs, to hospitals and doctor visits, to legal agreements and train tickets. The ID system is so effective that the government cannot, by law, ask for any single piece of personally identifiable information more than once. Taxes, voting, employment, and marriage records are all stored in the blockchain. Everything that defines who the person is and what makes up their legal persona is accumulated and attached in a permanent set of block chain transactions.

This isn't a futuristic scenario; the system we're referring to has been in use for ten years and during that time it has not suffered a breach or had a single identity compromised. If the ID card is lost, a new one is immediately reissued. However, the card is not sufficient to verify identity or to authorize transactions and legally binding contracts. This requires the use of one of two special PINs. One which authenticates who the holder is and another used to sign agreements. Because it's all stored in the blockchain there is never a possibility of alteration or identity theft.

Since every governmental process is digital, and uses this digital-self, everything from court proceedings to filing taxes happens in record-breaking time frames of days rather than weeks and months.

But all of this is just the tip of the iceberg. This same country was the first to offer an e-residency program that can be used by anyone in the world to establish an identity that allows them to start up a business, access global banking, and access thousands of business and personal services.

The country is not a super power; in fact, it's one few people have heard much about: Estonia, a former Soviet block country that has built what is arguably the world's most sophisticated governmental digital ecosystem.

Ironically, Estonia's digitalization came out of one of the worst cyberattacks ever reported. At the end of April of 2007 and through the early part of May, Estonia suffered a cyberattack that a spokesperson from their defense agency equated to the 9/11 attack on America. Triggered by Estonia's decision to relocate a Soviet era war memorial from its capital, Talinn, the attack crippled the he country's websites, banks, newspapers, and internet with distributed denial of service (DDoS) attacks from what appeared to be Russian government servers as well as more than one million public IP addresses from around the world, most of which were zombie computers that had been commandeered by hackers.

At the time, Estonia took great pride in being one of the most wired nations in Europe. But, for all intents and purposes, the attack took Estonia off the grid and set it back twenty years. A country in which 98 percent of all banking transaction happened online was brought to its knees without access to the web. It was the opening salvo of what's been called Web War I; the first time an entire nation had been disabled.[153]

It was after this cyberwar takedown that Estonia and NATO realized how incredibly vulnerable every nation was from a well-funded, state-sanctioned, or large scale global attacks coordinated by thousands of revenge-seeking individuals. It needed to both shore up defenses and also find something that would provide greater security for critical applications and transactions.

The stark truth is that we've barely begun to experience the magnitude of potential cyber risk. We'd estimate that if we stay on the current trajectory, we're less than five years away from a disastrous global cyber event that will take most companies by surprise and finally act as a wake-up call to all of us—a 9/11 category attack that will have a serious impact on the global economy and which will make what happened to Estonia seem paltry in comparison.

The root of the vulnerability is that most individuals, organizations, and nation states are still embracing an outdated mindset of "perimeter" defenses as the exclusive means of protecting their organizations. With a perimeter defense you can draw a line around the assets you need to protect. This is the way we once fought wars and barricaded our crown jewels from the enemy. This is exactly what Estonia did when they were unable to initially control the DDoS attack. They shut down all access to the any computer outside of Estonia. But no computer-based system and certainly no nation can shut itself off from the rest of the world for long.

This is the standard military response, from Windsor castle to NORAD's Cheyenne mountain complex to Fort Knox; it's how the physical world works. No matter how large the area to be protected, it was still surrounded by a single set of walls and defenses that created a perimeter; be it a border, a fortress, or a moat, if you post diligent defenders around the perimeter, you're safe.

There's just one problem with that approach in today's world. There is no perimeter.

Trying to define a cyber perimeter, whether it's a physical one around hardware or a digital one around software and data is like trying to fight a war with terrorists. Yes, we can lock down our borders, use analytics to sniff out the bad guys, and send them back home. But in the end, that only stops a small number of threats.

Antivirus software, firewalls, passwords, pretty much everything we've come to think of as the last line of defense against cyberthreats is defending us against an old enemy. Today's enemy is using social engineering, human weaknesses, the resources of a state player, and the exploitation of extended ecosystems to get well within the perimeter.

The now infamous breach of big box retailer Target, which has, by some estimates, cost the company nearly half a billion dollars, came from a vulnerability with its HVAC contractor! That's the danger of an ecosystem; it creates vulnerabilities where you would never, could never, have thought of defending yourself.

So, what's the solution? It starts by removing the notion of a perimeter in how we look at ecosystems and eliminating centralized administration.

Ecosystems are inherently complex and constantly evolving networks. The partners, processes, and people that make up the ecosystem are always in flux and do not form a well-defined perimeter. The inherent benefit of this, as we saw in Chapter 5, is that the ecosystem has visibility across its entirety, but that also means that the data it relies on is not centralized but exists throughout the ecosystem. In addition, the complexity and sheer size of many centralized systems make them incredibly vulnerable to human error.

For instance, a 2017 breach of the credit reporting agency Equifax exposed one hundred forty-three million Americans to cyberthieves who acquired their credit histories and the holy grail of personally identifying information, their nine-digit social security numbers. How did such a massive heist take place? Equifax was two months overdue installing a software patch for a known vulnerability!

At the same time, we are agreeing to Terms of Service (ToS) with businesses that are harvesting our digital-self with our permission. When you post to Facebook you're agreeing to around six thousand words in their ToS which includes, among other things, the following clause:

> *For content that is covered by intellectual property rights, like photos and videos (IP content), you specifically give us the following permission, subject to your privacy and application settings: you grant us a non-exclusive, transferable, sub-licensable, royalty-free, worldwide license to use any IP content that you post on or in connection with Facebook (IP License). This IP License ends when you delete your IP content or your account unless your content has been shared with others, and they have not deleted it.*[154]

As we pointed out in Chapter 3, trying to read all of the Terms of Service with every app that you use is simply impractical. However, we've barely begun to appreciate the magnitude of the challenge. As internet connected sensors become pervasive in our homes, vehicles, wearables, and workplaces (what's often called the Internet of Things or IoT) we will see orders of magnitude increases in the number Terms of Service for all of these devices. And it gets worse. Even all of this pales when compared to what we may soon be sharing through services that also capture our biometric, physiological, and genomic data. While some of this is protected when it is associated with a health record or a health provider, that's not always the case. Clearly, we share this information for some measure of value, whether that be the ability to share posts with friends or information about our heritage. Yet, as we've seen, the value of this information to whoever may ultimately own it is still unknown.

This is where a rather interesting dynamic, that's not often talked about, can amplify the risk of sharing this information. Recall that very early in Chapter 1 we talked about the fact that no one company owned the very dispersed nature of our digital behaviors. That's changing. Almost all the companies that are collecting this information have the same clause as Facebook, which states that your data is "transferable." This means that if the company is acquired your, data goes with the acquisition as part of the transaction. Given that the vast majority of small companies are ultimately sold, or their assets are sold, you may never know where your data ends up. But that's not as bad as the fact that as the data is acquired a funneling effect occurs in which this data can be increasingly connected with other data about you, amplifying its value with each new connection.

The challenge in all of this is that our digital-selves are being aggregated into massive collections that provide a more precise picture of who you are, something that you never explicitly agreed to. Trying to protect this by using a perimeter-based defense that builds a moat around our digital-self is fundamentally impossible No matter how well we legislate or protect access to private information, there is no way to adequately police it.

Our digital-self has exceeded our ability to protect it. The challenge becomes, how do you track and maintain ownership of your private data? The answer, in large part, is that all of this aligns precisely with the architectural objectives of blockchain to make data traceable with an indelible and immutable record of provenance. Without this your digital–self is neither traceable nor verifiable. The blockchain becomes both a means of maintaining the right of ownership as well as defending our digital-self from corruption.

An analogy that helps in understanding how blockchain is fundamentally different from any perimeter defense is the way our immune system fights off disease. Our bodies have great perimeter defenses, but we cannot exist without letting in all sorts of nasty bugs. Our bodies are constantly fighting off these intruders. The reason we do not succumb to them on a daily basis is that our immune system is built to deal with regular breaches of the perimeter. To do this it uses what's referred to as a Distributed Control System, meaning that it is not centralized; there is no one point of failure.

Not only is our immune system decentralized, but every cell in the human body also contains the entirety of our DNA. Liver cells differ from the cells that express themselves as eyeballs, but your complete DNA sequence exists in both.

The analogy between blockchain and how our DNA and immune systems work is significant in understanding how to defend against cyberthreats. In both cases the data needed to maintain the integrity of the system is distributed throughout every node or cell. Attacking any single node or cell, or any cluster, does not compromise the integrity of the rest of the system. In this scenario your digital-self is forever linked to you and can therefore be traced back to its owner.

Here's what this means for protecting our digital-self:

- Personally identifiable information should always be linked through the blockchain to its rightful legal owner.
- You should at any time be able to trace, view, and retract data which is linked to your identity no matter who currently stores or uses it.
- Personally identifiable information should always be auditable so that you can inventory where it is being used and how it is being used.
- Personally identifiable information can only be disclosed by its owner to a third party, however this information cannot be stored in any manner by that third party. Instead only a blockchain hash of the digital-self is stored by the third party.
- Any value derived from the use of a person's digital-self is subject to an agreement between that individual and the user of the data that spells out the exchange of value.
- The Digital-self is recognized as a legal entity to the extent that it has been authorized to conduct certain transactions on behalf of its owner.
- The Digital-self is granted protection as the property of its owner. Use of it by any unauthorized party is subject to laws similar to identity theft laws today.
- A universal e-registry is established for the optional participation of any citizen in any country (similar to Estonia's e-resident), which grants immutable identity and irrefutable property ownership rights to an individual.

Throughout the book we've been describing how industrial era models of business, factories, marketing, brands are all becoming unsustainable mechanisms of growth and progress as we move into the 21st century. It should be no surprise then that even the notion of defending and protecting ourselves, our organizations, and our nations has to change from the industrial era model of "define the borders and defend" to one of "open borders and protect." Ultimately, it's the only sustainable model of continuing to scale the ability to retain ownership over our data and digital-selves.

Robot Rules

We'd be more than negligent if we concluded without taking a final look at a controversy that we've been describing on-and-off throughout the book; the threat that many have claimed AI poses to civilization.

Elon Musk has called AI an "existential threat to humanity." Two years ago, he tweeted, "We need to be super careful with artificial intelligence. It is potentially more dangerous than nukes."

Stephen Hawking told the BBC early in 2017, "The development of full artificial intelligence could spell the end of the human race.... It would take off on its own, and re-design itself at an ever-increasing rate. Humans, who are limited by slow biological evolution, couldn't compete, and would be superseded."

On the other hand, Facebook's CEO Mark Zuckerberg has a more optimistic approach.

During a Facebook Live broadcast in July of 2017, Zuckerberg made it clear that he tried to oppose the spread of fear surrounding the potential of AI. "I have pretty strong opinions on this. I am optimistic...I think you can build things and the world can get better. But with AI especially, I am really optimistic. And I think people who are naysayers and try to drum up these doomsday scenarios—I just, I don't understand it. It's really negative and in some ways I actually think it is pretty irresponsible," he said. "In the next five to 10 years, AI is going to deliver so many improvements in the quality of our lives," added Zuckerberg.

So, who are we to believe—killer bots or compassionate companions? Our perspective is a much more balanced one. There's little doubt that AI will exceed our practical ability to understand all the variables that go into every decision an AV or any other sufficiently advanced AI-powered device will make. The fallacy in apocalyptic scenarios is that what we are dealing with in every current and planned case where AI is being included in devices is what's called narrow AI (We talked about this in Chapter 4). Your AV may be able to make decisions about how to drive but it cannot make decisions about anything else. It can't even play checkers with you. The concerns expressed by Musk and Hawking are only valid when you have general purpose AI, which also has the ability to set its own goals.

Still, we are not so naïve as to dismiss all of the concerns over AI's evolution. Vigilance is key, but so is a balanced perspective that looks objectively at the human cost of how we currently make decisions.

The ability to reason is the ultimate power. It is uniquely human. And the greater your power, the greater the impact of your decisions. We grant license to decide to our corporate, social, and governmental leaders with the hope that they have the capacity and the competency to use it correctly. And yet, if we are honest and accurate, how often are those decisions made in the clear? Rarely.

When the first atomic bomb was dropped on Hiroshima, the prevailing attitude on the part of most military leaders was that the war with Japan was already over. Others believe that the bomb had nothing to do with the end of the war. Gen. Dwight D. Eisenhower said in two separate memoirs that he, "disliked seeing the United States take the lead in introducing into war something as horrible and destructive as this new weapon." And later, in his memoirs, that "Japan was already defeated and...dropping the bomb was completely unnecessary." Over six decades later, it's still not clear if the decision to drop the bomb was necessary.[155]

As humans we are all constantly making decisions which have a very real human toll by calculating the odds of what a net positive outcome will be. Sometimes we can justify those decisions with clear and logical arguments, and other times we go on invisible intuition.

It may be the ultimate irony that the inevitable conclusion to revealing the invisible is that we are creating irrefutable transparency for what we do as humans while simultaneously creating AI that exists in a black box. This isn't an easy thing to grasp because it so far out of the reach of the mental models that have been ingrained in us since childhood. Machines are always predictable, people aren't.

In a May 2017 post to his blog, Mike Gault, Co-founder and CEO of Guardtime, one of the largest providers of blockchain platforms, looked at what irrefutable transparency might mean for the world by 2025:

> *Now here's a thought - imagine if that blockchain wasn't just for one cloud - but for all clouds, and all data - every transport, compute and storage of data across all networks in the world. Imagine what such*

as a system would imply for global society. It
would transform our society from one that
is trust based to one that is truth based, i.e.
humans can choose to trust each other, but
they can also prove what happened using
the Blockchain.[156]

The truth-based society Gault is describing sounds great in principle—who among us would not chose truth over lies? But do the technologies we've described in this book, behavioral observations, the irrefutability of ownership and identity constitute truth or simply affirm accuracy? We don't believe that the risk of AI is in its being able to evolve into a ruling class over humans. The risk we see is in our acceptance of its infallibility, that somehow, we will be lulled into believing that our decisions are not as good, as valid, or as valuable as those made by a machine.

In his book *The Digital Doctor: Hope, Hype, and Harm at the Dawn of Medicine's Computer Age*, Doctor Robert Wachter describes a scenario, that is unfortunately not at all atypical, which illustrates how this phenomenon of machine infallibility is already a risky proposition. [157]

Wachter talks about a young patient in a hospital pediatric unit who was prescribed an antibiotic at what appeared to the administering nurse to be an inordinately high dosage of 38 ½ pills. A normal single dosage would be a single pill. As Wachter tells it, the nurse's reaction was that it was, "a shockingly high dose." The dosage had been indicated by a computer-based system that the clinicians had all welcomed since it made the accuracy of dosing a dispensing pharmaceutical much safer and error free. Still the nurse questioned the dosage. Yet when she examined the medication that had been dispensed, the pills were all appropriately in the patient's medication drawer. According to the nurse, "I remember going to his drawer and I saw a whole set of rings of medications, which had come over from the robot. And there were about eight packets of it on one ring. And I was like, wow, that's a lot of Septra.... It was an alarming number."

Without anyone to turn to at the time to confirm the dosage, she rationalized it by thinking that perhaps this was a clinical trial. She even asked the sixteen-year-old patient if he felt the dosage was correct. Being accustomed to taking a variety of medication, he agreed and swallowed the half cup of 38 ½ pills. Six hours later, he was convulsing and had stopped breathing. Incredibly, the boy survived.

It's tempting to blame his nurse for what happened, or the prescribing doctor, or even the pharmacist who double checks dosages. But the error actually came down to a process that inadvertently interpreted an entered dosage in milligrams relative to the patient's weight, increasing it by thirty times what it should have been.

Tracking down the error was relatively easy. This was a straightforward problem with the application that operated the robot dispenser and the human interface. Still, it speaks to the other side of the problem we first described with Air France flight 447. While in that case the pilots ignored the computer's alarms, in this case a belief in its infallibility was to blame.

If we trust machines that are infinitely simpler to understand than those run by AI what's likely to happen to our trust when the computers are both the prescribers and the dispensers?

We find ourselves at the most incredible intersection of behavior and technology. On the one hand we have the irrefutability created by the blockchain, which has the capacity to record our lives with total transparency, and the belief in infallible computers. On the other hand, we have the black box of AI, which makes decisions in ways that are often impossible to understand.

If we circle back to the earlier point we were making about the creation of a truth-driven world, the connection to AI becomes fairly obvious. If a computer is right with irrefutable probability in 99 percent of all cases, does that constitute truth? What about 99.999 percent of the time? Keep in mind that in the other 0.001- percent it will be irrefutably wrong.

For example, Michal Kosinski, a Stanford University professor, has caused a fair amount of controversy by showing that facial recognition using AI can determine sexual orientation, political leanings, or even a person's IQ with an accuracy of between 83 percent and 91 percent.[158] What if facial recognition can also determine my propensity for criminal activity with 90 percent certainty? Again, keep in mind that in 10 percent of all cases it will be 100 percent wrong. Before you scoff at this ask how this scenario is any different from what Target was doing in profiling women who were pregnant. Knowing that no human or non-human decision-making process can achieve 100 percent certainty, at what point do we agree that there is an acceptably low error rate?

It's a Gordian knot of immense proportions.

The New Arms Race

We don't believe that the increased reliance or role that computers will play in autonomous decisions can be mitigated, stymied, or otherwise slowed. The economic and human benefits of both trends will soon begin to outweigh any attempts to hold them back. And even if we could we shouldn't. As Oren Etzioni points out in a Sept 2017 *New York Times* article, "The problem is that if we do so, then nations like China will overtake us."

We've obviously entered a new arms race, and this one has no finish line. So, what can we do? What should we do? What are the rules?

In 1942, Isaac Asimov introduced us to his three Laws of Robotics:[159]

1. A robot may not injure a human being or, through inaction, allow a human being to come to harm.
2. A robot must obey the orders given it by human beings except where such orders would conflict with the First Law.
3. A robot must protect its own existence as long as such protection does not conflict with the First or Second Laws.

Since that time these have been referenced in thousands of works and have become a mantra of robot proponents. The laws seem simple enough on the surface. So, is this the answer? Most definitely not. In a post for the Brookings Institution, Peter Singer points out the already absurd fiction behind these laws, "You don't arm a Reaper drone with a Hellfire missile or put a machine gun on a MAARS (Modular Advanced Armed Robotic System) not to cause humans to come to harm. That is the very point!"

A more practical view of the laws governing AI was proposed by Microsoft CEO Satya Nadella:[160]

- **AI must be designed to assist humanity**. Nadella says that machines that work alongside humans should do "dangerous work like mining" but still "respect human autonomy."

- **AI must be transparent**. "We want not just intelligent machines but intelligible machines," says Nadella. "People should have an understanding of how the technology sees and analyzes the world."
- **AI must maximize efficiencies without destroying the dignity of people**. "We need broader, deeper, and more diverse engagement of populations in the design of these systems. The tech industry should not dictate the values and virtues of this future."
- **AI must be designed for intelligent privacy**. Nadella asks for "sophisticated protections that secure personal and group information."
- **AI must have algorithmic accountability**. So that "humans can undo unintended harm."

Google also has its five laws, although it calls them challenges.[161]

- **Avoiding Negative Side Effects**: How do you stop a robot from knocking over a bookcase in its zealous quest to Hoover the floor?
- **Avoiding Reward Hacking**: If a robot is programmed to enjoy cleaning your room, how do you stop it from messing up the place just so it can feel the pleasure of cleaning it again?
- **Scalable Oversight**: How much decision making do you give to the robot? Does it need to ask you every time it moves an object to clean your room, or only if it's moving that special vase you keep under the bed and never put flowers in for some reason?

- **Safe Exploration**: How do you teach a robot the limits of its curiosity? Google's researchers give the example of a robot that's learning where it's allowed to mop. How do you let it know that mopping new floors is fine, but that it shouldn't stick the mop in an electrical socket?
- **Robustness to Distributional Shift**: How do you make sure robots respect the space they're in? A cleaning robot let loose in your bedroom will act differently than one that is sweeping up in a factory, but how is it supposed to know the difference?

Apple co-founder Steve Wozniak has said that we should add another law, that a human cannot harm a machine that "thinks." This challenges us to do something we have been suggesting throughout this book, to think of AI as a collaborator and to do what is so counter to our industrial era ethos: to anthropomorphize AI.

However, the problem with all these laws, challenges, or guidelines is that they are not intended for AI, computers, autonomous devices, or robots, but rather for humans.

Consider how you would enforce these three laws today. If you built a robot with the intention to harm another human, is there some sort of fail-safe built into every silicon chip that will prevent the robot from causing harm? Do programming languages such as Python have a standard piece of code that every software application must run to insure it isn't harming people? Of course not!

This is a ridiculous approach. It may soothe our conscience or calm our anxiety to believe that a simple set of three, four, or five rules can govern the evolution of AI, but it would be an illusion. Every one of the technologies we've talked about, from AI to AVs, blockchain to behavioral computing, will be used in some manner to cause harm, fight wars, enable terrorism, and break laws. We shouldn't tolerate that, but we need to accept it. The challenge isn't just finding ways to eliminate that possibility, which (unless we find a way to alter human nature) is futile, but to leverage these same technologies to the greatest degree possible so that we do significantly more good than harm.

So, what *are* we proposing? If we agree that the answer is not, and will not be, found in our ability to create perfect solutions, that the notion of truth is rarely as black and white as we'd like it to be, and that there is a measurable benefit to how we use these technologies, then the question becomes, "How do we create the greatest benefit from their use while minimizing their liabilities?" We'd like to propose the follow six global standards for any intelligent system or autonomous device:

1. In the absence of legal liability for AI, a human or a legally liable entity must ultimately be held accountable for the actions of any AI-powered device.
2. Robots, AVs, and any other AI-powered devices with the ability to make decisions must be developed to comply with the same laws that humans must comply with.
3. Any autonomous device must allow for the intervention of an authorized human to override any of its decisions, and there must always be at least one authorized human with an automatic line of succession.
4. Any decision made by an autonomous device must be auditable in a manner that is understandable by a human.

5. Any autonomous device that is involved in an incident that damages property, or which results in the injury or the death of a human must provide an auditable lesson(s) learned in a form that allows them to be understood by a human and shared with any other autonomous device.
6. Any general-purpose AI must be licensed to perform tasks only within a well-defined field of operation.

These standards establish a foundation for the legal and acceptable use of AI. Are they a panacea? Of course not. They are a starting point for a journey that will clearly take us to places we have yet to imagine.

In addition, we believe strongly that this is one area where international standards should be developed by which we can monitor, share, and ethically evolve AI. Recall our suggestion in Chapter 4, when we talked about how the data shared in an aviation incident is collected, analyzed, and widely shared across the entire aviation community in an effort to learn from the incident and increase the safety of the entire industry, not only one airline or manufacturer. The same is true with AI and intelligent devices, be they robots, AVs, or any other autonomous device. The establishment of a Global Artificial Intelligence Directorate is a necessary step toward ensuring that the use of AI conforms to an evolutionary path that benefits mankind.

Consider, for example, that while there are firm standards in place for conducting studies on human subjects, there are no such constraints on how research is conducted on publicly available data about human subjects. If our digital-selves become as robust a record of our behaviors as we are expecting, we will need to put in place ethical standards for their use.

Will any of these legal or ethical constraints eliminate criminal or nation state uses of AI for unethical or illegal purposes? We're not that naïve, but it will provide a means of sanctioning and otherwise pursuing actors who have nefarious intentions for the use of AI and our digital-selves. Don't discount this as unnecessary bureaucracy. This is one area where we need to play an active role in how we architect the future. Had we done something similar with the evolution of nuclear power we would likely have avoided much of the risk inherent in the rampant spread of nuclear weapons over the past seventy years.

The other side of this is defining the role of AI in situations where the ultimate authority still needs to be a human. It's one thing to use AI in narrow situations where risk can be contained and another to replace not only human judgment but human intuition, values, and ethics.

The behavioral goldmine that we've described throughout the book is open to anyone who wishes to grab a digital pick and shovel. It's a land grab without precedent, and without rules.

As the first full draft of the manuscript for this book was being finalized we were reminded of how important both of these points are (monitoring the applications of AI and the scope of its authority) when we came across a recent obituary for former USSR Lt. Col. Stanislav Petrov whose singular act of humanity may well have saved the world from nuclear holocaust.

Petrov was an unremarkable Soviet officer who on Sept. 26, 1983 was tasked with awesome responsibility of monitoring the Soviet's radar for incoming nuclear ballistic missiles launched from the USA.

Just three weeks prior, the Soviets had shot down a Korean Airways passenger plane, killing 269 people. This was the plane we talked about in Chapter 1, which spurred President Reagan to open up access to GPS. Tensions between the two super powers couldn't have been under more strain.

In the early morning of September 26th, Petrov's radar lit up with one after another blips. Five USA Minuteman intercontinental ballistic missiles were undeniably heading toward his homeland. The USSR was under attack. Red Army protocol was clear on what Petrov had to do; call in the strike, and quickly. In less than thirty minutes, the time it would take a ballistic missile to reach its target, Russia would lose any ability to launch a land-based counterattack. The sum of all fears was suddenly an unimaginable reality. Petrov recounted the anxious seconds,

"The siren howled, but I just sat there for a few seconds, staring at the big, back-lit, red screen with the word 'LAUNCH' on it," he told the BBC's Russian Service in 2013. The large backlit letters LAUNCH indicated that the missiles had indeed been launched from the USA. As Petrov watched and counted the seconds a second warning replaced the first, MISSILE STRIKE. "All I had to do was to reach for the phone; to raise the direct line to our top commanders."

Had Petrov made that call, we would—at least those of us who were left to talk about it—be remembering September 26th as the day the world nuked itself back into the stone age.

Clearly Petrov didn't pick up the phone. He sat there listening to his gut. A gut churning with the struggle to do what he'd been relentlessly programmed to do, without thinking, and with the very human intuition to prevent a nuclear holocaust, believing that his American counterparts could never initiate such an unthinkable act. Petrov's gut told him it couldn't be accurate, the computers had to be mistaken. And so, he looked at the undeniable data, listened to the screeching of the nuclear warning alarms, looked at the glaring red letters "MISSILE STRIKE" on the large monitor, and waited. He defied protocol and contacted the USSR satellite tracking stations to see if they had picked up anything. Nothing. Seven minutes had passed since the launch alarm. Twenty-three minutes later, Petrov knew his intuition had been right. The computers had been wrong. It was later determined that they had interpreted sunlight hitting a layer of clouds as incoming ICBMs.

Could AI have done a better job of correlating the necessary sensory data from radar and satellites? Would it have had the human reaction to freeze and consider the implications of following its stated objectives? Even Petrov conceded that his decision was based to a large degree on the fact that his background was not entirely military. Had AI been programmed by the military to use a military ethic would it decide differently than AI developed by a non-military contractor?

All impossible questions to answer, but that's precisely the point. There is no definitive linear or logical set of circumstances and no singular set of outcomes in cases where judgment and intuition play such a pivotal role.

We don't claim to have the answers to these questions. What we do have is an understanding of how each new generation of technology becomes simultaneously more powerful in its ability to construct and to destroy. We need to keep pace with the increased burden of vigilance that demands.

The last thing we've set out to do with this book is to instill fear. The benefits that we've laid out are well worth the cost of the vigilance they require. And, in any case, the choice is not between the evolution of AI or its destruction, but rather in how we learn to live with it by leveraging its benefits.

There Is No Finish Line

In all the conversations and interviews we conducted for this book, one comment made by Karl at nuTonomy stayed with us. Referring to the evolution of autonomous vehicles and AI in general, he said:

> *Who will get to the finish line and win this race? Races have ends [and] typically they have a single winner. Both of those are false in this industry. There'll be an initial version of an AV that someone will put on the road. It will be sufficiently safe and sufficiently humanlike, and people will use it. That'll be great, but that software will improve over time. Those advances will come through smart adaptation and imitation of humanlike behavior.*

Some challenges have a finish line—Neil Armstrong's first steps on the moon, the sequencing of the human genome. These are the clock problems that we introduced in Chapter 2. Other challenges require solutions that are constantly evolving, the cloud problems which are never totally solved. In many ways that's the kind of future we've been describing. A future in which humanity and technology will be evolving together.

One thing is abundantly clear. When we look back at the twentieth and early twenty-first centuries, we will be in awe at how we could possibly have survived in a system where so much of what we did was accomplished without a deep understanding of behavior. The dystopian society we talk about so often will not be the one we inhabit then but the one we are living in now.

We will feel immense compassion for the inhabitants of the past, how they were rarely recognized, anonymous faces housed in impersonal demographic buckets. They risked their lives in machines too primitive to drive themselves. The constraints they had to work under, the uncertainty and volatility that they encountered on a daily basis will be difficult to comprehend.

We began *Revealing the Invisible* by talking about the end of the industrial age and the beginning of a new era in which we will build our economy, our businesses, and our lives around a deep understanding of our behaviors and the behaviors of the intelligent machines with which we will cohabitate the earth—a new species that will be our collaborators and colleagues.

We've tried to be balanced in our views as we delved into the fear and the concern as well as the promise and the value of this uncertain future. We haven't been naïve about pointing out the risks of transparency and privacy. They are real and will require constant vigilance to be protected and preserved. However, we've been no less ambitious in describing the benefits of revealing our hidden behaviors, to each of us as individuals and to society as whole.

We could take another eighty thousand words to speculate on how all of this may play out but there is far more to learn from experiencing the future than by reading about it. We'll leave the science fiction to the science fiction writers. The truth is that we will all—individually and collectively—have to figure out the balancing point where we feel that the price of transparency is worth the benefits we receive. It's not a new discussion but it has clearly never had the potential to be as disruptive.

We began this book with a quote from Henry David Thoreau, "Men have become the tools of their tools." At the dawn of the industrial age, Thoreau was no doubt referring to the way in which humanity was becoming an instrument of commercialism, materialism, industry, and even war. Our tools were looming over us in ways we'd not yet experienced. The imposing images of factories, steamships overtaking sail ships, the burgeoning railroad system, all fueled global growth but also cast long shadows over the sort of humanity Thoreau envisioned. We probably need to be reminded that in 1850, 93 percent of the one billion inhabitants of our planet lived in extreme poverty. Today less than 10 percent of seven billion humans live below the line for extreme poverty.[162] Amazingly, that means that there are about four hundred million fewer people living in extreme poverty today! What Thoreau feared most, the industrial machine, is what has most raised humanity out of the depths of its despair.

There has never been a time of great progress when its opponents didn't speak of the threat it posed to humanity; the gloom and doom of our coming apocalyptic fall. It hasn't happened yet, but that won't stop the naysaying.

We'd like to end the book with a simple thought. "This is not the end." There are countless decisions, innovations, setbacks and leaps forward still ahead. We have come to the precipice of change countless times and will return to it countless more. Each time, we're faced with an apparent choice between two paths of action.

One is to focus on the risk of the future and grieve the loss of the past, the comfort of its familiarity and the certainty of its failings; for better or for worse, it's what we've known and how we've defined ourselves. Like ships' captains on a treacherous sea, we take pride in having become masters at navigating the obstacles of the past. Let the future wait for someone younger and more foolish with less to lose.

The other path is to risk passage into the future, unafraid, with full knowledge that much of what we know will be challenged by unimagined change and rewarded with equally unimagined benefits.

That choice is an illusion. We do not so much choose to enter the future as we are absorbed by it, swallowed whole. The choice is not in finding a way to avoid or delay it but rather to be observers or active participants in shaping it to our benefit.

In the same way that seeing the hidden mechanics of the subatomic gave us a deep and accurate understanding of how the universe works—leading to so many of the scientific discoveries that built the twentieth century—revealing the invisible patterns in our behaviors will lay the foundation for the transparency needed to build the 21st century.

Is there risk in that? Yes, and it will require all the vigilance we've described and more. But the greater risk is in doing nothing, in fearing that our ability to innovate and realize the promise of a future with ever greater value will somehow fall short of the risk. History has never borne out that fear.

It's inevitable: the invisible will be revealed, and with it, our future.

APPENDIX

List of data items collected by information brokers sourced from the Federal Trade Commission official website in May 2014.

Identifying Data
- Name
- Previously Used Names
- Address
- Address History
- Longitude and Latitude
- Phone Numbers
- Email Address

Sensitive Identifying Data
- Social Security Number
- Driver's License Number
- Birth Date

- Birth Dates of Each Child in Household
- Birth Date of Family Members in Household

Demographic Data
- Age
- Height
- Weight
- Gender
- Race & Ethnicity
- Country of Origin
- Religion (by Surname at the Household Level)
- Language
- Marital Status
- Presence of Elderly Parent
- Presence of Children in Household
- Education Level
- Occupation
- Family Ties
- Demographic Characteristics of Family Members in Household
- Number of Surnames in Household
- Veteran in Household
- Grandparent in House
- Spanish Speaker
- Foreign Language Household (e.g., Russian, Hindi, Tagalog, Cantonese)
- Households with a Householder who is Hispanic Origin or Latino
- Employed – White Collar Occupation
- Employed – Blue Collar Occupation
- Work at Home Flag
- Length of Residence

- Household Size
- Congressional District
- Single Parent with Children
- Ethnic and Religious Affiliations

Court and Public Record Data
- Bankruptcies
- Criminal Offenses and Convictions
- Judgments
- Liens
- Marriage Licenses
- State Licenses and Registrations (e.g.,Hunting, Fishing, Professional)
- Voting Registration and Party Identification

Social Media and Technology Data
- Electronics Purchases
- Friend Connections
- Internet Connection Type
- Internet Provider
- Level of Usage
- Heavy Facebook User
- Heavy Twitter User
- Twitter User with 250+ Friends
- Is a Member of over 5 Social Networks
- Online Influence
- Operating System
- Software Purchases
- Type of Media Posted
- Uploaded Pictures
- Use of Long Distance Calling Services
- Presence of Computer Owner

- Use of Mobile Devices
- Social Media and Internet Accounts including: Digg, Facebook, Flickr, Flixster, Friendster, hi5, Hotmail, LinkedIn, Live Journal, MySpace, Twitter, Amazon, Bebo, CafeMom, DailyMotion, Match, myYearbook, NBA.com, Pandora, Photobucket, WordPress, and Yahoo

Home and Neighborhood Data
- Census Tract Data
- Address Coded as Public/Government Housing
- Dwelling Type
- Heating and Cooling
- Home Equity
- Home Loan Amount and Interest Rate
- Home Size
- Lender Type
- Length of Residence
- Listing Price
- Market Value
- Move Date
- Neighborhood Criminal, Demographic, and Business Data
- Number of Baths
- Number of Rooms
- Number of Units
- Presence of Fireplace
- Presence of Garage
- Presence of Home Pool
- Rent Price
- Type of Owner
- Type of Roof

- Year Built

General Interest Data
- Apparel Preferences
- Attendance at Sporting Events
- Charitable Giving
- Gambling – Casinos
- Gambling – State Lotteries
- Thrifty Elders
- Life Events (e.g., Retirement, Newlywed, Expectant Parent)
- Magazine and Catalog Subscriptions
- Media Channels Used
- Participation in Outdoor Activities (e.g., Golf, Motorcycling, Skiing, Camping)
- Participation in Sweepstakes or Contests
- Pets
- Dog Owner
- Political Leanings
- Assimilation Code
- Preferred Celebrities
- Preferred Movie Genres
- Preferred Music Genres
- Reading and Listening Preferences
- Donor (e.g., Religious, Political, Health Causes)
- Financial Newsletter Subscriber
- Upscale Retail Card Holder
- Affluent Baby Boomer
- Working-Class Moms
- Working Woman
- African-American Professional
- Membership Clubs – Self-Help

- Membership Clubs – Wines
- Exercise – Sporty Living
- Winter Activity Enthusiast
- Participant – Motorcycling
- Outdoor/Hunting & Shooting
- Biker/Hell's Angels
- Santa Fe/Native American Lifestyle
- New Age/Organic Lifestyle
- Is a Member of over 5 Shopping Sites
- Media Channel Usage – Daytime TV
- Bible Lifestyle
- Leans Left
- Political Conservative
- Political Liberal
- Activism & Social Issues

Financial Data
- Ability to Afford Products
- Credit Card User
- Presence of Gold or Platinum Card
- Credit Worthiness
- Recent Mortgage Borrower
- Pennywise Mortgagee
- Financially Challenged
- Owns Stocks or Bonds
- Investment Interests
- Discretionary Income Level
- Credit Active
- Credit Relationship with Financial or Loan Company
- Credit Relationship with Low-End Standalone Department Store
- Number of Investment Properties Owned

- Estimated Income
- Life Insurance
- Loans
- Net Worth Indicator
- Underbanked Indicator
- Tax Return Transcripts
- Type of Credit Cards

Vehicle Data
- Brand Preferences
- Insurance Renewal
- Make & Model
- Vehicles Owned
- Vehicle Identification Numbers
- Vehicle Value Index
- Propensity to Purchase a New or Used Vehicle
- Propensity to Purchase a Particular Vehicle Type (e.g., SUV, Coupe, Sedan)
- Motor Cycle Owner (e.g., Harley, Off-Road Trail Bike)
- Motor Cycle Purchased 0-6 Months Ago
- Boat Owner
- Purchase Date
- Purchase Information
- Intend to Purchase – Vehicle

Travel Data
- Read Books or Magazines About Travel
- Travel Purchase – Highest Price Paid
- Date of Last Travel Purchase
- Air Services – Frequent Flyer
- Vacation Property

- Vacation Type (e.g., Casino, Time Share, Cruises, RV)
- Cruises Booked
- Preferred Vacation Destination
- Preferred Airline

Purchase Behavior Data
- Amount Spent on Goods
- Buying Activity
- Method of Payment
- Number of Orders
- Buying Channel Preference (e.g., Internet, Mail, Phone)
- Types of Purchases
- Military Memorabilia/Weaponry
- Shooting Games
- Guns and Ammunition
- Christian Religious Products
- Jewish Holidays/Judaica Gifts
- Kwanzaa/African-Americana Gifts
- Type of Entertainment Purchased
- Type of Food Purchased
- Average Days Between Orders
- Last Online Order Date
- Last Offline Order Date
- Online Orders $500-$999.99 Range
- Offline Orders $1000+ Range
- Number of Orders – Low-Scale Catalogs
- Number of Orders – High-Scale Catalogs
- Retail Purchases – Most Frequent Category
- Mail Order Responder – Insurance
- Mailability Score
- Dollars – Apparel – Women's Plus Sizes
- Dollars – Apparel – Men's Big & Tall

- Books – Mind & Body/Self-Help
- Internet Shopper
- Novelty Elvis

Health Data
- Ailment and Prescription Online Search Propensity
- Propensity to Order Prescriptions by Mail
- Smoker in Household
- Tobacco Usage
- Over the Counter Drug Purchases
- Geriatric Supplies
- Use of Corrective Lenses or Contacts
- Allergy Sufferer
- Have Individual Health Insurance Plan
- Buy Disability Insurance
- Buy Supplemental to Medicare/Medicaid

Individual Insurance
- Brand Name Medicine Preference
- Magazines – Health
- Weight Loss & Supplements
- Purchase History or Reported Interest in Health Topics including: Allergies, Arthritis, Medicine Preferences, Cholesterol, Diabetes,
- Dieting, Body Shaping, Alternative Medicine, Beauty/Physical Enhancement, Disabilities, Homeopathic Remedies, Organic Focus, Orthopedics, and Senior Needs

ENDNOTES

Introduction

1   Maria Popova, "The Vampire Problem: A Brilliant Thought Experiment Illustrating the Paradox of Transformative Experience," BrainPickings, accessed October 2, 2017, https://www.brainpickings.org/2017/09/13/transformative-experience-vampire-problem/?utm_source=Brain+Pickings&utm_campaign=8345b247c8-EMAIL_CAMPAIGN_2017_09_15&utm_medium=email&utm_term=0_179ffa2629-8345b247c8-234634073&mc_cid=8345b247c8&mc_eid=a59a59f2a9.

2   Bairoch, Paul. *Economics and World History: Myths and Paradoxes*. (Chicago: University of Chicago Press, 1999). Converted to 2016 US Dollars.

3   Bairoch, *Economics*...Converted to 2016 US Dollars.

4   We've affectionately named this Jetsonian after the futuristic Jetson family cartoon series of the 1960s.

[5] Lee Rainie and Maeve Duggan, "Privacy and Information Sharing," *Pew Research Center*, January 14, 2016, http://www.pewinternet.org/files/2016/01/PI_2016.01.14_Privacy-and-Info-Sharing_FINAL.pdf.

[6] Ranks as the leading cause of death when normalized for potential impact on total population against other leading causes of death as shown in Chapter 4.

[7] Michael Sheetz, "Technology Killing off Corporate America: Average Life Span of Companies Under 20 Years," *CNBC*, August 24, 2017, https://www.cnbc.com/2017/08/24/technology-killing-off-corporations-average-lifespan-of-company-under-20-years.html.

[8] J.M. Alston et al.,*Persistence Pays: U.S. Agricultural Productivity Growth and the Benefits from Public R&D Spending* (New York,: Springer-Verlag, 2010), http://www.springer.com/us/book/9781441906571.

[9] Dan Keldsen and Tom Koulopoulos, *Gen Z Effect: The Six Forces Shaping the Future of Business* (Brookline, Massachusetts: Taylor and Francis, 2014).

Chapter 1

[10] Keldsen and Koulopoulos, *The Gen Z Effect...*).

[11] John Gantz and David Reinsel, "The Digital Universe StudyIn 2020: Big Data, Bigger Digital Shadows, and Biggest Growth in the Far East—United States," International Data Corporation (IDC), February 2013, https://www.emc.com/collateral/analyst-reports/idc-digital-universe-united-states.pdf.

[12] Germany, ZEIT ONLINE GmbH Hamburg. "Http://opendata.zeit.de/widgets/dataretention/."

ZEIT ONLINE. Accessed October 08, 2017, http://www.zeit.de/datenschutz/malte-spitz-data-retention.

13 Emily Steel et al., "How Much is Your Personal Data Worth?" *Financial Times*, June 12, 2013, http://ig.ft.com/how-much-is-your-personal-data-worth/#axzz-2z2agBB6R; Facebook $24 billion yearly revenues / 2 billion users = $12/user.

14 Mayo clinic librarian.

15 Patrick Nelson, "Just One Autonomous Car Will Use 4,000 Gb Of Data/Day," *Network World*, December 7, 2016, http://www.networkworld.com/article/3147892/internet/one-autonomous-car-will-use-4000-gb-of-dataday.html.

16 Larry Dignan, "Apple's App Store 2016 Revenue Tops $28 Billion Mark, Developers Net $20 billion," *ZDNet*, January 5, 2017, http://www.zdnet.com/article/apples-app-store-2016-revenue-tops-28-billion-mark-developers-net-20-billion/.

17 Erick Schonfeld, "Zuckerberg Saves Face, Apologizes For Beacon," *TechCrunch*, December 5, 2007, https://techcrunch.com/2007/12/05/zuckerberg-saves-face-apologies-for-beacon/.

18 A full list of the data collected is included at the end of the book.

19 U.S. Naval Research Laboratory, "Father of GPS and Pioneer of Satellite Telemetry and Timing Inducted into National Inventors Hall of Fame," March 31, 2010, https://www.nrl.navy.mil/media/news-releases/2010/father-of-gps-and-pioneer-of-satellite-telemetry-and-timing-inducted-into-national-inventors-hall-of-fame.

[20] Julie Fancher, "Rowlett Mom Used GPS to Find Girl Who Was Sexually Assaulted," *Dallas News*, August 20, 2015, https://www.dallasnews.com/news/crime/2015/08/20/rowlett-mom-used-gps-to-find-girl-who-was-sexually-assaulted.

[21] US Department of Transportation, Federal Aviation Administration, "NextGEN," accessed October 2, 2017, https://www.faa.gov/nextgen//.

[22] US Department of Transportation, Bureau of Transportation Statistics, "Airline Fuel Cost and Consumption (U.S. Carriers - Scheduled) January 2000–July 2017," accessed October 2, 2017, https://www.transtats.bts.gov/fuel.asp?pn=1.

[23] Keldsen and Koulopoulos, *The Gen Z Effect.*.

[24] Geological Society, "Super-Eruptions: Global Effects and Future Threats," accessed October 2, 2017, http://pages.mtu.edu/~raman/VBigIdeas/Supereruptions_files/Super-eruptionsGeolSocLon.pdf.

[25] Steve Mirsky, "When Humans Almost Died Out; Earthy Exoplanets; And Scientific American's 165th Birthday," (podcast), August 12, 2010, https://www.scientificamerican.com/podcast/episode/when-humans-almost-died-out-earthy-10-08-12//.

[26] Debra Black, "Were Early Humans Close to Extinction?" *The Star*, January 27, 2010, https://www.thestar.com/business/tech_news/2010/01/27/were_early_humans_close_to_extinction.html.

Chapter 2

[27] "50 Years of Moore's Law," *Intel*, accessed October 2, 2017, https://www.intel.com/content/www/us/en/silicon-innovations/moores-law-technology.html.

28 Martin Lindström, *Small Data: The Tiny Clues That Uncover Huge Trends* (New York: Picador, 2017).

29 "John Vincent Atanasoff: The Father of the Computer," (obituary), accessed October 2, 2017, http://www.columbia.edu/~td2177/JVAtanasoff/JVAtanasoff.html.

30 We're using Newtonian/Einstein here specifically to show that while Einstein's physics were a significant leap forward in understanding why things happen, they did not negate Newton's explanation of how things happen. Both can co-exist and do.

31 The section on Toppler and his analogy of Clocks and Clouds was developed in collaboration with Jim Hays at aspiregroup.com.

32 Tibi Puiu, "Your Smartphone Is Millions of Times More Powerful Than All of NASA's Combined Computing in 1969," *ZME Science*, September 10, 2017, http://www.zmescience.com/research/technology/smartphone-power-compared-to-apollo-432//.

33 Adapted from Thomas Koulopoulos, *Cloud Surfing* (Brookline, MA: Bibliomotion, 2012).

34 "500 Billion Billion Moves Later, Computers Solve Checkers," *Chess News*, accessed October 2, 2017, http://en.chessbase.com/post/500-billion-billion-moves-later-computers-solve-checkers.

35 "Showdown," *The Economist*, March 12, 2016, https://www.economist.com/news/science-and-technology/21694540-win-or-lose-best-five-battle-contest-another-milestone.

36 Matthieu Walraet, "A Googolplex of Go Games," January 9, 2016, http://matthieuw.github.io/go-games-number/GoGamesNumber.pdf.

37 The way AlphaGo, and other deep learning systems work is not by playing all of these games against a human opponent, but against other computers and in many cases even itself.

38 Koulopoulos, *Cloud Surfing*.

39 Tom Bawden, "Global Warming: Data Centres to Consume Three Times as Much Energy in Next Decade, Experts Warn," *The Independent*, January 23, 2016, http://www.independent.co.uk/environment/global-warming-data-centres-to-consume-three-times-as-much-energy-in-next-decade-experts-warn-a6830086.html.

40 Research and Analysis by IDC, "The Digital Universe of Opportunities: Rich Data and the Increasing Value of the Internet of Things," EMC Digital Universe, April 2014, <https://www.emc.com/leadership/digital-universe/2014iview/executive-summary.htm>

Chapter 3

41 "H.R. 387 — 115th Congress: Email Privacy Act." www.GovTrack.us. 2017. February 3, 2018 <https://www.govtrack.us/congress/bills/115/hr387>

42 "RealAge," *Sharecare*, accessed October 2, 2017. https://www.sharecare.com/static/realage.

43 Chiara Palazzo, "Consumer Campaigners Read Terms and Conditions of Their Mobile Phone Apps...All 250,000 Words," *The Telegraph*, May 26, 2016, http://www.telegraph.co.uk/technology/2016/

05/26/consumer-campaigners-read-terms-and-con-ditions-of-their-mobile-p/.

44   Dianna Dilworth, "How Long Does It Take to Read Popular Books?: INFOGRAPHIC," *GalleyCat*, September 11, 2014, http://www.adweek.com/galley-cat/how-long-does-it-take-to-read-popular-books-in-fographic/91254.

45   Kashmir Hill, "Beware, Houseguests: Cheap Home Surveillance Cameras Are Everywhere Now," *Splinter*, February 18, 2015, http://splinternews.com/beware-houseguests-cheap-home-surveillance-camer-as-ar-1793845387.

46   Sam Biddle and Spencer Woodman, "These Are the Technology Firms Lining Up to Build Trump's 'Extreme Vetting' Program," *The Intercept*, August 7, 2017, https://theintercept.com/2017/08/07/these-are-the-technology-firms-lining-up-to-build-trumps-extreme-vetting-program/.

47   Kate Conger, "Despite Looming Jail Time, Gurbaksh Chahal Is Back as Gravity4 CEO," *TechCrunch*, September 1, 2016, https://techcrunch.com/2016/09/01/despite-looming-jail-time-gur-baksh-chahal-is-back-as-gravity4-ceo/.

48   United States v. Aaron Graham, Appeal 12-4659 (4th Cir. 2016), http://pdfserver.amlaw.com/nlj/GRAHAM_ca4_20160531.pdf.

49   Moxie Marlinspike, "Why 'I Have Nothing to Hide' Is the Wrong Way to Think About Surveillance," *Wired*, June 13, 2013, https://www.wired.com/2013/06/why-i-have-nothing-to-hide-is-the-wrong-way-to-think-about-surveillance/.

50 Marc Santora, "Order That Police Wear Cameras Stirs Unexpected Reactions," *New York Times*, August 13, 2013. http://www.nytimes.com/2013/08/14/nyregion/order-that-police-wear-cameras-stirs-unexpected-reactions.html.

51 Hearings of Subcommittee on Courts, Civil Liberties, and the Administration of Justice of the Committee on the Judiciary, 97th Cong. (1982), http://cryptome.org/hrcw-hear.htm.

52 Wikipedia, "Time Dilation," accessed October 2, 2017, https://en.wikipedia.org/wiki/Time_dilation#cite_note-HSWTime-2.

Chapter 4
53 Tesla has since modified lane switching so that it happens in a smoother and less "unnerving" fashion.

54 "Trends in Consumer Mobility Report," *Bank of America*, 2015, accessed October 2, 2017, http://newsroom.bankofamerica.com/files/doc_library/additional/2015_BAC_Trends_in_Consumer_Mobility_Report.pdf.

55 Geoffrey Mohan, "Is Playing 'Space Invaders' a Milestone in Artificial Intelligence?" *Los Angeles Times*, February 25, 2015, http://www.latimes.com/science/sciencenow/la-sci-sn-computer-learning-space-invaders-20150224-story.html.

56 "2016 Production Statistics," International Organization of Motor Vehicle Manufacturers website, accessed October 2, 2017, http://www.oica.net/category/production-statistics/.

57   Assuming 100 million vehicles at an average length of 10' / 5280' per mile / 24,000 mile distance at the equator = 7.89.

58   "Achievements In Road Safety," *International Organization of Motor Vehicle Manufacturers*, accessed October 2, 2017, http://www.oica.net/category/safety/global-safety/.

59   Daniel Tencer, "Number Of Cars Worldwide Surpasses 1 Billion; Can The World Handle This Many Wheels?" *Huffington Post*, August 23, 2011, http://www.huffingtonpost.ca/2011/08/23/car-population_n_934291.html.

60   "SeniorDriving.AAA," American Automobile Association website, accessed October 2, 2017, http://seniordriving.aaa.com/resources-family-friends/conversations-about-driving/facts-research/.

61   Zachary Shahan, "NASA Says: Automobiles Largest Net Climate Change Culprit," *CleanTechnica*, February 23, 2010, https://cleantechnica.com/2010/02/23/nasa-says-automobiles-largest-climate-change-culprit/.

62   Executive Office of the President National Science and Technology Council Committee on Technology, *Preparing for the Future of Artificial Intelligence*, October 2016, https://obamawhitehouse.archives.gov/sites/default/files/whitehouse_files/microsites/ostp/NSTC/preparing_for_the_future_of_ai.pdf.

63   Cari Romm, "Americans Are More Afraid of Robots Than Death," *The Atlantic*, October 16, 2015, https://www.theatlantic.com/technology/archive/2015/10/americans-are-more-afraid-of-robots-than-death/410929/.

64 Son, Khansari, Shastrula, Jarrahi, and Tomko v. Tesla, Inc., 8:16-cv-02282-JVS-KES (US District Court for the Central District of California 2016), https://assets.documentcloud.org/documents/3534570/Teslaamendedcomplaint.pdf.

65 By saying the claim is convoluted we are not passing judgment or implying anything about the merits of the lawsuit, but simply pointing out that AVs create all sorts of legal and even ethical challenges.

66 John Paul, "Cars Crashing Into Buildings," WHIOTV, November 4, 2014, http://www.whio.com/news/cars-crashing-into-buildings/2P23WGXgsGJzfoLavPj2HL/.

67 John Markoff, "Planes Without Pilots," *New York Times*, April 6, 2015, https://www.nytimes.com/2015/04/07/science/planes-without-pilots.html?mcubz=0.

68 "Flight Response," *The Economist*, September 15, 2016, https://www.economist.com/news/science-and-technology/21707187-artificially-intelligent-autopilot-learns-example-flight-response.

69 Jeff Wise, "What Really Happened Aboard Air France 447," *Popular Mechanics*, December 6, 2011, http://www.popularmechanics.com/flight/a3115/what-really-happened-aboard-air-france-447-6611877/.

70 J. C. R. Licklider, "Man-Computer Symbiosis," *IRE Transactions on Human Factors in Electronics* HFE-1 (March 1960): 4–11, https://groups.csail.mit.edu/medg/people/psz/Licklider.html

71 Garreau, Joel (2006). *Radical Evolution: The Promise and Peril of Enhancing Our Minds, Our Bodies—and What It Means to be Human*. Broadway. p. 22.

72 "Advanced Monty Hall," interactivate website, accessed October 2, 2017, http://www.shodor.org/interactivate/activities/AdvancedMontyHall/.

73 Susan P. Baker et al., "Pilot Error in Air Carrier Mishaps: Longitudinal Trends Among 558 Reports, 1983–2002," *Aviation, Space, and Environmental Medicine* 79, no. 1 (2008): 2–6, https://www.ncbi.nlm.nih.gov/pmc/articles/PMC2664988/.

74 Talk about egregious behavior of a director.

75 To be precise, more than 50 percent of the nodes have to agree.

76 Mark Russinovich, "Announcing the Coco Framework for Enterprise Blockchain Networks," Microsoft Azure, August 10, 2017, https://azure.micro-soft.com/en-us/blog/announcing-microsofts-coco-framework-for-enterprise-Blockchain-networks/.

77 "The Official Site of the Nobel Prize,"accessed October 2, 2017 https://www.nobelprize.org/nobel_prizes/lists/all

78 Tina Hesman, "The Machine That Invents," *St. Louis Post-Dispatch*, January 25, 2004, http://sl4.org/archive/0402/7882.html.

79 David Z. Morris, "Today's Cars Are Parked 95 Percent of the Time," *Fortune*, March 13, 2016, http://fortune.com/2016/03/13/cars-parked-95-percent-of-time/.

Chapter 5

80 E. L. Doctorow, *Ragtime* (New York: Bantam Books, 1976), 154–155.

81 David Halberstam, *The Reckoning*, reprint (New York: Avon Books, 1987), 73.

82   Halberstam, *The Reckoning*.

83   Max Roser and Esteban Ortiz-Ospina, "World Population Growth," OurWorldInData.org, accessed October 2, 2017, https://ourworldindata.org/world-population-growth/.

84   Roser and Ortiz-Ospina, "World…"

85   "Uber Movement," Uber Technologies website, accessed October 2, 2017, https://movement.uber.com/cities?lang=en-GB.

86   Georgios Achillias, "Phygital Platforms: Merging Physical And Digital," Wipro Digital, accessed October 2, 2017, http://wiprodigital.com/2015/09/15/phygital-platforms-merging-physical-and-digital/.

87   Pamela Paul, "Save Your Sanity: Downgrade Your Life," *New York Times*, August 18, 2017, https://www.nytimes.com/2017/08/18/opinion/sunday/technology-downgrade-sanity.html?smid=li-share.

88   Thor Berger, Chinchih Chen, and Carl Benedikt Frey, "Drivers of Disruption? Estimating the Uber Effect," Oxford Martin School of University of Oxford, January 23, 2017, http://www.oxfordmartin.ox.ac.uk/downloads/academic/Uber_Drivers_of_Disruption.pdf

89   "Map: The Most Common* Job In Every State," Planet Money, February 5, 2015, http://www.npr.org/sections/money/2015/02/05/382664837/map-the-most-common-job-in-every-state.

90   Johana Bhuiyan, "Uber for Trucks Is Here: Here's How It Will Work," *Recode*, May 18, 2017, https://www.recode.net/2017/5/18/15657862/uber-travis-kalanick-trucks-freight.

91 Paul A. Eisenstein, "Tesla Is Building a Pickup and a Semi-Truck," NBC News, April 14, 2017, https://www.nbcnews.com/business/autos/tesla-building-pickup-semi-truck-n746611.

92 "What's Next for Artificial Intelligence," *Wall Street Journal*, June 14, 2016, https://www.wsj.com/articles/whats-next-for-artificial-intelligence-1465827619.

93 International Management Congress, 1995.

94 Daniel Stamp, *The Invisible Assembly Line: Boosting White-Collar Productivity in the New Economy* (New York: American Management Association, 1995), 3.

95 US Census Bureau, *20th Century Statistics*, accessed October 2, 2017, https://www.census.gov/prod/99pubs/99statab/sec31.pdf.

96 In this case, the "incumbent" we will be referring to is the RIAA (Record Industry Association of America), an entity funded by the major music labels.

97 "RIAA v. The People: Five Years Later," Electronic Frontier Foundation, September 30, 2008, https://www.eff.org/wp/riaa-v-people-five-years-later.

98 While the record labels bought into Apple's vision, they also continued to pursue the three approaches we just mentioned until 2008.

99 David Holmes, "Who Killed the Music Industry?" *Pando*, August 5, 2013, https://pando.com/2013/08/05/who-killed-the-music-industry-an-interactive-explainer/.

100 MUSO" https://www.muso.com/market-analytics-global-music-insight-report-2016/.

101 "Introducing Pay-Per-Mile Car Insurance," Metromile, accessed October 2, 2017, https://www.metromile.com/.

[102] "Customer-Centricity in Insurance," Boston Consulting Group, accessed October 2, 2017, https://www.bcg.com/expertise/industries/insurance/customer-centricity-in-insurance.aspx.

[103] Tanguy Catlin et al., "Time for Insurance Companies to Face Digital Reality," McKinsey & Company, accessed October 2, 2017, http://www.mckinsey.com/industries/financial-services/our-insights/time-for-insurance-companies-to-face-digital-reality.

[104] "George Eastman," Eastman Kodak website, accessed October 2, 2017, http://www.kodak.com/corp/aboutus/heritage/georgeeastman/default.htm.

[105] "Obama Awards the National Medal of Science and National Medal of Technology and Innovation Ceremony: Speech Transcript," *Washington Post*, November 17, 2010, http://projects.washingtonpost.com/obama-speeches/speech/502/.

[106] Claudia Deutsch, "At Kodak, Same Old Things are New," *New York Times*, May 2, 2008, http://www.nytimes.com/2008/05/02/technology/02kodak.html.

[107] "Corporate Longevity," Innosight, accessed October 2, 2017, https://www.innosight.com/wp-content/uploads/2016/08/Corporate-Longevity-2016-Final.pdf

[108] Patrick Thompson and Caroline Viguerie,. "The Faster They Fall." *Harvard Business Review*, July 31, 2014, accessed October 8, 2017, https://hbr.org/2005/03/the-faster-they-fall.

[109] The Touch-point framework and much of the initial thinking about ecosystems was from conversa-

tions between Tom and Ralph Welborn, CEO of Imaginatik

110 Yossi Sheffi, "China's Slowdown: The First Stage of the Bullwhip Effect," *Harvard Business Review*, September 9, 2015, https://hbr.org/2015/09/chinas-slowdown-the-first-stage-of-the-bullwhip-effect.

Chapter 6

111 We believe that the story of Hastings' motivation has become somewhat folklore. Netflix co-founder Marc Randolph has claimed that the story is a fabrication.

112 Austin Carr, "Blockbuster Bankruptcy: A Decade of Decline," *Fast Company*, September 22, 2010, https://www.fastcompany.com/1690654/blockbuster-bankruptcy-decade-decline.

113 Mae Anderson and Michael Liedtke, "Hubris—and Late Fees—Doomed Blockbuster," *Associated Press*, September 23, 2010, http://www.nbcnews.com/id/39332696/ns/business-retail/t/hubris-late-fees-doomed-blockbuster/.

114 Alexis Madrigal, "How Netflix Reverse Engineered Hollywood," *The Atlantic*, January 2, 2014, https://www.theatlantic.com/technology/archive/2014/01/how-netflix-reverse-engineered-hollywood/282679/.

115 Madrigal, "How Netflix..."

116 "How Netflix Uses Analytics To Select Movies, Create Content, and Make Multimillion Dollar Decisions," Kissmetrics (web log), accessed October 2, 2017, https://blog.kissmetrics.com/how-netflix-uses-analytics/.

117 David Carr, "Giving Viewers What They Want," *New York Times*, February 24, 2013, http://www.nytimes.

com/2013/02/25/business/media/for-house-of-cards-using-big-data-to-guarantee-its-popularity.html?mcubz=0.

[118] Jay Moye, "Share a Coke: How the Groundbreaking Campaign Got Its Start 'Down Under,'" Coca-Cola Company, September 25, 2014, http://www.coca-colacompany.com/stories/share-a-coke-how-the-groundbreaking-campaign-got-its-start-down-under.

[119] "New Live-Design Experience Promises Custom Shoes in Less Than 90 Minutes," Nike, September 5, 2017, https://news.nike.com/news/nike-makers-studio.

[120] Andrew Seybold, "iPhone Passes BlackBerry, But The Race Is Far From Over," *Forbes*, November 9, 2010, https://www.forbes.com/sites/investor/2010/11/09/iphone-passes-blackberry-but-the-race-is-far-from-over/#b099396520fd.

[121] Dan Thorp-Lancaster, "Kantar's Latest Smartphone Market Share Report Sees Windows Phone Dip Below 1 percent in the U.S.," Mobile Nations, January 11, 2017, https://www.windowscentral.com/kantars-latest-smartphone-market-share-report-sees-windows-phone-dip-below-1-us.

[122] Eric McLuhan and Frank Zingrone, eds., *Essential McLuhan* (London: Routledge, 1997), 273.

[123] Nicole Ellison, Rebecca Heino, and Jennifer Gibbs, "Managing Impressions Online: Self-Presentation Processes in the Online Dating Environment," *Journal of Computer-Mediated Communication* 11 (2006): 415–441, http://onlinelibrary.wiley.com/doi/10.1111/j.1083-6101.2006.00020.x/epdf.

124 "Dove Real Beauty Sketches," YouTube, promotional video posted by "Dove US," April 14, 2013, https://www.youtube.com/watch?v=XpaOjMXyJGk.

125 By the way, there's also a YouTube spoof of the ad in which the subjects are men. We'll let you guess how that one turns out.

126 Retail Equation, *2015 Consumer Returns in the Retail Industry* (Irvine, CA: Author, 2016), https://nrf.com/sites/default/files/Images/Mediapercent20Center/NRFpercent20Retailpercent20Returnpercent20Fraud percent20Final_0.pdf.

127 Ray Smith, "A Closet Filled With Regrets," *Wall Street Journal,* April 17, 2013, https://www.wsj.com/articles/SB10001424127887324240804578415002 232186418.

128 A. Chopra and E. Skolnick, *Innovative State.* (New York: Grove Press, 2016).

129 "Patient Navigator Saves Clients Money," Patient Navigator, accessed October 2, 2017, http://www.patientnavigator.com/patient-navigator-saves-clients-money/.

130 Melissa Aldridge and Amy Kelley, "The Myth Regarding the High Cost of End-of-Life Care," *American Journal of Public Health* 105, no. 12 (2015): 2411–5, https://www.ncbi.nlm.nih.gov/pmc/articles/PMC4638261/.

131 National Human Genome Research Institute (NHGRI). (2017). The Cost of Sequencing a Human Genome. [online] Available at: https://www.genome.gov/27565109/the-cost-of-sequencing-a-human-genome/ [Accessed 7 Oct. 2017].

132 Dawn McMullan, "What Is Personalized Medicine?" *Genome*, accessed October 2, 2017, http://genome-mag.com/what-is-personalized-medicine/.

133 US Centers for Medicare and Medicaid Services, "NHE Fact Sheet," accessed October 2, 2017, https://www.cms.gov/research-statistics-data-and-systems/statistics-trends-and-reports/nationalhealthexpenddata/nhe-fact-sheet.html.

134 Electrolux has since introduced a robot vacuum cleaner.

135 "Human-Animal Teams as an Analog for Future Human-Robot Teams: Influencing Design and Fostering Trust," *Journal of Human-Robot Interaction*, Vol. 5, No. 1, 2016, Pages 100-125, DOI 10.5898/JHRI.5.1.Phillips

Chapter 7

136 Ron Grossman, "Sears Was the Amazon.com of the 20th Century," *Chicago Tribune*, May 12, 2017, http://www.chicagotribune.com/news/opinion/commentary/ct-sears-roebuck-homan-catalog-flash-back-perspec-0514-jm-20170512-story.html.

137 Barbara Maranzani, "The Mother of All Catalogs Ceases Publication," History.com, January 25, 2013, http://www.history.com/news/the-mother-of-all-catalogs-ceases-publication-10-years-ago.

138 Geoff Colvin, "Why Sears Failed," *Fortune*, December 9, 2016, http://fortune.com/2016/12/09/why-sears-failed/.

139 Natalie Zmuda, "Is Sears Holdings' Loyalty Program Helping or Hurting It?" *AdAge*, August 23, 2013, http://adage.com/article/cmo-strategy/sears-holdings-loyalty-program-helping-hurting/243796/.

140 Joe Cahill, "Another Thing That Hasn't Saved Sears: Loyal Shoppers," *Crain's Chicago Business*, August 23, 2013, http://www.chicagobusiness.com/article/20130823/BLOGS10/130829907/another-thing-that-hasnt-saved-sears-loyal-shoppers.

141 Jim Tierney, "Is the Shop Your Way Loyalty Program the Long-Term Answer at Sears?" Loyalty360 newsletter, May 31, 2017, https://www.loyalty360.org/content-gallery/daily-news/is-the-shop-your-way-loyalty-program-the-long-term.

142 Charles Duhigg, "How Companies Learn Your Secrets," *New York Times*, February 16, 2012, http://www.nytimes.com/2012/02/19/magazine/shopping-habits.html.

143 Franklin Foer, "Amazon Must Be Stopped," *New Republic*, October 9, 2014, https://newrepublic.com/article/119769/amazons-monopoly-must-be-broken-radical-plan-tech-giant.

144 "Americans Spend an Average of 17,600 Minutes Driving Each Year," American Automobile Association (press release), accessed October 2, 2017, http://newsroom.aaa.com/2016/09/americans-spend-average-17600-minutes-driving-year/.

145 Chris Isidore, "What's the Safest Way to Travel," *CNN Money*, May 13, 2015, http://money.cnn.com/2015/05/13/news/economy/train-plane-car-deaths/index.html.

146 Tesla has since moderated this behavior so that the lane change is not as abrupt.

Chapter 8

147 "Cryptocurrency Market Capitalizations," Coin-MarketCap website, accessed October 2, 2017, https://coinmarketcap.com/; and "Currency in Circulation: Value," Board of Governors of the Federal Reserve System website, accessed October 2, 2017, https://www.federalreserve.gov/paymentsystems-/coin_currcircvalue.htm.

148 Meaning it's not based on a gold standard or the value of any other commodity.

149 "Spend Anywhere, Without Fees," Monaco, accessed October 2, 2017, https://mona.co/.

150 Ben Dickson, "How Blockchain Can Create the World's Biggest Supercomputer," *TechCrunch*, December 27, 2016, https://techcrunch.com/2016/12/27/how-Blockchain-can-create-the-worlds-biggest-supercomputer/.

151 "The Golem Project Crowdfunding Whitepaper," Golem Project, November 2016, https://golem.network/doc/Golemwhitepaper.pdf.

152 "Vitalik Buterin: 'Putin Knows What Blockchain Is – This Is the Hype' [article translation from Russian]," Reddit web log post by "Treo123," accessed October 2, 2017, https://www.reddit.com/r/ethereum/comments/6xdsvr/vitalik_buterin_putin_knows_what_Blockchain_is/.

153 Patrick Howell O'Neill, "The Cyberattack That Changed the World," *Daily Dot*, May 20, 2016, https://www.dailydot.com/layer8/web-war-cyber attack-russia-estonia/.

154 "Facebook Statement of Rights and Responsibilities," last modified January 30, 2015, accessed October 1, 2017, https://www.facebook.com/terms.php.

155 Gar Alperovitz. "The War Was Won Before Hiroshima-And the Generals Who Dropped the Bomb Knew It," *The Nation*. August 5, 2015, accessed October 7, 2017, https://www.thenation.com/article/why-the-us-really-bombed-hiroshima/.

156 Mike Gault, "BlockCloud: Re-inventing Cloud with Blockchains," Guardtime website, accessed October 2, 2017, https://guardtime.com/blog/blockcloud-re-inventing-cloud-with-Blockchains.

157 Robert M. Wachter, *The Digital Doctor: Hope, Hype, and Harm at the Dawn of Medicine's Computer Age* (New York: McGraw-Hill Education, 2017).

158 Sam Levin, "Face-Reading AI Will Be Able to Detect Your Politics and IQ, Professor Says," *Guardian*, September 12, 2017, https://www.theguardian.com/technology/2017/sep/12/artificial-intelligence-face-recognition-michal-kosinski.

159 Isaac Asimov, "Runaround," in *I, Robot* (New York: Doubleday, 1950), 40.

160 James Vincent, "Satya Nadella's Rules for AI Are More Boring (and Relevant) Than Asimov's Three Laws," *The Verge*, June 29, 2016, https://www.theverge.com/2016/6/29/12057516/satya-nadella-ai-robot-laws.

161 Vincent, "Google's AI Researchers Say These Are the Five Key Problems for Robot Safety," *The Verge*, June 22, 2016, https://www.theverge.com/circuitbreaker/2016/6/22/11999664/google-robots-ai-safety-five-problems.

[162] Our World in Data, "World Population Living in Extreme Poverty, 1820-2015," 2017, accessed October 7, 2017, https://ourworldindata.org/grapher/world-population-in-extreme-poverty-absolute.

ABOUT THE AUTHORS

 **Tom Koulopoulos** is the Chairman and Founder of Delphi Group, a thirty-year-old global futures think tank which advises F500 companies and governments on technology trends. He is the author of ten prior books, past director of the Babson College Center for Business Innovation, an adjunct professor at Boston University, a columnist for Inc.com, and Founding Partner of Acroventures, an investment and advisory firm focusing on AI and leading edge behavioral technologies.

 **George Achillias**, MBA is a digital strategist focusing on AI led human-machine eco-systems. He leads strategy at an AI-focused investment fund and technology agency in Europe and works with FTSE250 companies to define their role, products and services in a decentralized blockchain-driven world.

Learn more at www.RevealingBook.com.